MY FORTY YEARS WITH FORD

GREAT LAKES BOOKS

*A complete listing of the books in this series
can be found online at http://wsupress.wayne.edu*

My FORTY YEARS
with FORD

CHARLES E. SORENSEN

with Samuel T. Williamson
Introduction by David L. Lewis

Wayne State University Press   Detroit

© 2006 by Wayne State University Press, Detroit, Michigan 48201.
All rights reserved. No part of this book may be reproduced
without formal permission. Manufactured in the United States of America.
10 09 08 07 06   5 4 3 2 1

Library of Congress Cataloging-in-Publication Data

Sorensen, Charles E., 1881–1968.
My forty years with Ford / Charles E. Sorensen ; with Samuel T.
Williamson ; introduction by David L. Lewis.
p. cm. — (Great Lakes books)
Originally published: New York : Norton, 1956.
Includes index.
ISBN 0-8143-3279-X (pbk. : alk. paper)
1. Ford Motor Company. 2. Ford, Henry, 1863–1947.
3. Automobile industry and trade—United States. I. Title. II. Series.
HD9710.U54F69 2005
338.7'6292092—dc22

2005028875

∞ The paper used in this publication meets the minimum requirements of
the American National Standard for Information Sciences—Permanence of
Paper for Printed Library Materials, ANSI Z39.48-1984.

Contents

Introduction

David L. Lewis

Charles E. Sorensen was an auto industry giant and one of the most important persons in Henry Ford's life. Surprisingly, he is the subject of only one book, this one, based largely on his oral reminiscences.

The reminiscences were taped at the Ford Archives in the early 1950s by oral historian Owen Bombard. Sorensen praised Bombard for having a "complete and accurate Ford chronology" that kept interviews on track.

At the time of the tapings, I was a Ford publicist working in the archives, located in Fair Lane, the Dearborn home of Henry and Clara Ford. Curious about the Sorensen interviews, I asked Bombard if the talks were going well. "Very much so," he replied. "Charlie plans to write his autobiography, and wants to cover every aspect of his Ford career."

Sorensen claimed to have known Henry Ford "better than any man dead or alive," and perhaps he did, although others have made the same claim. In any event, Sorensen's book makes it clear that he knew Ford very well indeed. He certainly was the most powerful of the men who served Henry Ford after Ford acquired control of the Ford Company in 1906.

Sorensen was born in Copenhagen, Denmark, in 1881, the son of a farmer/modelmaker. At the age of four, he emigrated to the United States with his family. He eventually became a patternmaker and worked in Buffalo, Milwaukee, and finally Detroit, where in 1904 he married a pretty bookkeeper, Helen Mitchell. Their first and only child, Clifford, was born in 1905, the same year Sorensen landed a job at Ford Motor Company's new Piquette Avenue Plant.

Tall, blond, and blue-eyed, Sorensen was so handsome that Percival Perry, head of Ford's English operations, called him an Adonis. Others said he had the profile of a film star. Not all of his early associates liked him though, for he had an explosive temper and often was grimly moody. But all respected his quick, keen mind, ability, and dynamism.

Sorensen gained Henry Ford's respect by translating Ford's design concepts into wooden parts that could be seen and studied. Advancing rapidly, he was second in command of Piquette production by 1907.

During World War I Sorensen was assigned to organize tractor production in Dearborn. Within three years his ability and force of personality had made him the untitled head of the Rouge Plant, destined to become the world's largest factory. By 1926 he presided over Ford's branch and assembly operations, and by the late 1920s he directed the company's worldwide manufacturing. In addition, he played an important role in sales affairs. He was completely loyal to Henry Ford, and, like Henry's son, Edsel, sometimes followed orders with which he disagreed.

Before moving to Dearborn, Sorensen played an important role in the development of mass production at the Highland Park Plant. Later, his foundry expertise and innovative use of castings in engine production, plus his brusque manner, earned him the sobriquet, "Cast-Iron Charlie."

"One-piece casting of the Ford V-8 engine block," the Early Ford V-8 Foundation stated in 2004, "probably was

Sorensen's greatest achievement. The impact of the engine was so great that Ford cars equipped with the engine became known simply as V-8s. With improvements, but not major changes," the foundation added, "the engine was manufactured for twenty-one years, two years longer than the Model T was produced."

Sorensen's "crowning achievement," Ford historian Ford R. Bryan wrote in 1993, was the "design of the production layout of the mammoth Willow Run Bomber Plant." Others have cited as Sorensen's greatest accomplishment his role in the development of mass production.

Sorensen had a domineering, almost tyrannical temperament, as illustrated by his treatment of Lincoln Motor Car Company founders, Henry M. Leland, seventy-eight, and his son, Wilfred. When Henry Ford bought failing Lincoln in 1922, he assured the Lelands that they would continue to manage the business. When the Lelands attempted to do so, Sorensen, who was charged with integrating the parent and subsidiary firms, set them straight. "You think of yourselves as exclusive," he informed Wilfred, "[but] you are no different from any other Ford plant." Sorensen's tactless takeover drove the Lelands out of the plant, to Henry Ford's considerable satisfaction.

In 1929 Sorensen was dispatched to the U.S.S.R. to advise the Soviets on vehicle production. Characteristically, he was as blunt as a pile driver. Asked by his hosts to evaluate Leningrad's highly prized Putilov Steel Works, he recommended that the plant be dynamited and rebuilt. While in the U.S.S.R., he arranged for Ford to help build and equip the Gorky Automobile Works and launch the 1932 GAZ, a clone of the Model A.

For decades, Sorensen, like almost all Ford employees, had no official title. In his book he described himself as "a viceroy ruling the production province of the Ford Empire." In 1941 he became a vice president and company director (Sorensen says executive vice president).

After playing a key role in Ford's pre–World War II defense buildup, Sorensen led the massive effort that made the company the nation's largest aircraft-engine manufacturer and the first mass-producer of bombers. His achievements were lauded in the press, and he became, second only to Henry Ford, a symbol of the company's wartime production prowess.

The most flattering of all the articles about Sorensen appeared in *Fortune* in April 1942 and hundreds of newspapers serviced by the Associated Press. *Fortune's* eight-page article, "Sorensen of the Rouge," was subtitled "Besides Making Engines, Tanks, and Guns, He Is Running the Biggest Bomber Factory in the World." He was, the magazine added, "the creator of Willow Run" and "a master of metals." That same year the Associated Press lauded Sorensen as the "manufacturing genius of the Ford Motor Company" and gave him major credit for developing the moving assembly line. Other articles described him as the "general manager" of the Ford Company, a "production genius," or simply "genius." The tributes were capped by newscaster Lowell Thomas, who, addressing Willow Run workers in the presence of Sorensen and Henry Ford, referred to the executive as the "legendary Charles Sorensen."

As Sorensen became a public figure, the press also reported on such matters as his racing yacht and salary—$225,000 in 1942, exceeded by only two Detroiters, Edsel Ford and General Motors's president, Charles E. Wilson.

Sorensen's publicity troubled Henry Ford, who regarded himself as the company's only general manager, genius, and legendary figure. Ford became abrupt and waspish toward his lieutenant, less attentive to his recommendations, and more uncommunicative. Sorensen, his arms pinioned, realized by late 1943 that his days at the Ford Company were numbered. In March 1944, Ford's secretary, Frank Campsall, informed Sorensen that the founder wished him to resign because he had been angling for the company's presidency. Furious, Sorensen instantly quit. Black two-inch headlines, "Henry Ford Fires Sorensen" and "Sorensen Quits Ford," streamed across the front pages of the *Detroit Free Press* and *Detroit Times*, respectively.

On May 7, 1947, a month after Henry Ford's death, Sorensen wrote his son, Clifford, that Henry Ford in 1940 had promised him and his wife a lifelong pension equal to half his salary. At Ford's request, Sorensen stated, the commitment was recorded by the founder's executive secretary, Frank Campsall. "Edsel also knew all about it," he added. But Edsel and Campsall preceded Ford in death, and Sorensen wondered if the document might have been removed from the latter's files and destroyed. He debated whether or not to broach the matter to the law firm having charge of Ford's estate. Knowing that he had "no papers to qualify" his assertions, he dropped the matter. No record of the promise has surfaced.

As Edsel's health deteriorated in 1942 (he died the following year) and Henry Ford's judgment became increasingly suspect, Sorensen looked to twenty-six-year-old Henry Ford II as the company's hope of the future. During the interregnum, he thought of himself as the company's "regent." Although he did not personally mentor Henry Ford II, he countenanced meetings between the Ford scion and his secretary, Russell Gnau, described by HFII as "sort of the Cholly Knickerbocker [a New York gossip columnist] of the Ford Motor Company. . . . By going to his office," he stated, "I'd get caught up on gossip and all that was going on," which included all of Sorensen's important decisions.

After leaving Ford, Sorensen accepted the presidency of Willys-Overland, Inc., of Toledo. But his Ford years were difficult to cast aside. While at Willys he was asked how he felt about leaving Ford. Tapping his chest, he replied, "It hurts here." "I never quite met anything of this sort before," observed Samuel Crowther, Henry Ford's former ghostwriter. "After all these years of almost dog-like service and loyalty, he is trying to find his own soul."

His chagrin notwithstanding, Sorensen vigorously directed Willys's postwar reconversion program. He persuaded a skeptical board of directors to offer a new utility line of civilian vehicles and produced the first civilian jeep only ten days after V-J Day. Clashes with Chairman Ward Cannady led to his resignation as president in 1946. Thanks to a five-year contract, he was named vice chairman, a virtually powerless position, and until retirement in 1950 continued to receive full pay—$220,000 per annum, slightly less than at Ford. Neither Cannady nor Willys-Overland is mentioned in his book.

Summing up Sorensen in 1970, Charles A. Lindbergh, who came to know the executive through his work at the Willow Run Bomber Plant, declared that he "was born for another era . . . he lived in the two-gun days of American industry, and shot it out with the best of them. He was a hard-boiled, hard-fisted fighter and probably would prefer to be known as such."

Conversely, Henry Ford II deprecated Sorensen. "I wouldn't give Sorensen any great kudos for brains," he told me in 1980. "I was never very impressed with his ability in any way . . . as for thinking things through and planning, I'd give him net zero." A grossly unfair assessment, I thought at the time, and still do.

Sorensen's lifelong passion for sailing and fishing began during his Buffalo childhood when he rafted on the Niagara

River. He owned a series of vessels, most notably a sleek 106-foot motor yacht, *Helene*, built for him in 1927. Although furnished with gorgeous wood, gleaming brass, and a large stateroom with a king-size bed, the *Helene* did have one draw-back: the owner and his guests had to walk on an open deck, regardless of weather, to get from the lounge to the dining sa-lon. Today the *Helene*, owned by Shamrock Chartering Company, Grosse Pointe, Michigan, serves as an excursion/cruise boat. Sorensen also had a racing yacht, *White Cloud*, which was well known in southern waters. He served as commodore of the Detroit Yacht Club and had membership in the Grosse Pointe Yacht Club and sailing clubs in Miami Beach and the Bahamas.

In 1927 the Sorensens built a large home at 5185 North Bay Road, Miami Beach, and spent Christmases there. "I can remember Novembers or Decembers walking around the Rouge and seeing Sorensen put his coat collar up," recalled Henry Ford II, "and I knew damn well that he would be going to Florida in a day or so. He loved it there."

The Sorensens resided in a Detroit Towers apartment at 8162 East Jefferson Avenue, Detroit, until 1944, after which they lived in Miami Beach. When visiting their Florida home in 1978, I scratched the following notes: "large and hand-some, red tile roof, attractive entrance door, beautiful hall with marble floor, magnificent living room, lovely dining room. Service entrance. Grounds immaculate in Sorensen era and now; Sorensens loved orchids."

Helen died in her home at age seventy-nine on March 4, 1959. At the time, Sorensen was president of the Miami Heart Institute. His book minimally comments on his married life, his only child, Clifford, born in 1905, and two grandchildren, Charles Mitchell, born in 1937, and Sharon. At the time of Charles M.'s birth, Sorensen was described by the *Detroit Times* as a "very doting grandparent . . . so doting that he can scarcely wait until young Charles is allowed to come out on his yacht, the *Helene.* He feels that the young man will be a fine sailing companion." In 1936 Clifford was described by the *Detroit Times* as "one of the most popular young men in Detroit's fashionable society" and "one of the most eligible bachelors in town." When film star Jean Harlow visited Detroit in 1932, the *Times* added, "she was seen often in Sorensen's company." In 1936, Clifford, then president of a Ford supplier, Continental Die Casting Corporation, Detroit, married the firm's secretary, Irene McLaughlin McGrane, twenty-eight.

Sorensen gave Clifford $20,000 on his twenty-first birthday, and later assisted him in business enterprises, including a Cuban venture. In the late 1940s Clifford was seriously injured in an alcohol-related private-plane crash, which left his face badly scarred. His drinking intensified and eventually damaged his liver. After being divorced, he moved to Florida and was largely supported by his father until his death in 1964.

After Clifford's funeral, Charles M. informed his grandfather that he had gone into debt to fly to Florida for his father's services and that he was surprised to have been billed by the funeral home. He also complained that his grandfather had done too little for Clifford, and that he himself had been persecuted by his grandfather. Offering to pay the funeral bill, the senior Sorensen observed that "your father has been quite a load for me . . . and I have helped him in many ways that you don't know about." "I have no feelings against you," he told Charles M., "so relax and let things take their own course."

Sorensen was offended by his grandchildren's neglect and behavior. Charles M., in and out of a half-dozen prep schools and unresponsive to adult guidance, severely tested the older man's patience. He operated a gas station, dealt craps in Las

Vegas, and worked on charter boats in the Bahamas. Judged incorrigible, he finally was declared persona non grata by the senior Sorensen and his second wife, Edith Thompson Montgomery. Nonetheless, he attended his grandfather's funeral service—and was banished to the church's back row by the widow. "After the service," Charles M. told me in 1980, "I hung around to take a look and see if the SOB was in the casket. He was." Asked to sum up his grandfather, Charles M. replied, "He was pretty damn cheap. He sold a lot of people down the river." Charles M. probably was thinking of himself. He had been led to believe, he said, that his grandfather had deposited $10,000 in a "safety box" for his sister and himself. "I never saw the money," he added.

Sharon was admonished by Edith Sorensen for not acknowledging gifts sent to her by her grandfather and for not informing him in advance of her second marriage in 1966. "Frankly," Mrs. Sorensen wrote, "your grandfather is a bit hurt that you did not let him know ahead of time, so a letter from you would help a lot."

Sorensen's will, dated March 22, 1968, left nothing to Clifford's first wife or his grandchildren. His entire estate, apart from a $10,000 gift to Miami Beach's Community Church, was bequeathed to Edith, whom he married at age seventy-eight (she was sixty-five) in 1960. Edith—Gigi, as she signed her letters—was worth $125 million, according to Charles M., who reckoned his grandfather's estate at $25 million. Neither figure could be more than a guesstimate.

Edith was considerate of her husband's family. Of Cliff, she wrote Sharon, "I was so sorry to hear of Cliff's death. I always liked him so very much and felt so very sorry for him. He tried so truly hard [to improve himself] since I've known him." Of Cliff's second wife, Addy, whom he met in Cuba and who spoke only Spanish, she wrote Sharon, "Charles and

I would like to keep in touch with her for Cliff's sake. Hard as she is to know or understand, she made him happy, and that is what we must remember."

The Sorensens lived in Edith's home on St. Croix, Virgin Islands, from November 1 until May 1, and also maintained a residence at 1525 North View Drive, Sunset Island 1, Miami Beach. They lived the rest of the year in the Washington area (their letters bear Washington and Chevy Chase and Bethesda, Maryland, addresses), and they also visited Cape Cod annually. Edith, who underwent an unsuccessful hip operation in Boston in 1964, was still on crutches in 1967. Even so, that year she and her husband were contemplating a trip to Spain until, as Charles wrote, "We were stopped by that area of the Mediterranean being full of naval vessels and airplanes."

Sorensen, interviewed by *Newsweek* in 1964 in St. Croix, professed to be in "splendid" health. He also observed that he shot his age [eighty-two] in golf and enjoyed driving his three cars—a Ford station wagon, a Lincoln Continental, and a Rolls-Royce. "The Big Three are having a great race," he wistfully remarked. "I wish I were still in it."

In 1967 Sorensen contracted mumps ("just think of it," he wrote his granddaughter), followed by phlebitis in his right leg. "They had it all cleared up in two weeks," he cheerily remarked. "I wish I could see you now and then," he added, "but I don't go to Detroit anymore."

Sorensen's health deteriorated during the last year of his life. "Cobalt treatments have left him limp," his wife wrote Sharon in March 1968. "I've not left your grandfather's side or sight, and I'm getting weary and thin with the tension."

Sorensen died at age eighty-six on August 11, 1968, and was memorialized in Community Church, where he had served as a vestryman. He is buried in Woodlawn Cemetery, Miami. Survivors included brother A. H., two sisters, Mrs.

Ida S. Backoff and Mrs. Ann S. Bardon, and his grandchildren, all then living in the Detroit area.

Sorensen was decorated a Commander of Danneborg by the King of Denmark in 1937, and he was inducted into the Automotive Hall of Fame in 2001, decades after the admittance of others less worthy. He once was thought to have inspired the "generalized foreman figure" in Diego Rivera's massive *Detroit Industry* murals in the Detroit Institute of Arts. In 1999, however, the DIA's Founders Society stated that the portrait of a grim-looking man peering out of the lower left portion of the south wall automotive panel probably is a representation of Mead L. Bricker, a Sorensen subordinate.

A Sorensen farm on the west side of Detroit was bought by the city and converted into Rouge Park, a large recreational area bisected by the Rouge River. For many years the farmhouse served as the office for a mounted police battalion.

In 1978, when I was asked by *Car Collector* to name the ten most important people in Henry Ford's life, it was easy to include Sorensen. Those cited, in the order in which Ford became acquainted with them, were Clara and Edsel Ford, Thomas A. Edison, C. Harold Wills, James Couzens, Sorensen, Ernest Liebold, Evangeline Côté Dahlinger (thought by some to have borne a son by Henry Ford), Harry Bennett, and William J. Cameron.

My Forty Years with Ford has been out of print for years; its original publisher, W. W. Norton & Company, knows not how many. It deserves reprinting for two reasons. One, Sorensen himself was a towering automotive figure. Two, his book offers a very revealing and most interesting portrait of the auto industry's best-known individual, Henry Ford. Serious Ford historians have delved into this book for half a century, and they and Ford-history enthusiasts will continue to do so far into the future.

PART
1

1

"All That I Saw"

WHEN Henry Ford was born, Abraham Lincoln had two more years to live. And about no other two Americans have more words been said, more ink been spilled. One preserved the Union and emancipated the slaves. The other evolved an industrial system which revolutionized American life and work and emancipated workers from backbreaking toil.

Both sprang from the soil, and one had what the other did not possess. One put into simple words the thoughts and aspirations of the plain man. The other sensed aspirations of the plain man and started them on the way to fulfillment. Men like Samuel Crowther, Ford's ghost-writing autobiographer, and W. J. Cameron, his radio mouthpiece, clothed in words what they believed were Henry Ford's thoughts. It was my good fortune to be able, where others couldn't, to translate his mechanical ideas into tangible, visual form. He used to say I could smell what he wanted.

Before I was twenty-four, I pinned my flag on Henry Ford and his "car for the multitude," which was then still a dream. I saw that dream materialize and change the face of America. It was the greatest industrial adventure in history—

from a backyard machine shop to a billion-dollar world-wide enterprise and creation of a magic name. "All *that* I saw, and part of which I was."

Beginning as a $3-a-day patternmaker, I made wooden models of parts which either were discarded or went into the early Ford cars. I shared in the secret preparation of Model T and in the production of 15,000,000 of the same model. My dedication to the use of cast metal instead of forgings, and to economies and short cuts in casting processes, won me from Henry Ford the nickname of "Cast-Iron Charlie." Before I left, thirty-nine years later, I had taken part in the making of 30,000,000 cars.

Six years before we installed it, I experimented with the moving final assembly line which is now the crowning touch of American mass production. Before the eyes of Henry Ford, I worked out on a blackboard the figures that became the basis for his $5 day and the overwhelming proof of the present economic truism that high wages beget lower-priced mass consumption. I laid out assembly plants to be set up both here and abroad; and a few weeks as consultant in Soviet Russia gave me a liberal education in how not to do things and forever erased from my mind the fear that bureaucratic communism can successfully compete with free man.

I had a hand in planning the mammoth River Rouge plant, where iron ore and other steel-making ingredients went in at one end and 10,000 cars a day came out at the other. A quarter century later, a pencil sketch I made in a California hotel room was the beginning of the mile-long Willow Run plant which ultimately turned out one B-24 bomber an hour during World War II.

For about twenty years I was in complete charge of all Ford production. Although by the late 1940's I had become a director of Ford Motor Company and its executive vice-president, it was agreed in the early days of the company that I did not need a title to get things done—better, indeed, that I did not have one. The understanding was that anything to be made would be turned over to me for final engineering drawings and production. One of the mysteries of Ford Motor Company was how I could do so many things that normally would be done by the owner or the head of the business. But no one disputed that authority; Mr. Ford had a saying which everybody in the plant seemed to understand: "Let Charlie do it." And when he was abroad, one of his postcards reached me with merely the address, "Charlie, Ford Motor Co."

During the nearly forty years I worked for Henry Ford, we never had a quarrel. If we disagreed on policy, or anything else, a quiet discussion settled things. I don't recall ever receiving a direct order, "I want this done" or "Do it this way." He got what he wanted by hint or suggestion. He seldom made decisions—in fact, when I brought a matter up for his approval, his usual reply was, "What are we waiting for? Go ahead!" That was his answer when, in the middle of the Great Depression, I showed him plans and small-scale models of a $35,000,000 steel plant I proposed to add to the River Rouge operation.

Although the authority I exercised was not defied, it was frequently a cause for complaint by others in the organization. And when an executive not in accord with my decisions went over my head with his grievance, Mr. Ford would listen patiently, then end the discussion by saying gently, "You go see Charlie about it."

Throughout the years, casualties at the top of the Ford organization were enormous. No one retained Henry Ford's confidence longer than I. None, not even his son Edsel, had or exercised greater authority. I believe there are three main reasons for my long tenure.

One advantage I had over others was that, from my pattern-

making days on, I could sense Henry Ford's ideas and develop them. I didn't try to change them. This was not sub-
servience. We were pioneering; we didn't know whether
a thing was workable until we tried it. So, Mr. Ford never
caught me saying that an idea he had couldn't be done. If
I had the least idea it couldn't, I always knew that the thing
would prove or disprove itself.

When designers were given Mr. Ford's ideas to execute,
the usual result was incorporation of some of their ideas, too.
But it was part of my patternmaking training to follow
through with what was given me. I suppose that was why Mr.
Ford turned to me. I started with him when he had no more
security in his job than I had in mine. He had nothing but
one single-purposed idea: a low-cost car in large quantities.
I helped make it. I helped make him; he made me. He gave
me a chance to make my own way, to see the world, to
mingle with the world's great, and to have a hand in working
up the miracle of American mass production that I probably
never would have had otherwise.

No two men could have been more unlike than Mr. Ford
and I. We had little in common, yet I never saw two other
men in any business anywhere who were so close to each
other as we were—in fact, we had a business relationship
closer than even his family had with him, and in many ways
I knew him better than did members of his family. It was
useless to try to understand Henry Ford. One had to *sense*
him.

Another reason for my long tenure was that I minded my
own business. Production—whether it was automobiles, tractors, aviation motors, or B-24 bombers—its planning, installation and supervision was a seven-days-a-week job. I had no
time for the outside interests of Henry Ford which arose as
he grew older. Labor matters were not in my province. I took

no part in his crusades like the World War I Peace Ship to "get the boys out of the trenches by Christmas." I was not involved in his miscast and fortunately unsuccessful candidacy for United States senator. I did not share his racial prejudices or his diet fads, except that by preference I am a teetotaler and nonsmoker. I might scour the country for automobile parts but not for antiques for Greenfield Village. He gave up trying to make a square dancer out of me.

By sticking to my job of production and not mixing in outside affairs, the white light of publicity fortunately did not beat down upon me until World War II, when I had been with Mr. Ford for more than thirty-five years. I avoided headlines by preference. My work, the ever-increasing dependence of Henry and Edsel Ford upon me, and the free hand they gave me in my chosen field of production were then and still are satisfactions far greater and more lasting than headlines and scrapbooks of news clippings.

But these conditions ultimately created another sort of publicity. My avoidance of the limelight made me somewhat of a legendary character at Ford. The myths about me, who remained in the background, were as fantastic as those about Henry Ford, who occupied the foreground.

Someone was always spreading stories about how hard and tough I was. There were yarns that I took sledge hammers and axes to desks of supervisors who had grown too big for their britches, that armed with crowbars three of us wrecked desks and computing machines of a useless statistical department. One story with more lives than a cat is that I kicked a box from under a sitting Detroit Edison repairman, believing him to be a Ford employee who should be standing up at his work, and that the Edison man got up and knocked me flat. For more than ten years I have had a standing offer of $1,000 to anyone able to prove that story true. Another $1,000 offer holds good for anyone able to prove that Harry Bennett, Ford's superpoliceman and pistol-packing errand boy, got Henry Ford to fire me in 1944. My money is safe; neither $1,000 offer will ever be claimed successfully.

Considering the fact that not all the people working at Ford were perfect little gentlemen who remembered their Sunday-school lessons, the truth is probably stranger than all the hard-bitten fiction about me. The truth is that during my thirty-nine years with Ford Motor Company I never laid hands upon a soul, no one ever laid a hand on me, and I never smashed a desk in my life. As for my departure from Ford Motor Company, I said to Henry Ford on January 14, 1944, "I'm leaving for Florida tomorrow, and I'm not coming back." Why I said this and why I did it are part of the story I shall tell.

My story is about the Henry Ford I knew better than any man alive or dead knew him. It is about the fabulous growth and preservation of Ford Motor Company, which, in his shaken old age, not even its owner could destroy. It is about the creation and birth in that company of what has been the miracle of the twentieth century: the modern American industrial system of mass production with its moving assembly line. It is not the story of Charles Sorensen. It is, however, the story of what I, Charles Sorensen, was privileged to see of Henry Ford and his works, and of what part I had in them. It is a story of Mr. Ford's greatest success and of his most tragic failure.

Henry Ford once said that "history is more or less bunk." Certainly that is true of much of what I have read about Ford and the Ford Motor Company. Some of it rivals the weirdest of fiction and the wildest imaginings of the comic books.

Many a write-up of Henry Ford was made after a few sessions with him under the watchful eye of his publicity staff, which then released further "desirable" material. He was both the victim and the beneficiary of this situation. He approved of the familiar saying that the best kind of publicity is the kind one gets for nothing; he played this up to the limit and he enjoyed it immensely. Such publicity had its effect upon him until it completely changed his character.

Various "interpretive" Ford biographies and write-ups remind me of the ancient fable of the description of an elephant given by four blind men. One ran his hands along the beast's side and said, "An elephant is like a wall." Another put his arms around the elephant's legs and said, "No, he is like a tree trunk." A third felt of his tail and said, "He is like a rope." The fourth blind man grasped the trunk and announced, "An elephant is like a snake."

In this story, I attempt neither interpretation nor speculation. I rely upon no recollections other than my own, and in many instances events as I narrate them differ from generally accepted versions. I do not intend to refute or take issue with those versions. My aim is not controversy but merely to set down the facts as I know them. It is true that after the lapse of years memory may be at fault; and psychologists and court trial lawyers tell us that even eyewitness accounts of the same happening vary widely. My own memory, however, is supported by diary entries I made at the time and by the complete and accurate chronology covering all phases of Ford Motor Company activity compiled by the able staff of the company's archives.

The Ford Motor Company archives consist of nearly a mile of boxed records and some five million words of reminiscence by Ford associates. They are housed in Fair Lane, the limestone home which Henry Ford had built in 1915 on the banks of the River Rouge at Dearborn. Here Ford roamed when a boy and continued to do so until, at Fair Lane, he died the night of April 7, 1947. A few days earlier, the Rouge had overflowed and put Fair Lane's powerhouse out of commission. That night, an emergency power plant short-circuited, and all electric lights went out in the house. A short time later, the man who had done so much to mechanize the world's work died as he had entered the world eighty-three years earlier, by the light of an oil lamp and a few candles.

2

What Was Henry Ford *Really* Like?

HE was unorthodox in thought but puritanical in personal conduct.

He had a restless mind but was capable of prolonged, concentrated work.

He hated indolence but had to be confronted by a challenging problem before his interest was aroused.

He was contemptuous of money-making, of money-makers and profit seekers, yet he made more money and greater profits than those he despised.

He defied accepted economic principles, yet he is the foremost exemplar of American free enterprise.

He abhorred ostentation and display, yet he reveled in the spotlight of publicity.

He was ruthless in getting his own way, yet he had a deep sense of public responsibility.

He demanded efficient production, yet made place in his plant for the physically handicapped, reformed criminals, and human misfits in the American industrial system.

He couldn't read a blueprint, yet had greater mechanical ability than those who could.

He would have gone nowhere without his associates, we did the work while he took the bows, yet none of us would have gone far without him.

He has been described as complex, contradictory, a dreamer, a grown-up boy, an intuitive genius, a dictator, yet essentially he was a very simple man.

He lived a life so secluded that few ever saw him in his own home. I know of only two members of the Ford staff who ever spent a night with the Fords. One was our English manager, the present Lord Perry. I was the other. On their first trip abroad, the Henry Fords visited the Perrys and traveled over England with them. Mrs. Ford became very fond of Lady Perry, and the two corresponded for years. When the Perrys came to Detroit they stayed with the Fords, first at their home on Edison Avenue in Detroit and later at Fair Lane in Dearborn.

Sometimes a boyhood friend or two would see him at his office, but I never knew him to look them up. His closest friend when a boy was his neighbor and schoolmate Edsel Ruddiman, for whom Henry and Clara Ford named their only son. Ruddiman went on to college, became a distinguished organic chemist, and later with his son Stanley joined Ford Motor Company to carry on soybean experimentation, in which they minded their own business without any pretense of Henry Ford's sponsoring them.

I knew all of Henry Ford's immediate family except his father, who died a few months before I joined the company. His sister Margaret married Edsel Ruddiman's brother John. I knew his two brothers William and John but never saw them in his home. They hated him, either because they envied him or because they expected him to do more for them. But Henry Ford's philosophy of "help others to help themselves" applied to his family as well as to all who sought his help, and he warned me not to do his relatives any favors. Two brothers-in-law had Ford agencies but were not allowed to use his name in any way to build up their prestige in the sales department. I, too, lived up to this philosophy. No one related to me ever sought or gained favors in the Ford organization.

I was astonished how poor Henry Ford was at spelling. I never saw him write or dictate a letter. His secretaries, Ernest G. Liebold and Frank Campsall, prepared replies to communications which he had not even read. I have seen Liebold hold letters that had to be answered on his desk for days before he could catch Mr. Ford and read them to him. Ford didn't sign a letter very often—even left that to his secretaries. He did enjoy autographing books and souvenir cards and he would hand out a signed photograph to anyone who asked for it. He signed his name in the Spencerian handwriting he acquired in a Detroit night school business course.

As a farm boy, he had no chance to go beyond the rural school, where reading and writing and arithmetic in simplest form were all a pupil could get. Even at that, he passed up much education that such a school could have offered. He was not too serious about his schooling; tinkering with watches and with machinery around the farm appealed to him more.

In engineering work in the drafting room, it was plain to the men to whom he gave his work that he could not make a sketch or read a blueprint. It was to his everlasting credit that, with his limited formal education, his mind worked like a modern electronic calculating machine and he had the answer to what he wanted. The trick was to fathom the device or machine part that was on his mind and make the object for him to look at. That was where I came in.

Although he neglected his education as a boy, the business he developed taught him much. "What I don't know," he used to say to me, "I can always hire someone to show me how to do. In that way I learn more than if I tried to do it myself."

Of course, he met and had contact with the foremost writers, educators, scientists, and statesmen. They visited him and talked with him, and he loved it. Experience was his school. I wonder whether anyone ever got more.

Nevertheless, he saw to it that the youngsters around him got the good practical education that he had neglected in his schooldays. In Greenfield Village he established a school for children of Ford employees living in Dearborn. They were started in early grades as in public schools; later the girls took up domestic science and the boys were given mechanical training. He believed this was enough for the great majority of young people. The rest was up to them and their ambitions. As for college, that was up to the individual.

Nothing about him indicated he was the richest man in the country, and world famous. He dressed simply and shaved himself every morning with an old-fashioned straight razor. An old barber in Dearborn to whom he had gone when he was a boy cut his hair. He wore very thin, light-soled oxfords which always looked the worse for wear. He could read without glasses until he was seventy-five. Social life and a lot of people around him had no appeal. He liked to be alone with Mrs. Ford.

Henry and Clara Ford were as close-knit and devoted a married couple as I have ever seen. She was ever loyal and ambitious for her husband. Though she appeared not in the best of health, she was always cheerful and bright and gave him the encouragement he needed. All her married life she was Henry Ford's balance wheel. When he would listen to no one else, he listened to her, partly because she didn't exert her influence so often that he got used to it but more so because he relied on her judgment. She had strong opinions about some of his associates. The roistering Dodge brothers were particular objects of her displeasure, and she thought James Couzens failed to appreciate her husband's efforts. She was what Henry Ford needed. She watched his health carefully, was always convinced that he worked too hard, and occasionally was able to get him away for a rest.

From the early days on I saw the Henry Fords often. When Mr. Ford left with me on trips to see suppliers or to test new cars, he always stopped at his home for a few minutes to see his wife. During the struggling days of the Ford Motor Company my wife and I saw much of Mr. and Mrs. Ford. Our houses were not far apart and in neither were there any servants. Everything was work to us. Holidays we knew nothing about. Sundays Henry Ford and I used principally for making long test drives.

Throughout all his early penny-pinching years, Ford never yielded to any temptation he might have had to sell the farm at Dearborn his father, William Ford, gave him when he was married and upon which he built a comfortable square house. On Sundays we used to run test cars out there, where we made any necessary adjustments or repairs. Gradually, however, Mr. Ford began taking his wife to the Dearborn farm for weekends, and I brought my wife and small son out on Sundays. We brought our own lunches and sat on the lawn and "visited." And when Henry Ford and I talked shop Mrs. Ford would perk up and direct a little friendly sarcasm at us for our seriousness.

Mrs. Ford's early married life was not easy. Shifting from one home to another, she and Henry just got by with their small income. Every penny they had to spare went for Henry Ford's experimental work. That was before I knew her. She told my wife about her struggles to make ends meet—the typical story of hard-working, ambitious young Americans. My wife and I followed the same pattern. A start with nothing makes good citizens.

As the years went on, Mrs. Ford had her garden club, the Ford hospital, and other charities, but she could not tie her husband in on any of them. He avoided these activities and made fun of them when his wife talked about them. By the time the Fords went to England after World War I, Henry Ford had become an international character. Perry, by then Sir Percival, showed them around. They met King George and Queen Mary, Lady Astor, Winston Churchill, and other leading Britishers. At one party Lady Astor noticed a pearl necklace Mrs. Ford was wearing. It is reported that she fingered it and asked, "Is that the best Mr. Ford can do for you? Why don't you make him give you a real one?"

Although Mrs. Ford never did have a desire to show off with jewels, I believe that trip went a little to her head. Her husband also noticed it and I heard him set her down rather sharply at times over some of her social aspirations. Ford had no fondness for society. If he went to any social affair it was because Mrs. Ford almost dragged him there. Afterwards he would tell me how So-and-so "made me sick" by playing up to him. He was certain that people who paid him these attentions did so because they wanted something.

Mrs. Ford had about the same education as her husband, yet she was a reader of good books. I never saw Ford with a book in his hand, but his wife used to read to him on the porch at Fair Lane, overlooking the River Rouge. Here they took their meals when they were alone, and this was where I usually found them when I got a call to come to the house. Just outside the porch was one of the bird-feeding stations that were scattered over the estate, and during bird seasons it would be some time before Henry Ford could get away from that subject to talk with me about other matters. The Fords would check the birds, their varieties and comings and goings, from pictures on the backs of small handbooks which Mr. Ford used to autograph and hand out to children. I still carry one of those books with me in my bag.

On Fair Lane's grounds was a deer park so laid out that the creatures could come near the house. When the deer occasionally got out of the enclosure, my place a mile and a half away had some strange attraction. They would cross the lawn and lie on the open terrace in front of our house; and when they got in our vegetable gardens, I was not too fond of them.

Fair Lane's downstairs porch was the most cheerful room in that big barn of a house. It and the bedroom and sleeping porch just above on the second floor were the Fords' favorite rooms. When Henry Ford was ill, I would visit him upstairs. The sleeping quarters did not impress me as being too well furnished. The bed was old and rickety and Mr. Ford sank way down in the mattress. I often told him I had a better bed at home, and as often he said he was going to do something about it, but he never did.

The Fords never seemed quite at home at Fair Lane. It was built in 1915 with swimming pool, game room, bowling alley, and billiard room designed for their son Edsel. But Edsel married within a year and set up his own establishment elsewhere, and thereafter the Fords did so little entertaining that few outsiders ever saw the place. It used to give me the creeps to go there.

Henry Ford was healthy, but not robust. He was wiry, slight of build, and his nervous energy was apparent to all who knew him. He was always complaining about his stomach and was forever trying different diets—nuts, raw vegetables, and milk from soybeans. He did not drink or smoke, and his prejudice against those who did was so violent that it affected his judgment of their abilities. I often wondered how he could live on the little food he ate. In all the years I knew him, he never weighed more than 148 pounds, but for a man who appeared almost frail, he had remarkable endurance. I walked the woods in upper Michigan and followed tractors on foot with him in the heat of summer days. On foot, he was tireless. He could run like a deer. Often when I was on a trip with him he would have the car stopped and say, "Let's take a run." He always won easily—even, when he was seventy, over active men half his age.

In later years when he was ill I saw him at home or in Ford Hospital. He might stay in bed for a couple of days, then defy the doctors and get up and walk. When he was operated on for a hernia, his appendix was removed at the same time, and he shocked nurses and doctors by getting out of bed the second day.

Simply by intuition, he had anticipated the modern surgical practice that gets patients up and walking around within a day or two. Probably he irritated M.D.'s most by taking up with a chiropractor, a Dr. Coulter, who had a way with Henry Ford. He would explain his treatments not in medical or physical words but in automobile terms: "adjust the carburetor . . . align the chassis." Ford loved it, recommended Coulter to his associates, and threatened Ford Hospital doctors with attaching the chiropractor to that institution. When his son Edsel was dying of cancer, he wanted Coulter to treat him.

While I, as I have said, knew Henry Ford better than did any other person now alive or dead, he never had a close, intimate friend. His annual camping trip with Thomas Edison, Harvey Firestone, and John Burroughs was a case in point. With squads of newswriters and platoons of cameramen to report and film the posed nature studies of the four eminent campers, these well-equipped excursions into readily accessible solitudes were as private and secluded as a Hollywood opening, and Ford appreciated the publicity. He admired Edison, who was a busy, retiring person like himself, and he was ever grateful for Edison's encouragement when as a young man he was experimenting with a gasoline motor. When they were together, they had much in common; but aside from this annual camp get-together and an occasional Edison visit to Detroit and Dearborn they seldom saw each other.

With Harvey Firestone, the relationship was of business origin. Firestone admired Ford and clung to him for obvious reasons. Since he was one of our large suppliers of tires, I saw much of him. He did a splendid job for Ford Motor Company and sought Ford's advice on future plans. But their relations were strictly business. In that way I believe I saw more of Firestone than Ford did.

Although Ford and John Burroughs had a common interest in birds, the naturalist was primarily Edison's friend. Henry Ford saw Burroughs only on the annual well-publicized camping trips.

After Ford started Greenfield Village and the Museum at Dearborn, he seldom came to the Rouge plant. I would lunch with him at the roundtable at the Dearborn Engineering Laboratories, where he had an office. I sat on his left; Edsel was on his right. Business talk was taboo. Occasionally there were guests and interesting talk, but after lunch was over it was the almost invariable custom to walk through the big room in the engineering department. If Ford had a problem and some engineer like Farkas, Zoerlein, or Smith was working on it, he would stop for a look-see and a chat.

In his later years he actually put more hard work into the Museum than he did into the Ford Motor Company. The Museum was to be his monument—a cross section of American industry, beginning with early times, and a visible, authentic record with tools and machinery of all arts of manufacturing originating in the United States. He loved this Greenfield Museum.

Many a writer has noted "contradiction" in the interest of

Ford, the apostle of machine production, in the old hand-crafts. I never could see this as a contradiction, but rather as another indication of balance and sense of proportion.

While building Greenfield Village, and seeking antiques to display in his museum, he became interested in the dress and costumes of Early America. He organized an orchestra and in 1925 hired the famous dancing teachers, Mr. and Mrs. Benjamin Lovett, to teach the old-fashioned dancing so that he could give parties and dress up in the fine old costumes he had collected. He searched the country for the music that had been played in the early days.

There was another angle to it—he saw that it was a good source for publicity. With his old fiddlers and old costumes came a new source of publicity to keep the name of Henry Ford in the spotlight.

He organized dancing classes in the schools around Dearborn. He had books printed with the music and calls for the old-fashioned dances. He bought an old tavern, Botsford Inn, on Grand River Avenue, a former toll gate and gathering place for herders when they drove their cattle into the Detroit markets. He restored it to its original state, with an upper room that had a 30 x 50 foot dance floor. The floor had a spring to it which he claimed was especially designed for the old-fashioned circular dances.

I soon tired of these dances. I was working hard and putting in long hours, so I began staying away. At first, he never failed to remark on my absence. Invitations were sent out by Campsall, his secretary. I always sent a note of regret when I knew I would not be attending, so he stopped reminding me when I did not come.

Mrs. Ford was bored with the parties. He tried to liven them up by asking Edsel's friends to come; the Grosse Pointe group came and he started them off as a class. A few took a real interest, but when some of them suggested addition of modern dancing, he brushed them off, so in time that crowd broke up.

He had a room in the Engineering plant fitted up for his dancing parties. Every day the orchestra came there to practice and work with Mr. and Mrs. Lovett. Every day after lunch Ford dropped in for a few steps with Mrs. Lovett. Some days he would have a class of young children from around Dearborn. It was just the place to take some of his friends of the press.

Mr. Lovett complained to me that Henry Ford never quite caught the rhythm of dance music. The dance seemed a mechanical thing to him. He had his choice of partners who could help him keep time and when he had a partner who did not dance better than he did he soon got rid of her.

Mr. Lovett knew just what dance to put on for certain partners. It was a well-managed affair, but I suspect the Lovetts got a few gray hairs in the process.

Mr. Ford was more benevolent than charitable. Although Ford Motor Company contributed to local charities, Edsel was behind that. Henry Ford took no interest in Community Chest drives or various national drives for special funds. He was interested in families and individuals—in cases in which he could encourage people to avoid or throw off poverty. The individual cases came to him through the Ford Motor Company's employment office or short-lived sociological department and sometimes he read about a case in the newspapers.

In the country near his farms he would find families in need. It might be a widow with children or a family where the husband was ill. When he found such cases he would lend aid directly. If there was a boy or girl old enough to go to work, he would arrange for the child to be paid as much in the plant as was the head of the family. Medical aid would be added if necessary.

While doing this, he observed how the family members

reacted to his help. He expected them to improve their ways of living. He did not call this charity. He did not like the word. He thought organized charity was too bureaucratic. He was never satisfied that charity could be doled out by system or that happiness and peace of mind could be bought. He preferred his own way.

One day on his way to Highland Park plant he saw a worn old man, a typical tramp, walking along the road. Ford stopped his car. "Where are you going?" he asked.

"Detroit," said the man.

"Do you have a job?"

"No."

"Well, what are you going to do?"

"I'm going out to see that fellow Ford and see if he will give me a job."

"What kind of a job?"

He didn't know. He would do anything. Ford invited him to ride into Detroit, then brought him to Highland Park and my office. "Charlie," he said, "I found this man looking for work. He looks like a good man. What can we give him to do?"

I talked to the man and learned he had done common labor work all his life. We could use him so we settled on what he would do. I learned that he had been all over the country, walking and riding freight cars. He had no dependents. Henry Ford talked to him about settling down and staying with us. The most he would say was, "Well, we'll see."

I suspected that he would not stay long. I had one of our employment office men come to my office and write him up for his employment record. Henry Ford gave him $10, and the man left us for his new job.

Ford asked me not to lose sight of the man for a while and to help him along. After he went to work in our paint shop, Mr. Ford looked in on him. He would shake hands with him and tell him he would be getting a raise soon. On his tool crib record and in the employment department I had a note reading, "If this man leaves his job, contact me before paying him off."

I gathered from his foreman that he was uneasy and would soon be moving on. After about six weeks he was through, and I got a call that he was being held for me to decide what to do.

It so happened Henry Ford was with me when I got word. We went to the office where the man was yelling his head off because of a delay in paying him off. When he saw Ford, he sailed into him saying, "I want to get out of this jail." I don't believe that even then he was sure it was the real Henry Ford who had picked him up.

3

Henry Ford's Man

Henry Ford was no mystic or genius. He was a responsible person with determination to do his work as he believed it should be done. This sense of responsibility was one of his strongest traits.

I often tried to persuade Mr. Ford to diversify his business; get into the food-producing field, because he liked farming, or take up something like Sears, Roebuck or Marshall Field. He would have nothing to do with the idea. "I don't want any more business," he said.

I also tried to get him to expand the auto field. I felt we could build a near monopoly. "Let us shoot at seventy-five per cent of market requirements," I urged.

"I don't want any more than thirty per cent," he replied.

How right he was! If Ford Motor Company had seventy-five per cent of the auto business today, it would be prosecuted as a monopoly. He actually welcomed the competition that was looming before us, though in later years he had suspicion amounting to hallucination that bankers and General Motors were out to ruin him.

This ability to sense signs of the times and to counteract forces that showed danger signals was almost uncanny. I would go to him with problems that looked insurmountable. Nothing appeared to frighten him. In the early days of the New Deal he was threatened with all sorts of government reprisal for defying the National Industrial Recovery Act, that the government would take over his company if he didn't sign up and display the Blue Eagle. He replied, "Go ahead. The government will then be in the automobile business. Let's see if they can manage it better than I can."

That stopped General "Iron Pants" Johnson and President Roosevelt.

There is no doubt that Henry Ford had courage. Probably he will never be glorified for his Peace Ship excursion; but no one can tell me it didn't take courage to undertake it. It took courage, too, to fight the Selden patent, to hold to his fixed idea of a cheap car, to battle dividend-hungry boards of directors, to build River Rouge plant in the face of stockholder opposition.

By nature he was a happy person. Despite his lack of close friends and the aloof life he lived, he enjoyed being with a group of his men developing some project. Up until his old age he delighted in practical jokes. Back in days when we were designing Model T, we set up a target range for 22-caliber rifles on the third floor of the Piquette Avenue plant, and Henry Ford used to join us Sunday mornings for shooting matches. We kept our rifles in a cabinet which I built in the drafting room. Sometime during one week Ford opened the cabinet and changed the sights on my rifle so that when I aimed at the target the bullet went galley west. It took me some time to realize what was wrong, but after I figured it out and we had our laugh, I readjusted my sights to accuracy by clamping the rifle in a vise, then firing it and setting the sights to bear on the bullet hole.

After World War I, and during our strange adventure in the railway business with the rust-streaked Detroit, Toledo

& Ironton Railroad, Mr. Ford pulled a monumental hoax on me. While we were on an inspection trip, I received a telegram stating that our tractor plant at Dearborn was on fire and about to burn to the ground. I was wild. I wanted the train stopped so that I might hire a car and drive to the disaster; but before I had bitten my nails down to the quick, Bill Cowling, D.T. & I.'s traffic manager, confessed that Henry Ford had put him up to sending the wire.

On a later trip Ford tripped Cowling on the same trick. On the outskirts of Springfield, Ohio, our train was flagged, and Cowling was told of a big wreck down near Ironton, our southern terminus. He, too, went wild and burned up the wires ordering all available wrecking equipment to the scene. Nearly two hours later we arrived: we found no wreck, only a convention-on-wheels of cranes and some angry crews blowing off as much steam as was coming from open safety valves of the wrecking train locomotives. Ford had had me fix up the wire to Cowling, who had a hard time living that one down.

This manifestation of slip-on-the-banana-peel humor had a more unpleasant side when Ford used to pretend in all innocence not to know why I had fired a man he had told me to fire. It parallels in a small way, but is only partially accountable for, his long-time habit of stirring up associates to see their reactions under stress. His lasting accomplishments were achieved when facing down opposition, such as when his directors opposed the Model T idea. When that opposition had been overcome and he ruled an industrial empire, other interests and projects shared his attention.

New things stimulated him. If a suggestion appealed to him, he first showed it in a quick flash of his eyes and an approving smile. I saw the same characteristic reaction in Henry Ford II. As soon as Mr. Ford saw an idea developed and at work, it was out of date. He never ran out of ideas. In his prime he was loaded with them, and it was impossible to keep up with him unless one had vision and initiative enough to anticipate them and stay ahead of him. Like all men in his position, he was pestered by inventors and cranks, all with ideas they wanted him to look at. His answer to most of them was, "I can't do it. I have so many ideas of my own that I can't keep up with them; so how can I devote time to yours?"

Constant ferment—keep things stirred up and other people guessing—was the elder Ford's working formula for progress. Initially, that lay behind his putting Harry Bennett on Edsel's neck, but what began with occasional harassment became a habit with Bennett, who in so doing drove a wider wedge between father and son. Henry Ford's greatest failure was in expecting Edsel to be like him. Edsel's greatest victory, despite all obstacles, was in being *himself*. I saw all this, but it is a story I must relate later because it needs greater detail and the background of events.

He was so much of an individualist that no one ever really knew him.

The most frequent question I've been asked about Henry Ford is "Was he modest?" According to Webster, modesty means decent reserve and propriety, a humble estimate of oneself in comparison with others, shyness and a sensitive shrinking from anything indelicate.

No, Henry Ford was not modest. He did a lot for people he liked, but he didn't want his staff to be in the public eye. No one else in the organization could stand out and above him. He pretended to be humble when with people who did not know him. But I knew this was an act. He never could be humble when around us. When I saw both sides of him, I knew that he lacked modesty.

He sought publicity. There was nothing shy about him in that. Shyness is a tendency to shrink from observation. He wanted to be observed. Henry Ford and Arthur Brisbane of the Hearst newspapers were friendly. Brisbane had a farm and was greatly interested in the tractors we were making. He wrote up our plant and experimental farm at Dearborn but neglected to play up Henry Ford, and he learned from the Detroit office of the Hearst papers that he had offended him. I told him that Henry Ford did not want his staff to receive publicity. It was dangerous for anyone to get newspaper notice. I was not exaggerating. After the name of Henry Ford became a household word, men in Ford Motor Company who might temporarily get more publicity than he did aroused his jealousy. One by one they were purged, a process familiar in personal dictatorships.

I was with Brisbane and Henry Ford one day following a tractor on the farm. Brisbane was particularly nice to me, asking me many questions, and he could ask plenty. And I was able to answer most of them. Suddenly the atmosphere got very chilly. I sensed the reason and abruptly left for the plant.

Brisbane later asked me about the incident. I reminded him of what I had told him previously. "Do you mean to tell me," he asked, "that Henry Ford resents my showing interest in you? Is he jealous?"

I laughed his question off, but he understood. My ability to keep out of the public eye was one reason why I stayed as long as I did at Ford while others left.

For a while Mr. Ford toyed with politics. At President Wilson's suggestion he ran against Truman Newberry in 1918 for United States senator from Michigan. He lost in a viciously corrupt campaign against him. He made no campaign at all. In the middle 1920's there was talk of drafting him for president. The late B. C. Forbes, founder of *Forbes Magazine*, visited Dearborn and had lunch with us at the roundtable. He said that with all the then current talk about

Henry Ford and the Presidency he wished to see the man and his organization.

"If you should be elected, Mr. Ford," he said, "whom would you choose for a Cabinet?"

I'm sure such a thought had never entered Ford's mind, but he had a quick reply. He turned to me and said, "Charlie here will be secretary of war."

I thought this a ridiculous answer and tried to pass it off. Forbes could see that I resented it but he picked on me with a lot of questions. Knowing what the result would be should I answer them, I walked out on him.

Had Mr. Ford been drafted for president, I know he would have gone along, but I would have hated to see him in the White House. He would not have lived through one term.

He could not make a speech. His few attempts to talk to a group of people were pitiful. Once on a visit with him to the Oliver Plow Company at South Bend we stumbled in on a sales meeting by mistake. The plow salesmen recognized him and Mr. Weed, the Oliver sales manager, asked him to say a few words. In introducing him Weed mentioned Ford as a presidential possibility. Mr. Ford didn't say more than a dozen words. He was so confused, no one could understand him. He turned to me, mumbled something, and walked out of the room.

Ford was frank enough about his inability to make a speech. He swore he would never be caught like that again. "I can hire someone to talk for me that knows how," he told me. "That talking thing is a gift. I'm glad I never acquired it and I'll never try again."

Nor would he listen to speakers on the radio. In the fall of 1938 came the meeting of the British Prime Minister Neville Chamberlain with Adolf Hitler at Munich. Upon his return Chamberlain spoke by radio—"Peace in Our Time." The world was eager to get his report on that memorable meeting, and we had a radio on the table at lunchtime to hear him. In the middle of the broadcast Henry Ford got up. I saw what was coming, so reached over and snapped off the radio, but he left the table and went straight home.

Next morning he asked, "Who put the radio in the dining room yesterday?"

I knew it was Edsel, so I said, "I did. But it's gone now, so please forget about it."

Henry Ford tried hard to persuade people that he was sincere. He was always on the lookout for something that would bring him to public notice. There were good intentions behind such sensational efforts as the Peace Ship, the $5 day, and sociological work among Ford employees, but they were overshadowed by his use of them to gain publicity.

He enjoyed all this publicity. Shortly after the $5 day announcement, critics denounced it as unsound and selfish. I chided him for the way he was playing this up. "Don't," I said, "destroy a good deed by talking about it."

"I don't care what anybody says," he replied, "so long as they talk about Ford."

"You can't be more than one hundred per cent good," I went on. "When you come through with a new idea, you will still be tops even if you're only seventy-five per cent. But if you continue to pose as being one hundred per cent on your good deeds, you'll be rated as a hypocrite."

I remember how Mr. Ford flashed back at me: "Since when have you become a preacher, Charlie?"

In criticizing him for this attitude, I went further than I ever had before. I told him that the public was beginning to believe that he was not sincere, that he was blowing his own horn too much, and that he was getting publicity for himself and not for his product or the organization behind it.

I am just as certain he didn't know what I was talking

about as I am sure that he never understood the meaning of sincerity. He could change his views on most things overnight. He told me one afternoon in 1941 that he wouldn't sign a contract with the CIO and ordered me to close down the plant; the next morning I heard over the radio that he had yielded and given the CIO more than it had asked for. Behind this sudden move was, as I shall reveal later, the biggest domestic crisis of his married life.

With the obvious exception of his single-purpose goal of a cheap car for the masses, a set policy was next to impossible with him. It was impossible because by nature he was an experimenter. This was one reason for the big turnover in his executive staff over the years. Old Detroiters will recall the speculation and stories about how and why top Ford officials left, and I doubt that they ever got the facts.

The official himself rarely knew just why he was out. Ford never explained. The insincerity about the whole business was that the man might feel that Henry Ford was his best friend and that everything was going along fine. Ford might tell him to pick out a car for himself, raise him up among the clouds; then when the man got into difficulties, he would be dropped overnight, but not by Henry Ford. If he wanted someone to resign, he didn't speak to the man. It was "Let Charlie do it." No one who saw this process working ever heard me pass the blame to Henry Ford. I assumed full responsibility.

When he wanted to size up a man quickly he loaded him with power. If the man took the least advantage of his new position he got some kind of warning, not from Henry Ford but from the least expected quarter. How he accepted the warning was what Henry Ford was watching. If he went to Ford to see if the warning was really coming from him, he would be encouraged to disregard everything. That would throw him off completely, but in a few days he was out, completely mystified over what had really happened. That was the way Bill Knudsen left the Ford organization, and probably he never knew why to his dying day.

Wills, Couzens, Flanders, and John Dodge were beyond the test. They all soon sensed that I could get along with Henry Ford. I got all the warnings from them. The pattern I have referred to was the same but soon I was being called Henry Ford's "man."

John Dodge stopped me one day in the Detroit Athletic Club and wanted to buy me a drink. I told him, "Sorry, I don't touch the stuff."

His quick comeback was, "What is the matter with you? Won't Henry let you take a drink?"

I used to deal with him on the parts Dodge Brothers made for Ford Motor Company. I would see him about parts that on inspection were rejected for faulty workmanship. Then the same defective parts would come back to us in the next lot. When I showed him a stamp we had put on these rejected parts, John Dodge professed not to know about them. Once they had been back six times and I had records to prove it. Dodge sailed into me and threatened to have me thrown out of Ford Motor Company.

"Go ahead and try it," I challenged. I hoped he would, for I was pretty sure that whatever he said about me to Henry Ford would help me. I told him I would stop payment at once and that we would get ready to make the parts ourselves. Within the next few days our people actually made some of the parts, better and for a lot less than Dodge prices. John got that news when he went to Couzens and Henry Ford about me.

I continued to call on him, but there was always a battle over whatever I brought to his attention. One Monday morning I was at the Dodge shop early. A secretary asked me into the office, saying that Mr. Dodge would be in any minute. I noticed a man sitting in the lobby when I went in. A few minutes later I heard a wrangle outside. The man stepped up to John Dodge as he was coming in and said, "You are the one who struck my horse and wagon yesterday with your automobile. You smashed up my wagon and I want you to pay for the damage you have done."

I heard John Dodge reply, "So you are the fellow who got in my way!" He hauled back, and slapped the man hard across the face, then threw him out the door. The previous afternoon Dodge had docked his boat after having a good time up the river, then climbed into his six-cylinder Model K Ford and went tearing down Jefferson Avenue. This fellow got in his way, and the climax of the incident I heard. John was ready for me when he found me waiting. And, I may say, I was ready for him.

I was always ready to tell him where he wrong. That is about all I ever had to tell him, so I wondered why he never tackled me and how I managed to get along with him.

After he got out of Ford Motor Company we were still good friends. I saw a lot of him, but he never had any love for Henry Ford, even when he got $12,000,000 for his Ford stock. It was incidents like these that helped give me the name of being Henry Ford's "man."

I learned not to take advantage of Mr. Ford or of his generosity. I could sense what he wanted and I did not need to be told what to do. Rumors and advice from outsiders didn't disturb me. Having joined Ford Motor Company in its formative period, I had an advantage.

Sometimes Mrs. Ford would ask me about a man who had left us. She never really figured out how people could leave or lose their jobs and she was shocked that such things could happen without her husband knowing about it. I gathered that Mr. Ford had not kept her posted on such matters, that he had given her the impression he did not know what had happened, and that I was responsible. This pleased him immensely, for it worked out the way he wanted it to.

Now, years later, I can sit down and reason it all out better than I could then. I never had the slightest desire to take Henry Ford's place, nor did I ever covet anything he owned. I certainly didn't try to imitate him. I went on in my own way, and he never criticized me for that in all the years we worked together.

I don't consider myself a victim of Henry Ford. I helped him build his empire. And I got as much experience and satisfaction out of it all as he did. Perhaps more.

Henry Ford was opinionated in matters about which he knew little or nothing. He could be small-minded, suspicious, jealous, and occasionally malicious and lacking in sincerity. He probably hastened the death of his only son. He came close to wrecking the great organization he had built up.

These were his defects. Taken by themselves, they were grave faults, and it might well be wondered how one could retain one's self-respect and still serve such a man. But when weighed against his good qualities, his sense of responsibility, his exemplary personal life, and his far-reaching accomplishments, these defects become microscopic. It is not for his failings but for his impact upon his time and his momentous part in liberating men from backbreaking toil that he will stand out in the future. It was because I understood what he was trying to do that I pinned my flag on Henry Ford and that I still hold him in respect and esteem and am proud to have had the label "Henry Ford's man."

4

What Made the Ford Organization Tick?

Two events of 1903 were of momentous consequence to the world. At a beach near Kitty Hawk, North Carolina, Wilbur and Orville Wright were the first human beings to fly a heavier-than-air machine, and transport became three-dimensional. In Detroit, Ford Motor Company was incorporated. It was destined to make motor transport universal, to attain mass production, to demonstrate the superiority of an economy of abundance over one of scarcity, and to begin the elevation of a standard of living to a height never before dreamed of. Of those still living I am the most intimately connected with that development.

Since 1893, when the Duryea brothers' gasoline buggy first clattered over the streets of Springfield, Massachusetts, there have been more than twelve hundred automobile companies and some two thousand different makes of cars. Today there are only six passenger-car makers. Why did the Ford company survive when twelve hundred others went out of business? It was born at the right moment. The time was ripe for a cheap car. Ford had one. An inexpensive car required revolutionary cost-cutting production. Ford evolved it. Both car and production methods were unorthodox in that day, and the organization that developed them was likewise unorthodox.

Its head was a single-purposed man who dominated yet at the same time delegated sweeping authority and responsibility. Its operations were intricate, yet experts were distrusted and virtually all executives came up from the ranks. When the music was not written, we improvised. When it was written, we had no time to learn to read—we played by ear. Judged by present-day standards Ford management was loose, eccentric, and as helter-skelter as a northwoods lumber camp. I shall abstain from claim or denial that such an organization would work today. My point is that no other would have done the job then, and my purpose is to indicate *how* it worked.

The history of the Ford Motor Company comprises four periods.

From 1903 to 1913 was the Couzens period. True, the company had Henry Ford's name, its product and production were his. There never would have been a Ford car without him. But the Ford Motor Company would not have made Ford cars long without James Couzens. He controlled expenditures, organized sales, and set the pattern for business operation. He drove Ford and the production side to produce cars to meet the public's demand. He yelled for plant expansion and drove us from the Piquette Avenue Plant into Highland Park. Everyone in the company, including Henry Ford, acknowledged him as the driving force during this period.

From 1913 to 1925 was the Henry Ford-Edsel Ford period. By 1913 the company was firmly established financially. Its problems were almost exclusively those of production and its expansion, of manufacturing, and of supply. No sooner were we established in Highland Park, with the world's biggest automobile plant and the most complete and efficient machine shop on earth, than both production and purchasing of cars expanded and we set our sights on a bigger plant. This period saw the moving assembly line and the flowering of mass production, the revolutionary $5 day, construction and operation of the mammoth River Rouge plant, and the peak of Ford automobile production. It also saw the Ford family become sole owners of Ford Motor Company through purchase of shares held by other stockholders.

From 1925 to 1944 was the Sorensen period. Henry Ford acquired other interests, and Edsel, as president of Ford Motor Company, confined himself largely to administrative work. I was in charge of production and plant operation. Model T was abandoned for Model A; and then the company entered the Great Depression and carried on up to the early days of World War II with the V-8. Then the entire Ford plant turned to war production work. At first, my position was that of a viceroy, ruling the production province of the Ford Empire. After Henry Ford had a stroke and Edsel lapsed into his fatal illness, my position as executive vice-president became that of regent. Besides the war program, I had the self-imposed responsibility of maintaining the organization until I could persuade a reluctant Henry Ford, failing both mentally and physically, to bring young Henry Ford II into the organization, so that I might be free to retire as I had planned.

The period from 1944 to the present is that of Henry Ford II control. Becoming a director in December, 1943, a month before I left, young Henry became executive vice-president when I resigned. He was elected president of the company in September, 1945, two years before his grandfather's death. Just turning twenty-seven, he had the task of converting the Ford organization from a war machine to a peacetime basis and of resuming civilian motorcar production, which had been suspended five years before. Under the will of the elder Ford, of which I was a witness, 95 per cent of the company's common stock was turned over to the Ford Foundation, a philanthropic trust which in 1956 sold the bulk of these securities to the public. Thus, no longer a completely family-owned affair, Ford Motor Company is now more of an institution, with 319,000 shareholders and management policies very different from those, which I shall describe, of its first three periods.

How Ford Motor Company ran its business and how it picked and promoted its staff was as great a mystery to the auto industry as it was to the public. An old Danish poet wrote, "To succeed is to realize what is possible." There speaks tradition, Old World respect for authority and reluctance to venture beyond the known fact. Henry Ford's philosophy was "We must go ahead without the facts; we will learn them as we go along." It was his working principle while designing his cars. He would have an idea, perhaps make a rough sketch, but he couldn't tell whether or not it was worth trying until he saw a model of it which had been worked up in our pattern shop. Thus he learned the facts by going ahead without them. And so it was that in reversal of the Danish poet's philosophy I arrived at this working maxim: *The only thing we can't do is something we haven't yet thought of.*

If experts and the positive voices of experience had been heeded, there would have been no Ford car, no Ford Motor Company, and its resulting impact on our civilization. Only the rich and the well-to-do could afford the automobile in its early days, and the industry, such as it was, catered to them.

The experts, to generalize a bit, come along and pick up where the pioneers leave off. Confronted with the unusual,

something beyond their rules and special knowledge, their reaction is "It's never been done" or even "It can't be done."
The pioneer says, "Let's try it." Ford was not an expert, and
he didn't rely upon experts, whether they were scientists,
engineers, railroad men, economists, educators, business executives, or bankers. He was an individualist who arrived at conclusions—both right and wrong—by independent thought.

One of our first bouts with the experts came in the pre-
Model T days. In 1907, Couzens brought in Norval Hawkins
on the sales and accounting end. When a member of his own
auditing firm, Hawkins had made an impressive inventory
of the Ford Manufacturing Company after that organization
had served Henry Ford's purpose—to manufacture parts—
and was about to be merged with Ford Motor Company. He
was a supreme example of a man whose contribution to success
of Ford Motor Company was in a field apart from the one in
which he was an expert. He was the greatest sales manager
the company ever had, and my hat is off to his natural-born
genius in this line. He also brought considerable order to office
routine. But the toilsome record-keeping of the cost-account-
ing systems he installed initially was a bureaucrat's heaven
and a production man's hell, and the latter is where much of
it went.

Under Hawkins's cost-time study, a part such as a piston
entered production bearing a ticket which covered every
operation. If ten operations were involved, an entry was made
on the ticket after each stage before proceeding to the next
one. If one piston was lost in the move, all progress stopped
until the missing piece could be found and accounted for.
The time consumed in each operation was computed in lots
of 100 or more, and results were tabulated on a card file which
ultimately found its way back to the foreman so that he
might check timing at each stage. Not only did the process
mean delay from one operation to another, but when a motor

assembler couldn't get pistons, all car production was held up.

This rigmarole did not appeal to Mr. Ford. While Couzens roared for more production and at the same time put the brakes on expenditures, costs were rising and production falling in the name of "efficiency." One Sunday morning Ford and I went into the record room Hawkins had set up. We found drawer after drawer of cards and tickets. Mr. Ford took one drawer, held it bottom up, and its contents spilled on the floor. We did the same with all other cards until the entire record system was thoroughly fouled up. Then Ford departed, leaving me to settle with Couzens and Hawkins the next day.

Bright and early Monday morning Couzens sent for me. He had heard Hawkins's report of the shambles in the record room, and he was boiling. All that Couzens knew about the system was what Hawkins had told him; he had never seen it at work. When he stopped for breath, I said to him, "Come out with me into the shop and let me show you what has happened to plant operation. This system can't adapt itself to our kind of manufacturing. Just spend half an hour in the plant and see for yourself."

When he refused but calmed down a bit, I gave Mr. Couzens the real story of how production was delayed by a system which had complicated instead of simplifying operations. I told him that, since reports from the Hawkins system were a week old, they were too late to help us keep on top of the job. Couzens thought we were spoiling work and losing materials and that there was no accounting for the loss. He then said that his idea of a proper operation was a good receiving clerk and an equally good shipping clerk in each department. I agreed with him, because that was what we already had. If what came out of a department didn't tally with what went in, the difference represented spoilage, which was all we needed to know. That ended my trouble with Couzens over excessive record-keeping. When he saw our daily checks on spoilage, he called me in to tell me that he now saw we had a simpler way to control costs.

Thus ended "efficiency red tape" with Ford Motor Company almost before it began, and Hawkins confined himself to sales, where he did a magnificent job. I have gone into this incident with some detail because it strikes me as a vivid illustration of the difference between two diametrically opposed shop management practices. One is rigid *system*, in which rules tend to be paramount; the other is flexible *method*, in which the objective comes first. And, so, our supervisors were not required to bury their noses in paper work; they were expected to watch the production lines where their eyes would tell them what might be going wrong before reports could be written.

One of the hardest-to-down myths about the evolution of mass production at Ford is one which credits much of the accomplishment to "scientific management." No one at Ford—not Mr. Ford, Couzens, Flanders, Wills, Pete Martin, nor I—was acquainted with the theories of the "father of scientific management," Frederick W. Taylor. Years later I ran across a quotation from a two-volume book about Taylor by Frank Barkley Copley, who reports a visit Taylor made to Detroit late in 1914, nearly a year after the moving assembly line had been installed at our Highland Park plant. Taylor expressed surprise to find that Detroit industrialists "had undertaken to install the principles of scientific management without the aid of experts." To my mind this unconscious admission by an expert is expert testimony on the futility of too great reliance on experts and should forever dispose of the legend that Taylor's ideas had any influence at Ford.

The way we built our initial organization was one of the soundest things we ever did. We didn't plan that way; we were compelled by circumstances. There weren't enough men with experience in this particular line of business. And our training of others had much to do with the rapid growth of the company.

This making of men was followed through so consistently that everyone in the organization understood it. It applied even to men hired to operate machinery. Trying to buy men away from another organization for that purpose was bound to fail because there were not enough of them around to amount to anything.

At times, it looked difficult to put into practice. One Easter Monday morning not enough men turned up at the Piquette Avenue plant to man the Potter & Johnson machines on which we turned out our flywheels. I was discussing the problem when Henry Ford came in and saw the long line of idle machines.

"What's the trouble, Charlie?" he asked.

"Plenty!" I said. "These machines are all down and the men aren't on the job. We'll be holding up the rest of the plant before the day is over."

"Why," said Ford, "that's an easy thing to fix."

I turned to him in amazement. "Easy to fix!" I repeated. "What do you mean? How would you fix it?"

"Just go ahead and make some more men for these jobs," he replied.

It all sounded perfectly simple: don't go out and hire more lathe operators; train the ones we've got.

We trained thousands of mechanics that way. When foremen or executive supervisors were needed, they were picked from men who showed ability in operating machines. This was a fundamental principle during the first three periods of Ford Motor Company.

Good managers at Ford had to have some of these qualities: (1) Refreshing simplicity. (2) Brains. (3) Education. (4)

Special technical ability. (5) Tact. (6) Energy and Grit. (7) Honesty. (8) Judgment. (9) Common sense. (10) Good health.

Men with four or five of these good qualities are rare; those with six or seven are almost nonexistent. So, an organization needing all these qualities in the aggregate must make some division of the responsibility load. Division of the responsibility load and functional responsibility are the basis of today's industrial management. They make possible the large-scale decentralization and specialization characteristic of modern American business.

Today, more than forty years later, I marvel how Henry Ford sensed this type of organization. He did not want to be informed just for the sake of being informed, for soon he would be doing nothing but getting information. He was decentralizing the major operation.

It is quite unlikely that our large corporations and industrial establishments could ever have reached their present size with efficiency if the principle of decentralized responsibility had not been adopted. In today's industrial organizations a situation rather than the personality is the dominant factor. The situation controls, and the true leader is the one who responds immediately and effectively to the situation. And, since a situation is always primary, authority derives from function rather than position. The responsibility is *for* and not *to*. Of course, I understand all this better today than I did in 1909. As I see it now, years later, I must say that of the two men, Ford and Couzens, who headed up our early organization Henry Ford had a much clearer conception of what organization meant and would mean in the future.

The paradox is that but for Couzens and his organization and domination of sales and finance Ford Motor Company would not have lasted long. He was a hard, shrewd operator with a whiplash temper and energy; but unlike Ford, he insisted that all details and facts in his field be brought to his attention and frequently for his decision. One morning in the fall of 1915, Mr. Ford came to my office. "Mr. Couzens has quit," he told me. "I've just left him. Charlie, he was one of the hardest men I ever had to work with, but I wish I had one just like him to take his place."

He never got that wish.

CHAPTER

5

Work Was Play

IN 1906, long before Couzens left, Henry Ford became president of the company after the death of John S. Gray. Although he headed Ford Motor Company and owned a majority of its stock, circumstances prevented him from exercising complete control. The obstacle was a financial one. The company was making money, the popularity of Model N, which had come out earlier that year, vindicated Ford's insistence upon an inexpensive car, but a large expansion program was necessary, and this would take more money. It was up to Couzens to provide the money, and therefore he dominated the situation.

A few days after Gray's death, Walter Flanders was brought in as a cost-cutting production manager. Couzens, Wills, and the Dodge brothers were behind this selection, and Ford was worried. He was aware of Flanders's ability, yet feared the man might take his place. There was a streak of jealousy here. Flanders, a forceful, boisterous man, was popular with the directors and got along well with men in the shop. In the nearly two years he was at Ford, his rearrangement of machines headed us toward mass production. Ford, a quiet, sensitive person, got a few gray hairs at this stage, but he learned a great deal from Flanders, and so did I.

This was the rare case of a man whom Henry Ford did not pick but who contributed greatly to getting Ford Motor Company under way. Another man not hired by Henry Ford but who made good was, as I have said, Norval Hawkins. These two were the exceptions, however. "Hereafter," said Ford, "anybody who goes along with us must come up from the bottom and work right through the organization."

That policy prevailed until Henry Ford II took over in 1945, and only a handful of the supervisory or executive staff came from outside the organization. Clarence Avery, who was Edsel Ford's manual training teacher at Detroit University School, came to us in 1912, and I made him my assistant in production planning. In 1916, Ernest Kanzler, Mrs. Edsel Ford's brother-in-law, joined the organization, and I shall deal with him in later chapters.

The largest additions to the staff from the outside came after 1911, when we acquired the J. R. Keim Pressed Steel plant in Buffalo. When we moved the whole equipment to Highland Park a year later we brought in William H. Smith, John R. Lee, William Knudsen, Charles Morgana, and a number of others. We built a new plant for pressed steel. Smith was superintendent, Knudsen was his assistant. Lee took over some of Wills's office work, and Morgana became a machinery buyer. The other men took over the press shop. There was no feeling of intrusion here. The Highland Park staff never lifted an eyebrow, and all but one of the newcomers from Keim fitted into their places naturally.

The one exception was Bill Knudsen—and I must correct extravagant stories told about him when he left Ford. He had nothing to do with major production or its planning at Highland Park. Few of the basic staff seemed able to get along with him. I thought he would step out, but eventually

I offered to use him in the assembly plant work I was developing. He was sent out to set up the knockdown assembly plants we were then establishing in cities over the country where we had important branches. Bill did so well in this that he continued to circulate among the branches and fit their materials and assembly programs to our sales office's yearly schedules. He reported to me on branch production problems, and any additional work or operations involving him cleared through my office. I also had handled foreign branch production problems since their inception, and when I left Ford Motor Company temporarily to go with Henry Ford to Dearborn and tractor development I turned my foreign division work over to Knudsen. World War I halted our foreign branch business, but with the coming of the Armistice Knudsen was given power of attorney to handle these operations, and this was his major job until he left Ford in 1921.

According to law, a corporation must have officers, a president, a secretary, and a treasurer and, if it is a public company, a board of directors. A set of bylaws specifies the duties of such officers. When Ford Motor Company was incorporated in 1903, John S. Gray was elected president. After he died, in 1906, Henry Ford was president until 1919, when he was succeeded by his son Edsel. Edsel died in 1943; Henry Ford again was president until 1947, when his grandson, Henry Ford II, succeeded him.

And, so, in fifty years there were four presidents, with three members of the Ford family holding that office for forty-seven years. But whether he or his son was president, Henry Ford ruled his company. He never regarded a corporation title as giving a man full exercise of what that title implied; he would have preferred no titles at all. It never could be said of Ford Motor Company that it had "too many chiefs and not enough Injuns."

When I had charge of production, for instance, I could advise, check up, or dip into the treasurer's affairs, watch capital investments, and hold up what expenditures I felt were unnecessary. I was not then an officer of the company, but anyone who had Henry Ford's confidence had the same privileges in his field that I had in mine. It was his way of keeping control of the treasurer.

In this way, he said, he knew more about how funds were handled than had he sat in with Klingensmith, who was one of Couzens' successors as treasurer and who, Ford felt, would hide details from him. Annoyed by this method, Klingensmith felt it was interference and that Ford did not trust him. A number of times I saw him almost in tears over the situation, and it only made matters worse when he ran to Edsel for sympathy. He didn't then grasp Henry Ford's determination that no one else would control finances the way Couzens had. No one was going to run off with his business.

By the time Couzens, Wills, and John Dodge were out of the way, the company was Henry Ford's empire in fact as well as in name. When Klingensmith became treasurer, he believed he was taking over all of Couzens' former duties, and some time later he announced to branch managers that, like Couzens, he was general manager, too. Riding with me one morning on the way to Dearborn, Mr. Ford said, "Charlie, Klingensmith is telling around that he is general manager. No one should be general manager who does not own the business. Kling knows that he was never given such an appointment, but he influences Edsel. I must stop that."

He said no more until we reached Dearborn and I was getting out of the car. "Wait a minute, Charlie," he said. "I want you to tell Klingensmith that I have appointed you general manager. Don't do anything more than that. Just tell him that and let's see how he takes it."

At that time Henry Ford had resigned the presidency of

Ford Motor Company in favor of Edsel and had organized and set up at Dearborn Henry Ford & Son, a new company with two purposes. One was to make farm tractors; the other was by threat of bringing out a new car to intimidate remaining stockholders to sell their Ford Motor Company shares. But, although no longer an official of Ford Motor Company, he never lost control. I, too, was out of Ford Motor Company and was working on the tractor in Dearborn, and making plans for the River Rouge Plant, but I went to Highland Park, where the motor company was, once or twice a week and usually with Mr. Ford. So, when he told me to see Klingensmith, I understood his purpose—also I never felt that Klingensmith measured up to being general manager.

The next morning I dropped in at Highland Park to see Klingensmith and found him in a flip, cocky mood. "And what are you doing in Highland Park?" he asked airily.

That was a perfect opening for me and my mission. "To see what you're doing," I said.

My reply sort of slowed him down. Then I let him have it. "Henry Ford has appointed me general manager," I announced coldly.

Now, Klingensmith was a capable, hard-working treasurer, but he was no Couzens. He evaded matters that Couzens would have fought for. Nor would he approach Henry Ford on policy questions. He knew enough to let him alone. The minute I told him I was general manager, he did nothing more in that direction—didn't even trouble Edsel. From then on Klingensmith knew that with or without title Henry Ford was general manager, and that was that.

Without titles and a tier of officials how could one build an organization? When Flanders resigned as production manager, taking with him his assistant Walborn, to work for a newly formed auto company, Henry Ford called Ed Martin and me to his office. "Ed and Charlie," he said, "Flanders and

Walborn are leaving, and I want you to take their places. You, Ed, will be plant superintendent and you, Charlie, will be assistant superintendent. Just go out there and run the plant. I know you can do it. But there's one thing I want to add: work together as one. I don't ever want to hear that you can't work together. And don't worry about titles."

And, so, with no further grant of authority and no specified division of it, Ed Martin and I worked together for thirty-two years with no real break in our relations. Too often the concern of corporation executives about their titles—even size and furnishings of their offices—deflects thought and energy from jobs they are supposed to do. That concern may whet ambition—but with a wrong emphasis. In the absence of a flock of titles, such things didn't worry us at Ford.

Except in personal morals, two men could hardly have been less alike than Peter E. Martin (whom we called "Ed") and I. There was complete difference in our dispositions, habits, and religious backgrounds. Ed was of French-Canadian descent and a devout, generous Roman Catholic. My parents were Danish, I was raised in the Lutheran tradition, and I did not find consolation in religion then as I found later. He had a friendly nature; I was more aloof, but our dissimilarities never affected our relations. Ed liked to be always on the job in the plant. I liked to get around—which broadened both my outlook and my experience. Therefore, Ed worked in the plant, overseeing production, while my job evolved into production organization and development. After Ed was forced to retire with a fatal heart condition, members of his staff and mine told me they marveled at how we stuck to our tasks with no discord. To me, the answer was obvious: We had a sense of achievement by association, by teamwork.

Selection is too narrow a word when thinking of building for leadership. Inside any company, some of the ablest men are never selected. They just get a job in the old-fashioned way and emerge on merit. A smart boss watches for them and does something about it as soon as they emerge. Some may have formal education but many do not. It is still the glory of our country that this doesn't matter. A man is doomed not by being uneducated but by remaining so.

Who can tell us what leadership is? It is a radiant quality which some men possess which makes others swing joyously into common action. What they do is wisely conceived and eminently fair. Such leadership, which is above all the characteristic of American production and the function of voluntary effort, springs from mutual understanding. The boss must know the worker and the worker must know the boss. They must respect each other.

It was Ford's good fortune that he could start with this right from the beginning. He knew every man on the payroll, most of them by first name. He did not gather them together and make speeches and show elaborate plans; individual contact meant more. Ford knew when to give praise when it was due and when to make fair criticism when that was due. These are two of the strongest attributes of wise leadership, particularly when dealing with the imaginative and creative personalities so much needed in industry. Yet all too few men employ them; a job well done is likely to be taken for granted.

It isn't the incompetent who destroy an organization. The incompetent never get into a position to destroy it. It is those who have achieved something and want to rest upon their achievements who are forever clogging things up. To keep an industry thoroughly alive, it should be kept in perpetual ferment. "The art of government," said Napoleon, "is not to let men grow stale." Henry Ford didn't let us grow stale.

He demanded and got loyalty and energy. After I began to understand his philosophy I became its disciple. I found no greater thrill than to hire or promote a young man of unusual promise, and then have my judgment justified. The men who rose to the top were a much surer index of the organization's competence than the plants we built. As the company expanded and men were hired not by the dozen but by the hundreds and thousands, Henry Ford necessarily lost touch with his work force. From then on, the basic group— men who were working at Ford between 1903 and 1909— became departmental superintendents and were the backbone of the Ford organization.

Ed Martin rose from machinist to general superintendent and vice-president. John Wandersee, who became head of metallurgy, began as a sweeper. Joe Galamb, hired as a draftsman by Ford's first chief engineer, Harold Wills, ultimately succeeded to that position. Fred Diehl, who answered a Ford want ad for a timekeeper, became head of purchasing and, before he retired in 1929, spent several billions for materials. Other "early birds" were Fred Rockelman, who managed the Ford-owned Detroit, Toledo & Ironton Railroad; Max Fredericks, superintendent of the tool department; August Degener, superintendent of inspection; Carl Emde, tool designer; Harry Hanson, plant engineer; William Klann, superintendent of engine assembly; Archie Tyrell, shipping superintendent. And I, whose fortune it was to go further than any other, started as a $3-a-day patternmaker.

I am often asked what made Henry Ford's organization click. I can probably best answer by explaining how I made Samuel Crowther understand it. Crowther had ghostwritten Ford's *My Life and Work* and *Today and Tomorrow*. He covered a lot of ground on detail operations, but either forgot or could not see what and who sparked all these operations. I found his books hard to read, and I've had another go at them since I began these reminiscences. Crowther realized that his collaboration with Henry Ford was an open

door for him to look around. Mr. Ford would not tell him
what to say, so he came to me to discuss points about which
he was writing.

I never felt that he was seeing just what made things tick.
His detail work was tremendous and perhaps useful as a
schoolbook. After he had finished *Today and Tomorrow*, I
did not see him for over a year. Then he came back to me
with a new slant. He had made a discovery. He had missed the
important thing in his first book. Now he wanted to analyze
the organization. It was then some twenty years after I had
pulled a chassis by rope on the third floor of the Piquette
Avenue plant and assembled the first car while moving; organization had stabilized.

I sent Crowther back into the plant and gave him a list of
men to see. I told him to forget mechanical details, because
many of them as covered in his book were already out of
date. What was up to date, and even ahead of it, was the organization.

After a look-around he told me that the organization was
a revelation to him. How easy it all seemed, but where did a
motive to do the things he saw come from? It looked orderly
to him. The difficult thing for him to understand was how an
organization of 100,000 workers functioned and was guided
and controlled.

Crowther had always worked on a one-man basis with
only himself to be concerned about. In this visit he had
learned that Henry Ford was not guiding any of these men,
that there were many foremen and some superintendents who
had never talked to him or even seen him. Still, here was the
wonder plant rolling along smoothly.

Once I kept him on the end of the assembly line nearly half
a day. He learned that I knew every superintendent and
foreman in the plant, as well as in the branches in the United
States and Europe. Superintendents and their assistants were

not the sit-down type. Our top men didn't hold down office chairs. Their formula, and mine, was, "You've got to get around." Then Crowther began to sense what organization meant to Ford Motor Company. He discovered that the "motive" came from a close-knit group of men who lived on the job and that there were ideas in every corner of the shop.

With this group, work was play. If it had not been play, it would have killed them. They were as men possessed. They often forgot to eat. They drove themselves much harder than they drove anyone else. As we designed new machines to meet our requirements, Charlie Morgana would give machine-tool makers our specifications calling for a machine to make so many hundred pieces per hour. When they read Charlie Morgana's specifications calling for output of so many pieces an hour, they usually thought we'd made a mistake: "You don't mean making so many hundred pieces per hour, you must mean so many hundred pieces per day."

Then the designer had to sit down and prove that we were right because we had made a machine ourselves to do exactly that. So it went on with the thousand pieces of machinery that we bought.

Even when we were doing things in our Highland Park and River Rouge wonder plants that were rated impossible, the group of men that we had around us was still sure it could do everything and even better than we were doing it. Even at that time anybody was welcome to come and see how it was done.

Rival motorcar makers studied our layouts but at best succeeded only in copying what we were doing. There was a pride in belonging to this famous industrial management crew —perhaps the most famous in the world, even though any one individual's part may have been small. The same as Ed Martin and I, a crew like this had a sense of achievement by association. They were not experts. When one man began to fancy himself an expert, we had to get rid of him. The minute a man thinks himself an expert he gets an expert's state of mind, and too many things become impossible. The Ford operations and creative work were directed by men who had no previous knowledge of the subject. They did not have a chance to get on really familiar terms with the impossible.

I am certain now that no other formula would have been successful. There was no one around who had had experience, and if one came along who had done well in any other business we had more of a problem to get him to drop his ideas and fall in with our progressive manufacturing and assembling. It was simple to start a man off with no experience. He could accept the formula without trouble. And if he became proficient he developed into a full-fledged Ford executive, a specialist but not an expert.

PART
2

6

I, Charles Sorensen

I OFTEN wonder where I would be today had my father missed the boat to America over seventy years ago. I was born in Copenhagen, Denmark, September 7, 1881. A short distance away at the time was the 18-month-old son of Customs Inspector Knudsen. Our paths didn't cross until thirty years later, and I had the good fortune to beat Bill Knudsen to the United States by fifteen years.

The name "Sorensen" is as common in Denmark as "Smith" is here, and the figure of "Herr Sorensen," an old man wearing a nightcap, is the Danish Uncle Sam. Soren Sorensen, my father, was a *modele sneger*, a modelmaker who worked in wood. For more than two centuries his people had been parish clerks and farmers whose descent through an old Danish noble family named Hoeg, meaning "banner," could be traced back to the Middle Ages.

My mother, who was Eva Christine Abrahamsen, came from a long line of farmers. Orphaned at an early age, she was adopted by an uncle, a construction engineer, who took her to Sweden, where he helped build the railroad between Stockholm and Oslo. As the work progressed, they moved from one location to another. My mother described this town-to-

town migration so vividly that long years later when I made
my first trip from Oslo to Stockholm I easily recognized places
and spots along the way that she had told me about. After the
road was built, my mother returned with her foster father-
uncle to Denmark and Copenhagen. Here she met and married my father.

My father, as a boy, lived on a farm close by the king's
farm and summer home. He knew King Christian I, who,
like most members of the Danish royal house, had no false
sense of dignity and freely mingled with commoners. On
entering young manhood my father went to Copenhagen and
apprenticeship in a woodworking plant. He took drafting
lessons which speeded promotion to modelmaking and the
fashioning of models of interiors, stairways, and wooden
household furnishings.

After work my father followed track and field sports and
helped in the training of several athlete friends. His particular
idol was not a relation, "Little Sorensen," then Denmark's
greatest professional distance runner. Shortly after I was born,
Little Sorensen went with a manager to the United States
to compete against top American milers. He met with great
success. "This is a great country," he wrote my father, reporting his triumphs. "Come on over."

Nothing could stop my father from following Little Sorensen to the States. He went on his own, leaving my mother
and two of us children—I was then about thirty months old
—to follow when he could afford it. A year and a half later,
when I was four years old, he sent for us. I have recollections
of preparations for the trip and of boarding the ship in which
we shared steerage quarters with several other families. There
were many youngsters on board, and I had a fight with one
who delighted in roughing up other children. I think I must
have licked him; at any rate, I threw his cap overboard, and
my mother had to replace it.

We landed in New York and went through the immigrant station at old Castle Garden down on the Battery. The steamship people put us on a train for Erie, Pennsylvania, where my father was working at Black and Germer Stove Works. He had become an accomplished draftsman and could lay out a complete stove—all views, top, bottom, and four sides, each in different ink—in one drawing.

Meanwhile, Little Sorensen, the human magnet who had drawn my father to America, was flitting about the country, running distance races and winning acclaim in sports news columns. Not quite two years after we had joined my father in Erie, Little Sorensen settled down in Buffalo, apparently for good. Although he was only ninety miles away, my father had to follow his fleet-footed idol to Buffalo. The move was impulsive, yet its outcome was fortunate, for there was a better opening for him at Jewett Stove Works, one of the oldest and best in the country.

My father did very well during his eleven years at Jewett. He rose from patternmaker to assistant superintendent. Before he left the old country he had learned enough English to carry on with the language. My mother also studied English in Copenhagen; and between them my parents had little difficulty in adjusting themselves to new ways, new people, and new speech in a new country.

I was six and ready for school when my father followed Little Sorensen to Buffalo. I began to read and figure at School No. 4 on Pine Street. When I was eight we moved to the outskirts of the city, where my father had built a home on Portage Avenue, and I attended Fillmore Avenue School No. 24. By this time there were seven of us, counting my parents. Two sisters and a brother were born in our new home, and two other children born there died in infancy.

In 1895, when I was fourteen, I went to work for the first time. An architect-surveyor near our home hired me during summer vacation to act as linesman while he surveyed and laid out building lots in outlying suburbs. We drove to work with horse and buggy, and then nearly walked our legs off lugging surveying equipment the rest of the day. Returning from this rugged work I helped to stable and feed the horse and the next morning currycombed and hitched him up before starting out. All this I enjoyed. It was good experience, and I suppose the leg work was equivalent to seventy-two holes of golf.

The second summer I had the same job. My employer showed me a few rudiments of mechanical drawing so that I might help him make up his plats and drawings. He would make an original, then I turned out a number of copies. Wanting to learn more technique of ruling pen, T-square, and triangle, I enrolled in night school and there an old German professor taught drafting mathematics.

That fall of 1896, I became an apprentice in the pattern shop at Jewett. My formal schooling ended at sixteen; my education in the school of experience had begun, and I had to spend most of my mature life doing things for which I had not been specially trained.

No man can help it if he has to leave school in his early years, but he can very much help it if he lacks an education thereafter. The man who carries on night study courses while doing a full day's work has the necessary determination and sense of values for self-advancement. There are never enough such men. We at Ford Motor Company rarely selected a man entirely for what he knew. It was his capacity to learn, particularly the capacity to learn that about which he knew nothing. Proved competence in some field plus intellectual curiosity and audacity are to me essential qualities. The trick is to detect them.

When educators visited us at the plant and were luncheon guests at the roundtable, Henry Ford would describe his

rural school education. Pointing at me, whose formal education never got beyond eighth grade in grammar school, he
would say, "Tell your college story, Charlie," and my story
went this way:

One day Mr. Ford brought a rather seedy-looking man to
my office and said, "Charlie, this is an old schoolmate of
mine. He has a son who wants to go to college and learn
to become a forester. See if you can find the proper school,
and I'll help to pay the boy's way."

After inquiry of our western branches, a forestry school
was found in a West Coast university. I bought the boy a
railroad ticket, a Ford West Coast manager met him on arrival, took him to the school, and helped him get settled. Mr.
Ford paid the bills until, after three years of study, the boy
passed his forester's examination and returned to Dearborn.

Again Mr. Ford came to my office with the boy's father.
Now we had to start the boy in his forestry profession. "See
if you can find a job for him," Ford told me. "The boy wants
to go west—California, Oregon, or Washington."

Again I queried our western branch managers, and a position was found with a big lumber company in Oregon. So,
again, I bought the young man a ticket—at Henry Ford's
expense—and put him on a westbound train. When he arrived
at Seattle, a Ford branch manager met him.

Having had direct instructions from me to see that the boy
got off to a good start, the manager put him on a train to
a small town. Someone from the lumber company met him
and put him and his baggage on a large, heavy wagon with
big, high wheels. It was quite a distance to the camp, over a
rough and bumpy road. Somewhere along the way the boy
fell off. The wagon ran over him, and he was killed.

I got the sad news from our branch manager. When I told
it to Mr. Ford, he was concerned as to how he should break
it to his old friend, the boy's father. He thought for a while,

then said, "Charlie, do you realize that they forgot to teach that boy in college how to ride on a wagon?"

At Jewett, where all stoves were made of cast iron, I continued drawing lessons with my old German teacher. As a patternmaker's apprentice I ran errands between departments —from drafting room to pattern department to foundry. Between my mechanical drawing at night school and my daytime visits to various departments in the stove works, I soon began to realize what it meant to be a good mechanic.

In addition, I had kept the pattern departments clean. I swept up sawdust and shavings as they accumulated during the day and during the half-hour lunch period I was sent to a neighborhood saloon to bring back beer for some of the patternmakers. I cut notches in two four-foot sticks and in each notch I hung a bucket of beer. When both sticks were at full capacity, I lugged twenty pails of beer in one trip. For each pail I delivered I got one cent. So, at about twenty cents each day, I did pretty well at this business.

A good patternmaker must be something of a clairvoyant. He must translate a designer's one-dimensional drawings into a three-dimensional wooden model of the object to be cast in metal. From this pattern is made the mold into which is poured the molten metal for the casting.

Patternmaking is neither a profession nor a trade but an exacting, highly skilled craft which requires understanding of both. A patternmaker must be able to read the most complicated blueprints, and he must have more than a cabinetmaker's meticulous skill and infinite patience to saw and plane, sandpaper and glue together an accurate wooden representation of what the designer or draftsman has in mind. More than that, his pattern must meet the particularly exacting requirements of the molders in the foundry where the castings are made.

After a short while I was assigned a bench all to myself

and began to help in patternmaking. My first job was to cut pine strips for the patterns. We had the most beautiful white pine in those days—straight and clear and dried in a kiln over our boiler rooms. I brought these planks into the department and to a saw which ripped off strips about six inches wide. I then cut these strips to 30-inch length and split them down to a $\frac{3}{16}$-inch thickness. Next I took them to my bench where with a long plane with a very straight, sharp blade I smoothed them down to between $\frac{3}{32}$ and $\frac{1}{8}$ of an inch thickness and suitable for use on the boards upon which the patternmakers built their patterns. This plane work had to be extremely accurate, and I was enormously proud when I could keep everyone supplied with these required pieces.

In the Jewett plant there were machine shops which kept the production-line machines in order. I was also keen on the foundry end. After a two-year apprenticeship my daily routine included two hours in machine shops, two hours in foundry, and the remainder of the 10-hour day in the pattern shop. Thus by 1898, when I was seventeen, I was familiar with all operations of the plant, from preliminary design to final product. The Spanish-American War had come and gone. I had tried to get into it, but remembering and avenging the *Maine* had to get along without me. Recruiting officers turned me down because of the typical identification of the true patternmaker—two missing finger tips on my right hand.

Buffalo in those days was a center of the bicycle industry and was also a mecca for bicycle racing. Like most youngsters, I had a bicycle. There were road races and track races of all types, also races for boys in which I took part. It was my father's interest in foot racing that brought him to this country. It was my boyhood fondness for bicycle racing that led to my first contact and ultimate association with Henry Ford.

One of the greatest of all racers was Eddie Bald, whose father had a butchershop in our neighborhood. I saw him win his first novice race, and he soon became a hero to all of us boys, who tried mightily to imitate him. Out Main Street at the corner of Delevan was a quarter-mile cement track, one of the first stretches of concrete in America, which attracted the country's fastest pedal-pushers, hopeful of breaking speed records on its unequaled smooth surface. Among them was the great Barney Oldfield, who was almost as famous as a cyclist as he was later when Henry Ford transformed him into a motor speed demon. Another was Tommy Cooper, a somewhat tricky rider, who came over frequently from Detroit to compete against Eddie Bald. Although reputed to be a high liver when out of training, Cooper had salted away most of his prize money and was probably better fixed financially than his competitors.

Haunting the track in my spare time, I got to know all the great bicycle racers. It was here that I saw my first motorcycles—French machines used for pacing the cyclists' practice heats—and their De Dion engines were the first gasoline motors I ever saw. They were serviced behind the track's training quarters, and I began to spend more time watching and occasionally helping these operations than I spent on my bicycle or among the daredevil professional riders. I discovered that intricate castings went into these motors. If these powered driving mechanisms ever attained general use, the field of patternmaking, in which I was becoming competent far beyond my years, would be greatly widened.

Before 1898 ended, the owner of the stove works, Sherman S. Jewett, died. He was over ninety. Neither of his two sons was interested in continuing the business. Sensing what was coming, my father looked for another job.

He found one in Milwaukee at the Linderman-Hoverson plant, which specialized in the newfangled gas stoves, then just beginning to challenge the coal-burning kitchen range. He began as foreman of the pattern division, then became foundry superintendent, and when the rest of the family followed him to Milwaukee, I went to work under my father. After work hours I went to night school and also took an International Correspondence School drafting course which included algebra, geometry, and trigonometry.

I saw no motorcycles in Milwaukee, but the shafting that drove machinery in the pattern shop was powered by a single-cylinder gas engine. This coughing, explosive, and unpredictable contraption became my pet and I tinkered with it, humored it, and kept it running during the few months I was at Linderman-Hoverson.

My father was uneasy in Milwaukee. After a little more than a year he decided to go to Detroit, where most of the major stove plants were located. The rest of the family remained in Milwaukee until he sent for us. On a smaller scale, the situation was a repetition of what had happened years before in Copenhagen, only now it was stoves and not Little Sorensen that beckoned.

After my father left I became foreman of the pattern shop. I was only eighteen. Today I sometimes wonder how I got away with that job, but I did, and it may have helped to give me perhaps more than my share of the self-assurance that I would need many times later.

Before my mother and the rest of the children were ready to leave Milwaukee, I went on ahead to Detroit, where I joined my father at the Detroit Stove Works near Belle Isle Bridge. Close by at the foot of Helen Avenue was a three-story structure which was the forerunner of things to come in Detroit. It was the first auto plant in the country and home of Oldsmobile, the little curved-dash runabout and pioneer low-cost car.

Farther up Helen Avenue was the spotless home of Mrs. Neibeling, an elderly lady who took in a few roomers. Besides my father and me, the only other lodger was a young

Oldsmobile tester named Roy Chapin. Within a year he would drive a merry little Oldsmobile to New York in six days, and the smoothest part of those 900 miles was not roadway but the mule-trodden towpath of Erie Canal. Chapin was destined to be one of the motor industry's greats and during the Hoover Administration was the first automobile executive to become a member of a president's Cabinet.

After six months at the stove works, I quit and took a job farther downtown at Bryant and Berry pattern works on Jefferson Avenue just west of Woodward. Here the work was more varied and interesting. Six years earlier, Charles B. King had driven the first car through Detroit streets. Curved-dash Oldsmobiles were a familiar sight, scurrying along like cockroaches. The horseless carriage had become so much of a craze that by 1900 nearly a hundred makes of cars had appeared. Most were electric, or steam; only a quarter were gasoline-engine driven. Few of them survived more than a year, but for every horseless carriage that eventually reached the road there were probably three backyard mechanics experimenting with motors and dreaming great dreams.

This was going on all over the country where there were imaginative mechanics. Industrial Detroit had perhaps more than its share of enthusiasts and within a couple of years would become the chief automobile manufacturing center. Most of the city's automotive designers brought their sketches and experimental work to Bryant and Berry. These included Charles King and Oliver Barthel, who had been working with gasoline engines for nearly ten years. Each new experimental casting had to be preceded by patterns which themselves had to be experimental because many of the designs were but rough drawings. This guesswork and trial-and-error pattern-making was a fortunate preparation for what I would be doing the rest of my active life. But I didn't know it then, for I had become restless.

Being young and active, I chafed at indoor work and I envied the fast-talking salesmen who got about the country and seemed to be on their own time instead of tied down to ten hours a day, six days a week. So, I got a job selling gasoline and oil stoves for the Sun Stove Company. My territory was Iowa, but I saw no tall corn growing; it was midwinter, and I nearly froze to death. After three months of roaming the snowy open spaces, I had enough and returned to the Detroit office, where I quit and handed in my accounts. The bookkeeper who went over my sales figures and expenses was a very pretty, unusually quiet girl who had a disconcerting way of looking at me with a half-smile which had me guessing whether it meant approval or inner amusement. Her name was Helen Mitchell. I wanted to change it, and it took me two and a half years to make her see the idea my way.

After I thawed out from my Iowa winter, I returned to patternmaking at Bryant and Berry, where, one spring morning in 1902, Tommy Cooper, my bicycle friend of Buffalo days, came in. He was through with bicycle racing, he told me. He had spent the winter managing a coal mine in Colorado, and he hadn't liked the weather there any better than I had in Iowa. With him that morning was a lean, sandy-haired stranger. "Charlie," he said, "meet Mr. Henry Ford. I'm interested in a gasoline engine which he's building and we are going to put in a racing car, and he wants to see some of his ideas in pattern form."

CHAPTER

7

I Go to Work for Ford

WHEN Tommy Cooper brought him to my patternmaking bench that spring morning, I had heard about
Henry Ford but had never seen him. He had won considerable local fame as an automobile racing driver—Detroit
newspapers, then wrestling with French terms in the motorcar field, referred to him as a "chauffeur." The October before I met him there had been great doings at Detroit's first
automobile race. A parade of more than one hundred gas-,
steam- and electric-driven vehicles to Grosse Point Race
Track was almost as spectacular as the speed events. Alexander
Winton, a Cleveland auto pioneer, clipped a second from the
world's record for the mile (1 minute, 12.4 seconds) in an
exhibition spin around the track, only to lose the final race
of the afternoon against Henry Ford.

That was about as much as I knew. Although I was interested in gasoline motors and had haunted the Buffalo bicycle race track when I was a boy I was not one of the speed
nuts around Henry Ford in Detroit. I did not join the thousands who trooped out to Grosse Point that October afternoon. I had to work for a living. Besides, much of my spare

70

time was spent in trying to persuade Helen Mitchell to take the name of Sorensen.

For the Grosse Point contest, Ford had been coached in racing technique by Tommy Cooper, who had pedaled bicycles faster than autos could be driven in those days; and when Cooper returned from his Colorado mining experience he was ready to back Ford in the construction of another racing car. Meanwhile, Ford was at work in a little shop on Park Place with a couple of mechanics, one of whom was a part-time worker named C. Harold Wills.

Childe Harold Wills (he never used the Byronic first name favored by his poetry-loving mother) was as handsome as his name. He was a trained mechanical engineer and a good draftsman, and he began bringing patternwork to me at Bryant and Berry. Ford and Wills were designing two racing cars, "999" for Cooper, and "The Arrow" for sale. Cooper's car was named for a New York Central locomotive which had made a record train run between New York and Chicago. Cooper and Ford found the "999" too skittish to handle with throttle wide open, whereupon Cooper thought of his old competitor, Barney Oldfield. He came on from Utah to Detroit and launched his career as daredevil auto racer by driving "999" to an American record of a mile in a few seconds more than a minute.

Meanwhile, I changed jobs. Preston Henry, a young patternmaker I knew and a man named Frank started the Standard Pattern Works. This plant was on the third floor of a building on Randolph Street, and because they wanted more automobile design work they hired me. Early the next year Harold Wills and John Wandersee brought in some of their patternwork. They told me that Alexander Malcomson, a prosperous coal merchant who had watched the performance of Ford's racing car, wanted to form a company to put out Ford-engineered cars. This led to formation of Ford Motor

Company, with Malcomson and Ford as equal stockholders.

Malcomson's banker uncle, John Gray, was president, Henry Ford was vice-president and chief engineer, James Couzens, Malcomson's peppery-tempered bookkeeper, was treasurer. Other stockholders included the Dodge brothers, John and Horace, who in return for motor parts made in their machine shop got a block of stock. Wills was Ford's assistant.

Ford and Wills brought much of their experimental work to me. It was interesting work, and I liked it, but I wasn't happy at Standard Pattern Works. Preston Henry did a great deal of running around, partly calling on the trade looking for work, but partly in gay young bachelor doings. He was away from the plant so much that Mr. Frank, his partner, who did not know the engineering or patternmaking side of the business, turned to me to help him out. This didn't set well with Preston Henry, and soon I was in the middle of battles between the business partners.

Henry ended the situation in a particularly spectacular and heartless way. On Christmas Eve he sent me a telegram saying that my services were no longer required. I'd been married only six months, and I didn't show the telegram to my wife. I didn't want her to see that kind of Christmas present. The next day I went back to Bryant and Berry and remained there until the spring of 1905, when I went to Ford Motor Company.

Several times in the previous year I had asked Mr. Ford to let me work for him, but his reply was the same. "We're not well established. You're making a living as it is. I don't know how long it might last if you came here. Wait a little while until we're further along."

I continued to press him for a job. By 1905 the company had outgrown its Mack Avenue quarters and had built a three-story brick plant on Piquette Avenue. A short time after that Mr. Ford offered me a job in the pattern department. The pay was $3 a day and pretty good in those times for a young married man going on twenty-four.

And so, for the sixth time since Buffalo, I moved my tool chest to another job. I still have that chest, big as a Saratoga trunk and full of patternmaker's woodworking tools—some of which my father brought over from Denmark when he followed Little Sorensen to America.

The day I went to work at Ford and was dragging my chest into the pattern shop, an old enemy of mine, one Mc-Williams, blocked my way.

Months before we had clashed in meetings of the pattern-makers' union. I had joined the union because Bryant & Berry and Standard Pattern Works were union shops for awhile; any man hired must join the union. For one term I was elected union secretary. This experience was useful, because not only was I soon able to get up and make a red-hot speech but I got to know most of the really good mechanics in Detroit. But McWilliams was a trouble-maker, always looking for a chance to strike and stir up hard feeling against employers. Since I opposed his schemes at union meetings, we weren't on good terms.

By 1904, I had lost interest in the union and dropped out. But on my first day at Ford, there stood McWilliams. "If you want to work here," he said, "you'll have to be a union member again." I brushed him aside and told him to mind his own business and that I'd mind mine. I expected trouble, but Mc-Williams wasn't popular in the shop and left Ford soon after I joined; and that was my last personal experience with unions.

Then one of the most up-to-date automobile works, the Piquette Avenue plant became obsolete in a couple of years. The first floor was James Couzens' domain where he controlled accounting and sales, traffic and parts department, also timekeeping, payroll, and other business details. Purchasing, manufacturing, and design were all on the second floor. Cars were put together on the third floor.

Across the north end of the second floor was a heavy wall to keep out as much noise as possible. Here was the pattern department and a combined office and drafting room with a large blackboard and half a dozen drafting boards. The work in this room was done under the direction of Harold Wills. Henry Ford had no private office; he had a desk in this room, where he usually spent the first hours of the morning before circulating through the plant.

Soon after my assignment to a bench Mr. Ford came in. He was most friendly and expressed pleasure that I was now working for him. The head of the pattern department was Fred Seeman, who had been at Standard Pattern Works. I found that he spent much of his time watching production in the different foundries. Soon he began delegating me to look after the department while he was away, and this brought me in almost daily contact with Mr. Ford.

At first my work was much the same as at Bryant and Berry. It was apparent that Ford never quite understood what a design looked like until it was put into a three-dimensional pattern. I also discovered that he was not a draftsman and couldn't make a sketch that was any too clear, and much engine-design work was done in the office of Oliver Barthel. Now he found that when he explained to me what he wanted he could get some of his ideas developed and worked out in the plant. I began making sketches of his ideas and final drawings for some of their details, and when I couldn't finish them at Piquette Avenue I took them into the pattern shop. I would make a quick rough model form but according to dimensions. Mr. Ford would give this a final look to determine whether there should be changes or corrections in the design. I found that one problem in getting things the way

Ford wanted was Wills, who at times was extremely critical of his boss and his ideas. I must say that Wills was a clever, able designer. But like many gifted people he was high-strung and impatient. He did not credit Ford with the ability he fancied he himself possessed, and instead of giving him what he asked for, frequently tried to mold the Ford ideas to his. Because of this, I was afraid I was in for trouble working with both Mr. Ford and Wills. But it wasn't long before I got along well with Wills, who turned some development work over to me. He was always very pleasant and easy to work with, and I think that many times I helped him get exactly what Mr. Ford wanted. On the other hand, he did much to help me in making progress in the company and particularly with Mr. Ford.

I caught Ford's ideas more quickly than Wills did and could soon put them into some form or other so that the matter could be settled. This suited Wills perfectly, because he could devote more time in the plant to speeding up production.

Basically, differences between Ford and Wills were temperamental. There were other, more serious difficulties with which Mr. Ford had to contend. He had a board of directors which, paradoxically, was split three ways over a two-way issue: high-price or low-price car? With a few exceptions, the motorcar of those days was like a box at the opera, a showpiece for the wealthy and socially elect. The chief exception was the curved-dash Oldsmobile which Ransom E. Olds was then turning out by the thousands at $650 each, and, like Ford, he was in trouble with financial backers who fancied costlier, more luxurious cars. In Ford Motor Company, Malcomson, who had the heaviest cash investment in the enterprise, headed a group which favored a big, expensive car. Ford believed the company should stake its future on a low-cost, quantity-produced machine. It was fundamentally Ford's idea and *only* his idea. Whatever the record may disclose, I did not hear of anyone on the administrative side who was fully in accord with it. Couzens wanted a car that would sell—sell fast and for more than it cost to build—but tended more to support the frugal Ford than highfalutin' Malcomson. The Dodge brothers advocated a high-cost car. Being expert mechanics, they had great influence with the directors, but they disliked Malcomson and supported Ford and Couzens when the showdown came.

Here, then, was Henry Ford's situation: He had in Wills a chief engineer who was a perfectionist; in Couzens, a dragon at the cashbox; in himself, a man with a strong stubborn hunch for a cheap car for the average man, yet unable to describe its execution; and a board of directors out of sympathy with his aim and driven almost to hysterics by the groping and fumbling toward a low-cost car. For Ford merely had the idea; he had no picture in his mind as to what that car would be like, or look like.

Board meetings were usually held in Couzens' office. The minutes do not show how tense they were, but when the sessions were over Mr. Ford usually came by to tell me about the troubles he was having with this group. I could see that at times he was discouraged over the way things were going.

The first automotive products of Ford Motor Company were Models A, B, and C. A and C were Henry Ford's first gropings toward his dream of an inexpensive car. They were two-cylinder, chain-drive runabouts priced at from $800 to $950, and during 1903 and 1904, the first two years of the company's operation, some twenty-five hundred were sold. But his directors would not allow Ford to concentrate upon these two models; he must also design a vehicle for the high-priced field. Accordingly, he brought out in 1904 a heavier car, Model B, to sell for $2,000. Unlike the two lighter models, Model B had four cylinders and, instead of chain drive, it had torque or rotating-shaft drive. By the time I went to work at

Ford, another model had been added to the Ford line—
Model F, a touring car version of Model C, which sold for
$1,000.

Ford had now produced two light, comparatively inexpensive cars as well as a four-cylinder torque-driven automobile.
He was on the way but was still far from his dreamed-of goal.
His directors still demanded production of heavier, high-
priced cars. They couldn't shake Ford from his stand and
Ford couldn't shake them from theirs, but since it was their
money that started the company, he had to compromise. The
result was Model K, six cylinders, torque drive, and priced at
$2,800. The Dodge brothers were the ones really behind pro-
duction of this car, and though I know that Ford was never
in accord with it, Model K enjoyed a good reputation among
people of means.

My first pattern work at Ford was for Model K. I would
drop in at the drafting room on the second floor to make my
own sketches from the drawings on the blackboard and
drafting boards. Then I went to the pattern shop to get some
wooden form or model under way so that Mr. Ford could see
what his idea would look like. Shortly after my arrival at
Ford, designs which plainly were parts for a lighter car began
to show up on the blackboard and drafting tables. Mr. Ford
was applying to this car ideas he had worked out with Models
B and K. He was seeking a successor to Model F which would
have four instead of two cylinders and torque instead of chain
drive, and yet could be made to sell under the $800 minimum
for his earlier runabouts. This would be Model N, the success
of which was the curtain-raiser for Model T.

As Model N neared production stage, Malcomson became
so troublesome that he alienated even the Dodge brothers.
There were rumors that he was backing another motorcar
company, whereupon Ford, Couzens, the Dodges, Wills, and
two other Ford Motor Company stockholders organized the

Ford Manufacturing Company, which would make parts for Model N, while the Dodges continued as suppliers for Model K. This move had three results: First, it brought the manufacture of motorcar parts under Ford control. Second, it enabled stockholders to take two profits, one from manufacture of parts and the other from sale of cars. Third, it forced Malcomson to sell Ford Motor Company stock. Fourteen years later this same strategy forced remaining stockholders out of Ford Motor Company, when Ford organized Henry Ford & Son.

About the same time that Ford Manufacturing Company was formed there was a change in the pattern department. Fred Seeman left to go into business for himself, and Mr. Ford put me in charge of the department and of following up progress in foundries that turned out cast-iron and malleable work for us. I also got a nice little increase in pay and really began to feel I was getting somewhere.

Model N and its modifications, Models R and S, all had the same chassis. They were definitely Henry Ford's creations and approached the type of car that he always had in mind. It was to be a light car so standardized that it could be produced at the rate of at least a hundred a day. It was Ford's idea that Model N's four-cylinder motor could be cast in one block.

At that time all cylinder block castings were made from mahogany patterns reinforced with brass on the wearing parts. Even by skillful molders, these patterns got rough handling in the molding process and often had to be replaced. Stimulated by Henry Ford's dream of making the motorcar in large volume, I discussed with foundrymen the possibility of making metal instead of wooden patterns for cylinder blocks and mounting them on the molding machines. When I outlined this idea to Mr. Ford, he sensed immediately that it would mean not only a tremendous saving in foundry costs but also much better castings. But, since metal patterns would call for quite an investment, he asked me to see Mr. Couzens. And thus began my first contacts with the administrative side of the Ford Motor Company.

James Couzens was on the job every day in his office on the ground floor at Piquette. In all the years I knew him, I doubt that he went into the plant more than a dozen times. He was a shrewd, hard operator who had to be driving someone all the time. It made no difference who it was, and he rode everyone, including Henry Ford, as hard as he drove himself. He was a man of quick decision, so when Mr. Ford asked me to talk to him about metal patterns for our motor-block casting I realized that I had to have some real facts. That night at home I worked out my story. I checked my figures and made notes on everything I wanted to tell Mr. Couzens. The next morning I went downstairs primed for battle, but within ten minutes Couzens seemed completely satisfied and authorized the expenditure. "I don't mind spending money," he said, "so long as I get something back; that's what's going to make us successful in our line."

By this time the company had put a car at my service. I put in long hours to keep up with the program. We were running the pattern department ten hours a day, but many times I put in extra hours and even after that carried some of my work home with me. I was so absorbed with my work that time meant nothing to me.

I had married Helen Mitchell in June of 1904. We now had one son, Clifford. We moved to Medbury Boulevard, which was three blocks away from Piquette Avenue plant.

The Henry Fords lived close by, on Second Avenue, about three blocks from the plant.

In this new job I saw a great deal of Mr. Ford. He was much interested in my casting work and often accompanied me to the foundries to see how the work was done. Although there was sixteen years' difference in our ages, he didn't seem any older to me than I was. We were the closest friends.

We did not have Saturdays off in those days. Every day was a workday, and even Sunday mornings I would go to the plant. Mr. Ford often came, too, and we'd talk over last week's work and next week's plans. And all this helped me to understand better what he was trying to do.

He was determined to build the car for the masses and he sensed that there had to be a great development in the technique of manufacturing the parts that went into a car. This was constantly on his mind, and there never was a day we got together that this subject wasn't before us. That, of course, was the reason he was so interested in producing better, higher grade castings.

As I began to see the picture more clearly I wanted to make more things out of gray iron. It was becoming perfectly clear to me that we needed better development of the melting processes, a laboratory for analyzing our materials, better metal patterns, and mechanical devices for the sand.

Mr. Ford, sensing how keen I was on this work, gave me the nickname of "Cast-Iron Charlie." All these ideas that we had in our minds were finally realized when we got into the Model T. The real Model T never could have got to the stage in production that it did if we hadn't had the picture earlier of what the requirements for that car would be.

The first Model N wasn't completed in time for the New York Automobile Show early in 1906. But we showed it anyway. The little runabout was sent to New York without an engine in it, and nobody at the show was allowed to lift the hood. This didn't make any difference with the customers; what struck them most was the car's price tag: $500.

Model N's immediate success astonished everybody from Mr. Ford down. It proved, of course, his stubbornly held theory that a low-priced car would have a tremendous demand. But before this car went to the show, not much thought was devoted to its manufacture and cost. With Model N advertised to sell for $500, everything must be sharpened up to get its production costs down to under that figure.

About the same time that we sent the incomplete Model N to the New York show we began negotiations with C. R. Wilson Body Company for the carriage work on Model N. After Mr. Wilson left with the specifications, I got Mr. Ford's approval to build a model body in my pattern shop. It would be all wood with a few standard fittings such as locks, hinges, and forge brackets for fastening down a top, which was a separate piece contracted for and made elsewhere. As work progressed, I noted down each item of expense—labor and materials. As I recall, the total cost came to about $50. This low figure astonished both Mr. Ford and Wills, and it was a perfect ace in the hole to have when Mr. Wilson came back with his estimate.

Accompanying him was his superintendent, Fred Fisher, who with his brothers later won fortune and a deserved place in the automobile hall of fame as makers of "Bodies by Fisher." The Wilson bid stunned those of us in Mr. Ford's office into temporary silence. He wanted $152 for each unit!

"Now, Mr. Wilson," Mr. Ford began, "you've built a good many bodies for the carriage trade, and you must know what these things cost. We've made a cost study ourselves, and I must say your price is very high."

Bridling, Wilson said he knew exactly what he was doing and Mr. Ford must understand that this was the price of the body.

"Come out with us into the plant," Ford replied, "and

we'll show you a body that we have made exactly to design and specifications. Charlie here, who did this job, kept track of all labor and materials and figures that this body should only cost fifty dollars."

Now, I had learned to know Mr. Wilson because he was a neighbor of mine. His two sons were about my age, and we knew each other well; but he turned on me in a flash and said, "Sorensen, my wife and I were talking about you a few nights ago and what a smart young fellow you are. But we were wrong; you don't know what you're talking about."

"Mr. Wilson," I replied, "we have the facts and we know exactly what such a body should cost. I'm sure Mr. Ford wants you to have a reasonable profit for your work on this body, but he'll pay on the basis of what material, labor, and overhead costs are."

So far as I know, this was the beginning of the Ford purchasing formula. That evening when I was at home Fred Fisher, who lived close by, came over. "Charlie," he said, "you don't know how close you were to being right on the cost of that body. I worked it out the same way, and I can't find any fault with your figure. But Mr. Wilson has always made about a hundred dollars profit per unit, and he hasn't got the idea of making a great number of bodies like you people want. After we left you, I had quite a battle trying to convince him that we could make a lot of money if we set up for a large production and sold at a very narrow price. We should never ask more than seventy-five dollars for this body."

P.S. They got $72.

Some of our cost cutting in Model N production came by accident. All painting and trimming was done on the second floor at Piquette. Painting the wheels was considered a highly skilled job, for stripes on the spokes gave a star effect to the center of the wheel. It was quite an expensive operation until one day we refused the painters' demands for more pay per wheel, and they went on strike. That settled stripes on wheels. We gave them up, so, in a way, the painters helped us lower costs. But costs really began to decrease when Ford Motor Company acquired for a few months a roistering genius named Walter Flanders.

8

Couzens, Wills, and Flanders: Three Ford "Greats"

IT was Henry Ford's good fortune to have at his side three "greats" in the early days of his company. They were James Couzens, C. Harold Wills, and Walter Flanders, all three of whom left Ford Motor Company for one reason or another. Without the bulldog driving energy of Couzens in handling the purse strings and in constant nagging of dealers and branch agencies, the Ford company would have fallen apart almost before it had been put together. Without Harold Wills's perfectionist mind, the early Ford cars would not have had sufficient mechanical excellence for evolution into Model T. Without the genius of Walter Flanders in arranging production machinery and in cutting supply and inventory costs, the way would not have been paved for economical production of Model T, and the moving assembly line, upon which American mass production depends, would have been long delayed.

When Model N, Model T's immediate predecessor, was put on display at the 1906 Detroit Auto Show, immediately after its partial unveiling at New York, this item appeared in Detroit newspapers: "Early in 1904, I was convinced that the future of the automobile as a staple and permanent industry was dependent upon the production of a car for the ordinary man. I considered that I was an ordinary man and I wanted what ordinary people wanted, and I put my efforts towards developing a car that would meet what I conceived to be the ordinary man's car. I have since that time given the matter a great deal of thought, time and effort. I am convinced that such a car has got to be built of the best possible material obtainable and that it has got to be built light. I believed that I had conceived such a car, and the next question was to build it within the reach of the ordinary man.

"I then had to set about to design automatic machines to build in large quantities, and this I have succeeded in doing. Every piece that is produced by this machinery is inspected after each operation, which assures a thoroughly reliable machine. It is well known that quantities of anything reduce the cost of producing, and by getting out this car in such quantities I not only reduced the cost, but I am able to secure the best possible workmanship, because the man working so long and so steady on one piece becomes so proficient that there is not nearly the opportunity for mistakes which cause waste and expense. I have no doubt but what the public will recall the carriage business, and that it did not become very large until some manufacturer took a hold of it and produced them in large quantities and at a low price."

There are noteworthy things about this item. It is one of the earliest public statements on record of Henry Ford's ideas for a low-priced car and its manufacture. Its description of production methods anticipated their use by nearly a year. It is not a quotation of Henry Ford but is signed "James Couzens, Secretary Ford Motor Co.," and Miss Rosetta Couzens, the school teacher sister who invested half of her

$200 savings in Ford Motor Company, could have pointed out grave errors in her brother's syntax.

Published statements like this were largely responsible for stories, even now persistent, that Couzens was the originator of the Ford car. To say that Henry Ford did everything in the company would be an exaggeration. He was very much in the background on sales and commercial control. Couzens was the field general. He pushed everybody aside and ran us like a dictator. Mr. Ford did resent some of the Couzens statements that he, Couzens, was a creator of the product. But Couzens did this not to bolster his own ego but to keep the agents in line. He assumed responsibility for sales and service. He stressed service. Everything had to center around him in that field.

He worked fast, and I might say ruthlessly. No one could or would try to stop him, and more credit than he has received is due him for making a success of the company in its creative period, which I have already designated as the "Couzens Period."

He, more than anyone else, battled with Henry Ford to see that a suitable product was produced. I was present at several of these battles. He could really make Henry Ford do what he wanted. He had no ambition to head Ford Motor Company. His real ambition was to enter politics, a field in which his fiery temper and other qualities that contributed to the success of Ford Motor Company would ordinarily be liabilities.

Couzens was the driving force during the early years, dominating sales, service, advertising, and dealer and branch territory allotments. Although he had a blind side to almost everything mechanical, he was relentless in keeping after Henry Ford. When he could not see clearly what Mr. Ford was doing, Couzens jumped on him with both feet. For Ford was temperamentally the exact opposite of Couzens. Ford was always relaxed, whereas Couzens drove himself to the limit. Ford did not put in long hours regularly, though when some problem came up within his field of interest, unlike Couzens, he might work around the clock. Ford's patience, perhaps more than Couzens' driving, inspired the rest of us to work long hours to clear away problems. The many extra hours I put in, nights and Sundays, were part of that pattern. Although Couzens knew nothing about mechanics, when some development work was delayed, such as the Model T magneto, he would lash out at Henry Ford with hurricane force. Many times at the height of an argument I saw Mr. Ford walk away. But that did not stop Couzens. He would follow him out the door, then come to me to urge putting a firecracker under Mr. Ford.

There was a continuous stream of visitors from branch offices coming to Detroit to see Mr. Couzens; and when supply problems came up I would invariably be sent for to discuss the subject with branch managers. I got along splendidly with him, and I wonder sometimes how I did so, for even in those days I had acquired a reputation of being a battler, particularly in the branch offices. I think this was exactly what Couzens wanted—at any rate, our good relations continued as long as he was in Ford Motor Company.

Couzens surely put the fear of God into his branch managers. Several of them told me that when a letter came from him they wondered how it ever got there, it was so hot. Usually they hesitated to open it, and some preferred to read it in the confined solitude of the men's room rather than in their offices.

Despite his aggressive, domineering nature, I knew of no one in Ford Motor Company who didn't respect Jim Couzens. Most of the battles we had with him were over matters in which he gave way when the real situation was explained to him. Nearly all these arguments might have been avoided had the question been taken to him in the first place so that he could determine the course to pursue. Couzens had a gentle side when it came to his family, and his charities were many, but when it came to business, sentiment went out the window as Walter Flanders, one of the most rugged individuals to join the Ford organization, found out.

Flanders joined us after production of Model N had started and remained with us the better part of two years, then suddenly left to team up with Barney Everitt and William Metzger, two top salesmen of that era, to build the E-M-F car. He gave only ten days' notice that he was going to leave. He told Couzens of his plans and said he would be quitting the first of the next month. Couzens pulled out a checkbook, filled out a check and handed it to Flanders, remarking, "This will pay you up to today. If you are going to leave, you might as well go right now."

"Not bad logic," Flanders told me later. "That was one of the best business lessons I ever received."

It was a lesson, however, from which Flanders did not profit, for his E-M-F company soon sold out. Like two thousand others that entered the automobile business, E-M-F was short-lived because it had no one like Couzens around. And when Couzens left Ford, there was no one to replace him.

In contrast, Harold Wills, though he outlasted both Flanders and Couzens, was replaceable long before he left the company. He was an example of a man who, once almost indispensable, became softened by prosperity and high living. Wills was associated with Henry Ford a couple of years before there was a Ford Motor Company. Back in the late 1890's, when Ford was chief engineer at Edison Illuminating Company, all the steam-engine equipment carried oiling systems from the Detroit Lubricator Company, of which Wills's father was manager. When Henry Ford began making racing cars, he took on the younger Wills, first on part time and then on full time as a designer.

As the first designer for Ford and then in his metallurgical work, Wills was an important factor in the success of Ford Motor Company. He did not team up with Couzens at all. The basis of their discord was primarily costs, Couzens feeling that Wills was too extravagant in everything he did. However, Mr. Ford backed Wills in what he was doing until he became too independent to handle. I always got along with him very well, and he was exceedingly kind to me.

When Ford Motor Company was formed, Wills had some understanding whereby in addition to salary he received a share of Henry Ford's dividends. After I joined the company and went to work under Wills, I always knew when he got one of those dividends, for he would look up Ed Martin and me and hand each of us a nice little check. The first one, I remember, was for $100. The size of the checks increased as Will's income rose, and the last one he gave me was for $1,000. I was doing very well then myself, but I've never known the time when, nor the person to whom, an extra thousand dollars is not acceptable.

Wills was both generous and extravagant. He was a hard worker in the early years. Hours, holidays, meant nothing to him then. But as the fortunes of Ford Motor Company improved, so did his scale of living, the enjoyment of which drew him away from his work. He moved into a house on Jefferson Avenue in the Indian Village area with a waterfront and a dock for a fine yacht. He liked to hunt, so did I, and particularly in the spring of the year we spent many a weekend duck hunting.

As time went on, Wills specialized less in development work and more in metallurgy and tool design. He set up a laboratory in the Piquette plant to develop new steel alloys and their uses. From then on he was away from the plant a great deal, and we saw little of him for long spells. Eventually all the engineering work was in Joe Galamb's hands.

Wills liked fine jewels. This was, I think, a part of his perfectionist nature. After he could afford it, he always carried some around in his pockets and liked to display them to his friends. Divorced and happily remarried to a beautiful young girl, he showered jewels on her. One day he gave me a handsome diamond ring.

As the years went on, it was apparent that he and Henry Ford were drifting apart. He was proud and independent and often would not come to work before eleven o'clock. This indifference did not sit well with Henry Ford. One morning in the late nineteen-teens, Mr. Ford asked me to come to his office. Wills was waiting there, apparently summoned. In plain language Ford told him he would have to change his living habits or he would be dropped if he did not do so. He also said that Wills should stop giving Ed Martin and me a share of his dividend payments and that he should quit giving presents to the staff.

"Charlie here has a ring you gave him. You get that back from him and stop that sort of thing. And one thing more; get to work every morning at eight o'clock like the rest of us."

Ford walked out of the office leaving Wills alone with me. I took off the ring and gave it to Wills, and there wasn't much more to say. Ford was determined to put Wills to work the way he wanted, all of which was a shock to Wills, who always before had had a free hand. Instead of complying with the Ford ultimatum, Wills remained away more than ever. In 1919 he left the company. Ford paid him what was coming to him, and soon after Wills formed the Wills-St. Clair Company. Because of his reputation as a metallurgist and engineer, the new auto was launched as a superior car for particular customers who wanted the best.

I saw Wills only twice after he left. The first time was on a trip up the river to Lake Huron with the Fords on their yacht. As we passed, I pointed out the new Wills plant to Mr. Ford, who said, "Why not stop and see Wills?"

We docked at a pier close by where I got Wills on the phone at his home, and he came aboard. We sat on the deck for about an hour. Wills was sure he was on the road to success. He had a blueprint of his engine with him. It was an overhead valve, and the drive to the overhead camshaft was by a train of gears from the crankcase. It was so completely different from the simple L-head engine and Model T design with which Wills had grown that I was astonished that he would build such a complicated engine. I criticized it from a service and parts requirement angle, but he laughed at me. His car was the reverse of our thinking at Ford, which, it was apparent, he wanted to forget.

We left him with best wishes. I realized more than ever that Henry Ford was better off without him. The Wills-St. Clair was a beautiful piece of engineering but utterly unsuitable for the times, and a prime reason for its failure was that few garage mechanics of those days knew how to service it.

After Wills failed in his business venture he was hired by Chrysler Corporation for a while. In the later 1920's, George Holley, an old friend of Wills, asked Henry Ford to take him back. "See Charlie about it," he was told.

When Holley came to me, I was so astonished I could scarcely believe it. Wills was broke, Holley told me, and he would do anything.

"I doubt that very much," I replied, "but I'll see Wills and discuss the matter from a purely personal point of view."

When Wills called he said he needed a job, but I suspect he thought he would be welcomed with open arms and given a top position. We discussed the matter thoroughly. There was no opening for him in engineering. That division had been moved to Dearborn and under the eye of Henry Ford.

I suggested the purchasing department and handling of our special steel and metals, starting at a nominal salary. This meant reporting for work at 8:30 A.M. and punching a time-clock card. He had said he would do anything. I wanted to see if he meant it. Wills turned pale and stammered and could not tell me what he wanted to say. He left, and I never saw or heard from him again.

There was never any doubt in my mind about Wills's inherent ability. He was an individualist who sooner or later was bound to clash with Henry Ford, an even stronger individualist. So, even though he was a valuable man at Ford Motor Company, I knew there would be an end to his usefulness when Henry Ford set out to control him. I anticipated the end, but I had thought it would come from a clash with Couzens, the most combative individualist of the three. Nevertheless, Wills contributed immeasurably to the early success of Ford Motor Company, so in my book he remains one of the "greats."

Walter Flanders was a different sort of individualist. He played hard and rough, but he was a driving, hard-working production genius, an expert in the development and use of machine tools.

Machine tools were as wondrous in the industrial world of fifty years ago as automation, the ultimate in machine-tool use, seems today. Without them, automobiles could not have been put out in any quantity, costs would have been prohibitive, and replacement of worn and defective parts would have been next to impossible. Without them there would have been no such thing as mass production. They were the most obvious of answers to the production problem that came with the surprising rush of orders from Model N. Ford and Wills saw the necessity for more of them—and quickly—in both the Piquette plant and the newly opened shop of Ford Manufacturing Company on Bellevue Avenue, where Model N engines and transmissions would be turned out.

Outstanding of machinery salesmen calling upon us was Flanders. This burly, 35-year-old Yankee represented not one but three manufacturers and was not only a superlative salesman but a top mechanic. He was always on hand to see that machines we bought were properly set up when they arrived, and either he or one of his demonstrators was ready to train our people in their use.

With more orders coming in than Model N cars going out, Flanders appeared to Ford, Couzens, and Wills like an answer to prayer. He was engaged with the entirely unofficial rating of works manager, and his hiring arrangement included an understanding that he could continue to sell machinery elsewhere with an organization of his own.

Flanders liked to be on the move, so his plans for the future did not contemplate a lifetime of work at Ford. But in the twenty months, beginning in August, 1906, that he was with us he showed Ford Motor Company how to lay out production programs which fitted other phases of its operation. When he left in April, 1908, a month after the first announcement of Model T, he had created greater awareness that the motorcar business is a fusion of three arts—the art of buying materials, the art of production, and the art of selling.

Such an enlarged program at first threw a scare into the administrative side of the company. I well remember one morning when I was leaving the plant to go to one of the foundries to push along some castings that weren't coming fast enough to keep up with our stockpile. At that time we believed that castings should be left outdoors to age and rust for about thirty days before we machined them. The idea was done away with in later years. On going out into the yard to pick up my car I ran into Mr. Ford. "Where are you going?" he asked.

I told him.

"Guess I'll go with you," he said.

After we got in the car we sat quiet for a minute. I saw he had something on his mind, so I waited. Finally he talked. He had just come from a hot session with Couzens, and he was wrought up.

Couzens had impressed upon him that the expanded program Flanders wanted to undertake meant that they would be running out of money before they knew it. He must have poured it on hard, for this was the first time I had seen Mr. Ford discouraged. The thought of borrowing for operating costs frightened Ford. I never knew anyone who had greater horror of debt than he had. And he expressed himself very strongly to me, even hinting that he wouldn't be in business very long. Although I couldn't make out too well what all the trouble was about, I expressed sympathy. "I have some money in the bank," I said. "Of course, it isn't very much, but if you need it, you can have it anytime and—"

"No, Charlie," he interrupted, "when I have to do that, you and I will go somewhere else."

Well, we sat there quite a while, and again he stressed to me his determination to build a car at a low price. I had heard that from him many times, but he went on: his ambition was to build a car that his workers could afford to buy. This was an entirely new slant. He began to describe the great benefits to the country of this type of transportation in a vehicle that could be owned and operated by everybody including the workingman. I could not reply to this or draw any conclusions from it too quickly, but I remember so well I said to him, "Mr. Ford, that is a magnificent idea. If you are determined to do that, I'm sure that in time you will accomplish it. Of course, as I see it, it will take a lot of hard work, a lot of development work, and of course a lot of money to go with it."

He slapped me on the back. "Charlie, I'm going to do that job, and you're going to help me." Then, instead of going with me to the foundry, he left me with a little casual remark: "You go on, Charlie, with what you were going to do. I'm going to see that this job is finally accomplished. *I'm* determined to do it and nobody, Couzens or anyone else, is going to stop me on it."

This conversation has remained clear in my memory ever since. It seems to me to mark the real turning point in Ford Motor Company's future. The anxiety about money was merely temporary. What it inspired was a no-turning-back determination of Henry Ford to realize his vision of a car for the masses.

Flanders brought that vision nearer to reality. He was a large, heavy man with a great head of curly hair and a voice that could be heard in a drop-forge plant. Some of his personal habits and off-hours recreation were not in accord with Henry Ford's code of morals, but they never interfered with his work; he could carouse and hell-raise half the night and be on hand the next morning as fresh as a daisy in one of his native Vermont hayfields. He didn't care what people thought of him as long as he had his rough fun. In the plant he was a ball of fire, and men worked their heads off for him.

And so did I. My work in the foundry and in supplying materials soon attracted his notice. It was a great break for me. I now got help and guidance from a man who knew all phases of machine production and requirements of a motorcar. Without joining his after-dark amusements, I became strongly attached to him, and we were friendly all the time he remained at Ford. Flanders largely ignored Model K, devoting his time and planning to Model N. He realized that, if the selling price was to be $500, he had a real job to organize production to get within this price range.

Until Flanders came there was no such thing as fixed

monthly output. The large demand for Model N changed all that. When the sales department found it could get the agents to contract to take a certain number each month, it was possible to set up year-round delivery schedules.

This was the situation that Flanders needed in order to prepare the plant for a steady output to meet this demand. But he soon found that the demand was in excess of capacity, an ideal situation for a manufacturer to have, and under such conditions could set up a production program for twelve months ahead. This enabled the purchasing department to get better prices with fixed deliveries. Instead of our carrying inventories, he got the foundries and other suppliers to do it. Our stockkeepers were told not to have on hand more than a ten-day supply of anything to meet our production requirements. Previously the funds locked up for this purpose had been very large. Now, thanks to Flanders, those funds were freed and much of the confusion of hand-to-mouth operation that Ford Motor Company had been working under was now ended. The results were a revelation to all of us and led to the next step.

Early one morning in the winter of 1906-7, Henry Ford dropped in at the pattern department of the Piquette Avenue plant to see me. "Come with me, Charlie," he said, "I want to show you something."

I followed him to the third floor and its north end, which was not fully occupied for assembly work. He looked about and said, "Charlie, I'd like to have a room finished off right here in this space. Put up a wall with a door in big enough to run a car in and out. Get a good lock for the door, and when you're ready, we'll have Joe Galamb come up in here. We're going to start a completely new job."

The room he had in mind became the maternity ward for Model T.

9

Model T

IT took only a few days to block off the little room on the third floor back of the Piquette Avenue plant and to set up a few simple power tools and Joe Galamb's two blackboards. The blackboards were a good idea. They gave a king-sized drawing which, when all initial refinements had been made, could be photographed for two purposes: as a protection against patent suits attempting to prove prior claim to originality and as a substitute for blueprints. A little more than a year later Model T, the product of that cluttered little room, was announced to the world. But another half year passed before the first Model T was ready for what had already become a clamorous market. Besides my regular patternmaking and foundry work in connection with Model N production, I had especially keen interest in developments from this more or less secret room. The only ones allowed in it were Mr. Ford, Galamb, Gene Farkas and Louis Halmesberger—his two assistants—and me. For some reason which I can't account for now Mr. Ford didn't want Harold Wills in on this work, but he did tie Wills in on the vanadium steel development, which without question furnished the real impetus for abandoning the sensational success of Model N for the evolution of

Model T and ultimate realization of Henry Ford's dream of a car for the masses.

The summer before Mr. Ford told me to block off the experimental room for Joe Galamb, a momentous event occurred which would affect the entire automotive industry. The first heat of vanadium steel in the country was poured at the United Steel Company's plant in Canton, Ohio.

Early that year we had several visits from J. Kent Smith, a noted English metallurgist from a country which had been in the forefront of steel development. It took the American automobile industry to change the habits of our steelmakers and inspire them to produce new alloys. When Smith came to the United States, he made his first contacts at Canton, then traveled about the country with samples of his new type of heat-treated steel. Thus it was that he came to Detroit and saw Henry Ford.

Ford, Wills, and I listened to him and examined his data. We had already read about this English vanadium steel. It had a tensile strength nearly three times that of steels we were using, but we'd never seen it. Smith demonstrated its toughness and showed that despite its strength it could be machined more easily than plain steel. Immediately Mr. Ford sensed the great possibilities of this shock-resisting steel. "Charlie," he said to me after Smith left, "this means entirely new design requirements, and we can get a better, lighter, and cheaper car as a result of it."

It was the great common sense that Mr. Ford could apply to new ideas and his ability to simplify seemingly complicated problems that made him the pioneer he was. This demonstration of vanadium steel was the deciding point for him to begin the experimental work that resulted in Model T.

We wanted to be the first to take advantage of this new type of steel, but many things had to be ironed out and proved. Mr. Ford wanted to be sure that the steel could be uniformly made in successive heats. Accordingly, he tied in Wills with the program. From then on, Wills spent much of his time in Canton, where J. Kent Smith had his laboratory. As soon as he was convinced that the material could be handled commercially the same as other types of steel, Mr. Ford had the Canton plant follow through and make forgings for some of the Model N parts.

When forgings were brought to the plant they were machined in the toolroom. Then it was discovered that, in order to use these types of steel, better drills as well as cutting tools would have to be devised, and that meant more pioneering.

Meanwhile we experimented with other steels for such purposes as gears and the rear-axle drive shaft. Various good-sized heats were worked into forgings, then brought to the Piquette Avenue plant, where we set up a heat-treating and testing plant in a small building in the yard.

Wills had taken John Wandersee on his staff. John was an example of how in the early days we developed our own experts from our own people. He first came to work with us as a sweeper. He was without previous engineering or chemical or metallurgical experience, but Mr. Ford wanted him because he felt he could rely upon any figures John brought him. It was a happy choice, for Wandersee was always able to come up with facts and not opinion. Wills was inclined either to give his own interpretation of the facts or to exaggerate some of the details.

Taking Wandersee's figures, Joe Galamb worked out transmission engineering and design. Mr. Ford had decided upon planetary type of transmission. Joe would make a drawing which I would take down to the pattern shop and make in wood a true model size of the gear—even put the teeth in it. First designs were way oversize on what Mr. Ford thought they should be. It was astonishing to see how closely he sensed the sizes required for the different gears, and it was a great experience for me to see all this developing.

Gearshifts in those days were brutes. An absent-minded or an overeager driver could strip gears toothless quicker than you could say "Excuse my dust." In his determination to bring out a car that the ordinary man not only could afford to buy but could drive without being an expert or a high-toned chauffeur, Mr. Ford turned his back on the gearshifts of the day and experimented with planetary transmission. To get everything simple took a lot of fussy work. Before any experimental types were installed we first had to work out size and ratio. The first models were built out of wood, first to see their size and have Mr. Ford clear them. Finally we arrived at three foot pedals. One was the brake. Two others operated the transmission: one was reverse pedal; the other locked into low gear when pressed forward. When the foot was lifted from pedal the low gear was released and you went direct into the rear-axle drive.

This was a remarkable transmission. I'm sure many old-timers remember the stunts they could perform with it. It was possible to teeter the car back and forth simply by stepping first on the low and then on the reverse pedals. By releasing the low and then reversing that motion a man could do almost anything he wanted to get the car out of difficulty when in danger of bogging down in a rough country road. No transmission in today's cars could give that type of performance.

During World War II, when Henry Ford had become a querulous, suspicious old man who looked upon our government war contracts as a New Dealers' plot to take his business away from him, I aroused his momentary interest at a demonstration run of a Pratt & Whitney aviation engine. He examined the reduction unit, which could cut propeller speed to half that of the engine. After a moment's study he looked up and exclaimed, "Charlie, this has a planetary gear; it's Model T transmission!"

And so it was—the same principle, the same balanced pressure in all directions. It was remarkably efficient. Mr. Ford felt more kindly after that toward the Pratt and Whitney and our building it. I had one of the engines laid out in Dearborn for him to toy with and show to his visitors.

The aviation engineers were right in adopting the planetary gear principle. And so, I might add, were the tank designers. For a cross-country vehicle capable of going where even our Model T couldn't go, they employed the simplest, most dependable transmission of all. And when I mention "tank designers" I include Joe Galamb, who drew the first Model T transmission designs and whose renderings of tank transmissions were finally accepted a year later. Automobile history is full of strange parallels, of once-discarded ideas picked up years afterwards and used again. A year and more passed before planetary transmission could be worked out for Model T. Almost the same time elapsed before the transmission principle of a generation earlier could be accepted a generation later.

The first steel that we were to use on experimental Model T transmission was the carbonizing type. When the gears were cut and finished they were packed into heavy cast boxes and surrounded with a carbon material, then put in furnaces and brought up to heat and held for some time at that temperature. We wanted to find out how deep this carbon should go into the steel.

A small tight little group watched and checked out this process. Busy on the manufacturing end, Flanders wasn't too concerned about these experiments. He just wanted to get at it when the results had been determined.

It was primarily these new types of steel that would determine what Model T would look like. Every day it became more evident that soon Mr. Ford would come up with something revolutionary.

Of course, with his mind working the way it was at that time, there was no reason why he should be involved in administration or production. The current Models N, R, and S were to be steppingstones for the future car. The funds had to be found and the sales program had to be enlarged to the point where there was large enough volume to accommodate the change. I could see a big difference in Mr. Ford after he got into Galamb's room and began development work for Model T.

He kept saying to me, "Charlie, we are on the right track here now. We're going to get a car now that we can make in great volume and get the prices way down."

Mr. Ford did not want others in the plant to know anything about this until it had been thoroughly worked out and, of course, he was perfectly right in this. Had anything like what he was anticipating been exposed to the operating group, they would have held up production awaiting this new development, which Mr. Ford was not then ready to introduce.

Twenty months passed between the first heat of steel that was made in Canton and the announcement of Model T in March, 1908. But the real introduction of the car did not take place until October, 1908.

Actually it took four years and more to develop Model T. Previous models were the guinea pigs, one might say, for experimentation and development of a car which would realize Henry Ford's dream of a car which anyone could afford to buy, which anyone could drive anywhere, and which almost anyone could keep in repair. Many of the world's greatest mechanical discoveries were accidents in the course of other experimentation. Not so Model T, which ushered in the motor transport age and set off a chain reaction of machine produc-

tion now known as automation. All of our experimentation
at Ford in the early days was toward a fixed and, then,
wildly fantastic goal.

It could not be blueprinted. Today's engineers believe they
can design by coming up with just what is right on a piece of
paper. But Model T could not be designed that way. A blueprint didn't mean much to Henry Ford. He wanted to see
the finished size of the product; and that, as I've already said,
was where I came in. It was because of our constant tinkering
that we were so right in many of the things we made. By whit-
tling away at the wooden models of each part, and at the same
time calculating the probable tensile strength of it in a few
alloys of steel, we eventually came up with what was Model
T.

Throughout 1907 I continued to work with Mr. Ford on
Model T development, still retaining my dual jobs as foreman
of the pattern shop and as follow-up man for Flanders in
foundry castings. My foundry work also included jobs for
Model T. Obviously before Galamb could get to work on
planetary transmission, the engine and preliminary dimensions
had to be determined. The engine was to be an entirely new
four-cylinder design with a rating of about 25 horsepower.
Ideas were flying thick and fast, and Gene Farkas began rough
sketches on the blackboard. One of the first suggestions by
Mr. Ford was that its casting should be a four-cylinder block
instead of single unit blocks as on our earlier models.

I spent considerable time with Farkas on this particular
cylinder block. We decided that one-half of the crankcase
should be part of the block itself. Then Mr. Ford came along
with the idea of making a loose cylinder head jointed at the
point where the top of the piston came flush with the joint.
This simplified the design of the engine block. The casting
would be open on both ends and would be ideal for the
foundry work because the supporting cores could go through

the full length of this block. The whole crankcase core and cylinder barrels would then be in one unit.

I believe this was the first time a gasoline engine was designed to have a separate head. Later it would be adopted by other auto makers, and it prevails to this day. How to make a gasket that would hold against the compression was a nice little problem in itself. Galamb and his engineers had some doubts about it. Nevertheless, we stuck to the design and let the gasket development go until just before going into production.

This being an L type of engine, the camshaft was set on one side with its center in line with the valve chambers above it, and we built out a wall sufficient to enclose the valves within the casting. To seal this off, we made a steel stamped cover with a gasket. We did this because in our other engines a great deal of dirt came up off the roads. Dust and oil collected around the front of the valves, which were very hard to clean. With the valves enclosed, there was no possibility of dirt.

We opened up the valve chamber into the crankcase. Plenty of oil could be flying around, and we balanced this oil outlet so that we got perfect lubrication.

For the first casting of our new-type cylinder block we had to make patterns, flasks, and core boxes so that accuracy could be maintained in placing the water jackets as well as the main cores and the valve chamber core. While the drawings were being finished, I began making a pattern that included a flask in which we could set the core without depending upon sand for finding its place. Even for our first trial casting, I made metal instead of wood patterns and machined correctly to all dimensions. The making of these patterns in the flasks and the accuracy of the core boxes were what spelled the success of the casting.

We had to be sure that we could do this before we would

let the design go. If it couldn't be done, we would have had to fall back on the old type of engines and cylinder blocks. Everything turned out even better than we had hoped for. We made repeated castings in this same mold, and the accuracy was astonishing. The casting problem was solved.

We were now designing with the higher types of steel in mind for use in crankshafts, connecting rods, piston pins and valves. The crankshaft was to be made of our new vanadium steel and according to calculations would be very light and small. This didn't look quite right to us because we had much heavier cranks in our other engines.

Nevertheless, we went ahead on a forged crankshaft with very close dimensions and then machined it. We put it on a testing machine to ascertain its physical qualities and how much load it would carry before twisting. Next we gave it a shock test equivalent to double the load it would get in the actual operation of the engine. And when we had finished we knew that our small, light crankshaft was more than capable of meeting any demand the road and motor would place upon it.

We also came up with something entirely new in the design of the connecting rod. Our light crank made it essential not to have any more revolving weight than was actually needed, so we forged the rod with the bolts on the crank and integral with the forging. That spelled lightness in itself. Had we drilled the rod for a bolt to go through it and then put a head on the bolt on top of the rod, obviously that would take quite a bit more material.

In our first design the crankcase stopped at the end of the block. Block and crankcase would be cast so as to cover the full diameter and the depth of the flywheel. We studied this with a one-piece transmission and flywheel cover. Then we had the idea of making a crankcase extend to the end of the transmission housing. A half cover would sit on the end of the block to go the full length of the crankcase. In this space we could get all the transmission and the flywheel. In front of the flywheel there would be a dry multiple-disk clutch entirely of steel plates.

While we were experimenting with patterns and castings for the lower crankcase, I proposed to Joe that instead we use a steel stamping which would be merely a cover with no point of strain within the case itself. A caller from Buffalo had only recently shown us the possibilities of using pressed steel in auto parts as well as in frames. He was William H. Smith, manager and part owner of the John R. Keim mills which was then making steel stampings of ball housings for the telephone receivers then in use. Mr. Smith thought the same process on a larger scale would do for automobile axle housings. Mr. Ford immediately sensed that this would be just what we wanted for cost-cutting operations in current production as well as in our experimental developments for Model T. Accordingly, he sent Wills and me to look over the Keim plant and its facilities.

It was an amusing experience for me to go back to Buffalo because the Keim mills were near where I had lived as a boy and at that time they made bicycle crank hangers and pedals. With other young bicycle enthusiasts, I used to go to the back of the plant where there was a scrap pile of rejected ball bearings. I had quite a boxful of those bearings, which I kept around our home.

When Wills and I dropped in at Keim we found a press running to prove it could turn out the housings we wanted. Everything looked splendid until the press stopped. Out of the pit came a supervisor who had been handling the press-work. The operation needed a lot of lubrication and a heavy type of oil, and the man from the pit, a tall, lanky fellow, was covered with grease from head to foot. And that was my first, but not my last, sight of my fellow Dane, William H. Knudsen.

Wills and I packed up a pair of the housings and took the night boat back to Detroit. When we showed the housings to Mr. Ford, they made a great hit with him, for if these stampings could be made, almost anything of this type we wanted could be done.

So it was that we applied pressed steel whenever possible in place of castings. Perhaps when I suggested its use for transmission cases, Henry Ford might have altered his nickname for me from "Cast-Iron Charlie" to "Steel Stamping Charlie," but I would still have much to do with foundry work from then on, and more than a score of years later I would be the first to turn out a V-8 engine block in a single casting.

Within our pressed-steel transmission case we proposed to place a flywheel magneto. A cast plate, with sixteen copper coils set over the core and a part of the main casting, was to be the magneto's field. This was bolted against the end of the block; then we mounted U-shaped magnets on the face of the flywheel nearest the coils. The magnets were of steel which had been properly electrically charged.

What we had was a direct-current generator supplying electric sparks to ignite gasoline in the compression chambers. As long as the flywheel turned, sparks were produced. Until then dry batteries had supplied the sparks for auto engines. Use of a magneto was a revolutionary development in the industry. But it was not a novel idea. For generations it had been described as the "Faraday principle" and electrical textbooks of the day showed this type of magneto. It was the exact reverse of today's ordinary generator, which has a revolving armature and a standing field.

One of Henry Ford's earliest associates, Ed ("Spider")

Huff, was delegated to develop this d.c. generator. Spider Huff didn't come along quite as fast as we did in our other development work, so we had to wait awhile until a prototype could be made and tested. In our first checkups, the magneto seemed to work very well. Its coil was timed satisfactorily so that it delivered a spark to each cylinder at precisely the right instant. We saw no immediate problems, but we ran into plenty a little later.

In our first test cars the magneto failed completely after just a short run. Checking into the fault, we found where insulation on the coils was breaking down. This was in an area where the oil going around with the flywheel got very warm. We hadn't given this serious thought in our first designs and now we had to do something about it. If we couldn't have done so, there would never have been any Model T.

Early one morning Mr. Ford came to me and said, "Charlie, the trouble with that plate is that we have not insulated it properly. We are using the wrong materials. Now you get some standard impregnating varnish, the kind that you use for electrical impregnation. I have several large syrup kettles at the farm that will be just the thing for dipping the magneto in that stuff, and I'll go out and get one." In about two hours he was back with a syrup kettle that was about thirty inches wide with a heavy flange on its top face. We set this up on a lathe and cut off the flange, making a nice true face. Then we drilled a hole near the center of it at the height of the varnish level that we would use. Above the varnish level we drilled another hole. With a grinder disk we made a thin rubber gasket the same diameter as that of the kettle. This we put on top of the kettle and pulled it down good and tight with a whole series of clamps. Next we took the kettle down to the engine room and hooked it up at the top to a vacuum pump. At the bottom we put another fitting for blowing in high-pressure air.

We could now put the magneto base in our improvised combined pressure-vacuum tank. The process of repeated dipping in varnish, first applying pressure and then pumping a vacuum, did not take very long. Then we removed the magneto from the tank and hung it in an enamel baking oven for about six hours. Mr. Ford and I worked about forty-two hours without letup, from the time we started until the job was complete. We were terribly anxious to see whether we were right because, if we weren't, we couldn't go ahead with that type of magneto; and if we had to change magneto designs, or give up the magneto idea entirely, we had a chain of alterations which would go back to patterns for the original cylinder block.

After we removed it from the oven, the varnish was hardened between all the coils. When we put the magneto into the car and tried it out, it was an absolete success. We kept the car running night and day for weeks to prove that we were right. From then on to the last of the millions of Model Ts there was no more leakage on the magneto plate. I cite only this particular job to show the hard work we put in to lick countless seemingly minor problems. Among the many others, however, none was so scary as this magneto one.

I could add a great deal about problems that had to be worked out before Model T was evolved, but detailed recital of them is not important. The real importance is what came out of them.

We worked through the whole year of 1907 on these problems. By early 1908 we had built several test cars which we tried out on the roads. I did a lot of driving myself. Mr. Ford invariably went with me, and we made trips as far away as Indianapolis and northern Michigan. Most of the roads were terrible, which was one reason why we took them; a car which survived them met the acid test. There is no better comparison of highways then and now than today's elaborate proving grounds which cost the big auto companies millions of dollars to produce synthetic hazards that, back in 1908, we got for free.

By March, 1908, we were ready to announce Model T, but not to produce it. On October 1 of that year the first car was introduced to the public. From Joe Galamb's little room on the third floor had come a revolutionary vehicle. In the next eighteen years, out of Piquette Avenue, Highland Park, River Rouge, and from assembly plants all over the United States came 15,000,000 more.

What are the prospects today for a light, cheap car, one in the tradition-shattering role of Model T? After World War I, Vice-President Marshall remarked that "what this country needs is a *good* five-cent cigar." After World War II, it might be said that what the *world* needs is a car that can be bought for under $1,000. That car is possible today, but only under certain conditions. One is a reversal of the present trend in auto design and in public preference. Today's cars are more wasteful of power and fuel than any that have gone before. Examine the torque charts of current models in relation to the ever-increasing horsepower. As horsepower rises, so does the gas consumption in ever-greater ratio. For speed and power the American people are paying dearly, not only in safety but in unnecessarily inefficient operation and gas consumption. It is true that higher octane ratings have bettered fuel efficiency, but what price this advantage when it is offset by higher horsepower?

The most economically operating cars today are the light, small, low-horsepowered ones of foreign make. They come from countries which tax horsepower instead of the size or weight considerations that prevail in our forty-eight states. Even with import duties, some of them can be sold in the United States for less than the Fords, Chevrolets, and Plymouths in the American low-priced field. Ironically enough, they are not bought by the great American public which Henry Ford first enabled to become automobile owners. Instead, they are largely the second or third cars in the garages of the rich and the wellborn whose preferences in the early 1900's dominated the young automobile industry, which fact inspired Ford's dream of a car for the multitude.

The multitude now expects in its automobiles the accessories which in Model T days would have been the exclusive, costly idiosyncrasies of the rich—automatic transmission, power steering, besides radios, heaters, defrosters, and a bewildering variety of body styles. We at Ford brought the automobile within the reach of the common man whose demands and satisfactions are no longer on the Model T scale.

Production of a good car selling for under $1,000 in this country appears to me possible under these eventualities:

1. Reversal of the popular preference for higher powered cars by government taxes upon horsepower, a levy which would be fought bitterly by oil companies and auto dealers.

2. A return to hard times or international complications interfering with the flow of foreign oil to this country.

3. Readiness of an automobile company to disregard dealer opposition and to spend $200,000,000 for redesigning and retooling in a gamble to popularize the $1,000 car and persuade the American public to buy it.

Nevertheless, there is a future market for a present-day version of Model T. There is still a large section of the globe and a big proportion of the world's population as deficient in motor transport as the United States was a half century ago. Economically and in scale of living their deficiency may be even greater. But most of them are stirring with new hopes and aspirations. There are great areas of Asia, Africa, and South America, comprising perhaps half the people on earth, that sometime, and perhaps sooner than we expect, will open up. Only American methods of mass low-cost production can bring those people what they will want at what they can afford—methods which I first experimented with back in 1908 at the Ford Piquette Avenue plant.

PART
3

CHAPTER

10

The Birth of
Mass Production

W<small>E</small> have seen how Model T slowly evolved. An equally slow evolution was the final assembly line, the last and most spectacular link in mass production. Both "just grew," like Topsy. But, whereas the car evolved from an idea, mass production evolved from a necessity; and it was long after it appeared that the idea and its principles were reduced to words.

Today, we do not hear so much about "mass production" as we do about "automation." Both evolve from the same principle: machine-produced interchangeable parts and orderly flow of those parts first to subassembly, then to final assembly. The chief difference is that mechanized assembly is more complete in automation; where men once tended machine tools, the job is now done electronically, with men, fewer of them, keeping watch over the electronics.

Interchangeable parts were not new in 1913. Johann Gutenberg, the first printer in the Western world to use movable type, employed that principle five hundred years ago. Eli Whitney used interchangeable parts when making rifles in the early days of the Republic; and in early days of this century Henry Leland, who later sold out to Ford, applied the same principle in the first Cadillac cars. Overhead conveyors were used in many industries, including our own. So was substitution of machine work for hand labor. Nor was orderly progress of the work anything particularly new; but it was new to us at Ford until, as I have already described, Walter Flanders showed us how to arrange our machine tools at the Mack Avenue and Piquette plants.

What was worked out at Ford was the practice of moving the work from one worker to another until it became a complete unit, then arranging the flow of these units at the right time and the right place to a moving final assembly line from which came a finished product. Regardless of earlier uses of some of these principles, the direct line of succession of mass production and its intensification into automation stems directly from what we worked out at Ford Motor Company between 1908 and 1913.

Henry Ford is generally regarded as the father of mass production. He was not. He was the sponsor of it. And later, in an article over his initials in the *Encyclopedia Britannica* and written, I believe, by Samuel Crowther, he gave what is still the clearest explanation of its principles. Another misconception is that the final assembly line originated in our Highland Park plant in the summer of 1913. It was born then, but it was conceived in July of 1908 at the Piquette Avenue plant and not with Model T but during the last months of Model N production.

The middle of April, 1908, six weeks after public announcement of plans for Model T, Walter Flanders resigned. I have already reported how Mr. Ford told Ed Martin and me to "go out and run the plant, and don't worry about titles." Ed, as plant superintendent, ran the production end. I was assistant plant superintendent and handled production development. This was a natural evolution from my patternmaking, which turned out wooden models of experimental new parts designs.

My daily routine was to arrive at the plant at 7:30 and look over the shipping department's record of the previous day's output. Any bugs in production would show up in those records. Next, I made a round of the second floor where Model N bodies were being readied for bolting to the chassis. At that time all our cars were put together on the third floor on the east side of the building. Joe Galamb's little room where Model T was designed was in a corner at the north end. On the west side of the third floor was an elevator; all the parts were brought up and stored until needed for assembly.

As may be imagined, the job of putting the car together was a simpler one than handling the materials that had to be brought to it. Charlie Lewis, the youngest and most aggressive of our assembly foremen, and I tackled this problem. We gradually worked it out by bringing up only what we termed the fast-moving materials. The main bulky parts, like engines and axles, needed a lot of room. To give them that space, we left the smaller, more compact, light-handling material in a storage building on the northwest corner of the grounds. Then we arranged with the stock department to bring up at regular hours such divisions of material as we had marked out and packaged.

This simplification of handling cleaned things up materially. But at best, I did not like it. *It was then that the idea occurred to me that assembly would be easier, simpler, and faster if we moved the chassis along, beginning at one end of the plant with a frame and adding the axles and the wheels; then moving it past the stockroom, instead of moving the stockroom to the chassis.* I had Lewis arrange the materials on the floor so that what was needed at the start of assembly would be at that end of the building and the other parts would be along the line as we moved the chassis along. We spent every Sunday during July planning this. Then one Sunday morning, after the stock was laid out in this fashion, Lewis and I and a couple of helpers put together the first car, I'm sure, that was ever built on a moving line.

We did this simply by putting the frame on skids, hitching a towrope to the front end and pulling the frame along until axles and wheels were put on. Then we rolled the chassis along in notches to prove what could be done. While demonstrating this moving line, we worked on some of the subassemblies, such as completing a radiator with all its hose fittings so that we could place it very quickly on the chassis. We also did this with the dash and mounted the steering gear and the spark coil.

The only ones in Ford Motor Company who looked at this crude assembly line idea were Mr. Ford, Wills, and Ed Martin. Mr. Ford, though skeptical, nevertheless encouraged the experiment. Martin and Wills doubted that an automobile could be built properly on the move. Wills was particularly hostile. That way of building cars, he said, would ruin the company.

If it was proved in 1908 that an auto could be put together while moving a chassis past a sequence of waiting parts, why did five years elapse before this technique was adopted? Why so long between conception and birth?

First, remember that while Mr. Ford encouraged the experiment he did not necessarily accept it. Second, recall the layout and manufacturing operations of the Piquette plant. Parts were elevated from the ground and second floors to assembly on the third floor. Once a car was put together, it descended by the same route that its component parts had come up.

This, of course, was an unthinking rejection of the aid of

the long-accepted principle of gravitation. But to reverse the procedure would have turned Model N production literally upside down during the last few weeks of its life. Moreover, the time needed to accomplish that reversal would have indefinitely delayed Model T production and the realization of Mr. Ford's long-cherished ambition which he had maintained against all opposition.

Although Model T was announced in the spring, it was not shown until October. Production did not start until December, and first delivery of cars was made in February, 1909, eleven months after the first announcement. Nevertheless, the advance orders pouring in indicated that Piquette Avenue, the last word in auto plants from years before, was too small to meet the demand.

Our situation was the reverse of the familiar saying, "All dressed up and no place to go." We were going places but couldn't get dressed up. Even before the new car went into production there was talk of a new plant. Couzens, who would have to find the money, was all for it. He could look at three sides of a nickel before spending it but anything that increased production had his support. More cars meant more sales, and more sales meant more money for the company.

Decision to build a new plant at that time was one of the most courageous steps ever taken by Ford Motor Company. It was not uncertainty of the success of Model T that made this decision hazardous. It was the risk that went with the sale of each Ford car, and that risk increased as the number of sold cars rose.

For five years the shadow of patent litigation with possibility of ruinous damages had hung over the company. Infringement suits against Ford and two French motorcar manufacturers were filed in behalf of the Association of Licensed Automobile Manufacturers comprising companies paying royalties to holders of the Selden patent. In 1877, George Selden, a Rochester, New York, patent lawyer, had applied for a patent for a horseless carriage driven by an internal-combustion engine. Although he never built that vehicle, Selden and his associates claimed that the patent was a basic one under which no manufacturer could make autos without a license. Mr. Ford denied that Selden's patent was basic, and he refused to join the A.L.A.M.

When I went to work for Ford Motor Company in 1905, Mr. Parker tracked down a description in a French technical magazine of a vehicle driven in 1862 by a gas engine made by a Belgian, Jean Lenoir. It was decided to build an engine according to Lenoir's specifications; if it worked it might upset Selden's claim. From drawings made in the Ford drafting room, I made patterns, produced the castings, and brought them into the plant. Mr. Ford delegated Fred Allison to build the engine and set it up on a Ford chassis. This took a year and a half and many tests before the contraption ran and was ready for demonstration. On September 15, 1909, Judge Charles M. Hough of the Federal Court for Southern New York announced his decision: Selden's patent was upheld.

If this decision held, Ford Motor Company faced ruin. Nearly ten thousand Model T cars had been turned out, each car being a potential addition to damage suits for infringement of the Selden patent. Nor was this all; nearing completion were the first shops of the new Ford Motor Company plant at Highland Park.

Mr. Ford's answer to this threat was to increase production and extend plant facilities. The Hough decision was appealed and Ford stood ready to take the case, if necessary, to the Supreme Court of the United States.

A year passed. In late November, 1910, the Circuit Court of Appeals began hearing arguments on the Selden patent. On

January 11, 1911, decision was announced: Selden's patent was upheld, but it did not apply to the cars of Ford and other auto manufacturers.

The Ford fight against the Selden patent is a milestone in the history of the automobile industry. I believe it is one of the greatest things Mr. Ford did not only for Ford Motor Company but for everybody in the auto-making business. All of us around him took only minor parts in this long-drawn-out case. He carried full responsibility for success or failure on his own shoulders with little or no encouragement from members of his board. He rarely had a pleasant moment inside or outside his organization as long as this uncertainty lasted. Yet the affair did as much to inspire him as anything that had occurred up to that time. He knew that he could battle with the best there was in the country and not be stopped. And the outcome of the case removed another barrier on the road to mass production.

One of the forgotten men in organizing for mass production had nothing to do with output and sales but with the reverse. He was Fred Diehl, who, as head of the Ford purchasing department for twenty years before his retirement in 1929, probably spent more money than any other man in American industry. He joined the company in 1906 as a $75-a-month timekeeper. A year later Mr. Couzens put him to work purchasing supplies. Until then large requirements like tires would be handled as an individual job by Mr. Ford and other large items would be handled by Couzens. Buying was on a hand-to-mouth basis, generally in quantities no larger than were actually needed for short periods. Flanders had stabilized some of this helter-skelter buying by setting production schedules of fixed monthly output. Diehl raised buying from a method to a science and finally supervised every bit of material that was bought for the company.

As volume buying increased with rising production, Diehl required large suppliers to submit prices covering six- and twelve-month periods. In these large buying ventures he had to prove his case to Mr. Couzens, who was watching expenditures as suspiciously as Henry Ford later eyed General Motors and the New Deal. It wasn't a simple matter to convince Mr. Couzens, an endeavor in which I had plenty of experience, and Diehl had many battles with him over the new purchasing plans.

Diehl saw to it that material requirements and specifications were drawn up so plainly that each of his buyers knew exactly what he was buying. His buyers were instructed to look for at least two sources of supply and then be sure of competitive bidding. Next, he required each bidder to submit prices based on material, labor, and other overhead, and even the amount of profit. Under such a system there was no question about costs being kept down, and the savings were tremendous. Instead of being resented, Diehl was very much respected by suppliers, for although their prices were kept in line they were assured of profit. Even suppliers who had no particular desire at first to do business with Ford Motor Company under such conditions were soon sitting on its doorstep when they sensed the volume of purchases and saw how fair Fred Diehl was in his buying.

All this required close cooperation between purchasing and manufacturing divisions of a sort in which both chicken and egg came first. Assured of dependable production figures, Diehl could buy in quantity and space delivery, which assured not only properly spaced parts for Ford assembly but lower costs because suppliers could plan more economical output. Without carefully planned supply, assembly line mass production would have been impossible. Without cost-cut buying, Ford car prices would not have stimulated the mass consumption upon which mass production depended. And

that is why I say that Fred Diehl is one of the forgotten but
key men in development of Ford mass production.

Until 1908, Couzens had been a sort of one-man band. He
was not only treasurer but in charge of sales. He chose Ford
agents, established sales branches in most of the larger cities,
and appointed branch managers. Betweenwhiles, he kept an
eye on costs and purchased supplies. As business grew, he had
to delegate. He put Fred Diehl in charge of purchases and
transformed Norval Hawkins, a top-flight accountant with
an auditing firm of his own, into a top-flight sales manager.

Mr. Ford was not too pleased with the appointment of
Hawkins but agreed that he was a good man for the job. For
quite a while we didn't see much of Hawkins. He was out on
the road lining up his sales and his staff in each of our branches.
But if we didn't see him we heard plenty from him. For the
first time, sales were setting a hot pace for production and
Hawkins was yelling his head off for more cars.

Once he returned from a trip to Texas with a great stack
of orders and blood in his eye. He came straight into the plant
looking for me. Henry Ford was there, too. Hawkins sailed
into me right and left. Why couldn't we produce the cars to
meet his orders?

We all knew what the program was. Mr. Ford was not enjoying this constant reminder of how we were behind. I
stepped up and said, "Now, Hawkins, look here, those orders
are all right. That's just what we want. You keep them right
where you've got them. If ever I catch up with you, you'll
find me on your neck and you'll be out on the street."

Further explanations were not necessary and Hawkins
walked away. Years later, when our production averaged
better than eight thousand cars a day for a year, I dropped
in on Hawkins and reminded him of the talk we'd had some
years before.

"I guess you better move on," I told him. "We've caught up with you."

He did. He went to work for General Motors, where he didn't last very long. Nevertheless, he was a great salesman and I take my hat off to him.

Hawkins knew how to get around to see that the cars were properly distributed. By May, 1909, his people had lined up a backlog of Model T orders that would equal our entire output up to August. It was necessary for Ford Motor Company to instruct dealers to stop taking orders and "We will give thirty days' notice when dealers may resume taking orders."

This was revolutionary. Nothing like it had ever happened before in the auto industry. In June the company announced that it would again accept orders for Model T beginning July 7. In August another announcement stated that the company's business had outgrown its eleven branches and that six to ten more would be established during 1910. In October new Model T prices went into effect: fully equipped touring car, $950; roadster, $900. Unequipped, prices were $75 less. Equipment included brass windshield, two gas headlights with generator, two oil side lamps, one tail lamp, and a tubular horn. Fourteen years later prices were $269 for roadster and $298 for touring car.

The pattern for pricing Ford cars was based on apparent comparative prices for 1909 and 1910: the greater the volume the lower the price. Hawkins and his people brought us our first challenging volume. That challenge had to be met by faster production. True, it was the car that made the salesmen, but it was the sales organization that sparked the growing production organization.

In describing the Selden patent case, Diehl's buying, and Hawkins's selling, I may seem to have gone on a tangent from the main topic of this chapter. I did so purposely, for evolution of the Ford mass production system came from just such a series of tangents. The function of the final, moving assembly line, first tested in 1908 and first installed in 1913, is to put together a number of pieces or parts arriving at that line in orderly sequence. And these pieces had to be put together before there could be any final assembly.

Naturally, the biggest of all developments leading up to Ford mass production was building and equipping the Highland Park plant. Decision to erect that plant was made, as I have said, in 1908 while the Selden suit was still pending and Ed Martin and I were rearranging the Piquette Avenue layout for production of Model T. The Highland Park tract was a former racetrack along Woodward Avenue and comprised some sixty acres, all of which by 1914 was covered by Ford Motor Company buildings. In other words, the entire plant had to be functioning before the Ford mass production and assembly system could be completely worked out into one great synchronized operation from one end of the place to the other.

It was that complete synchronization which accounted for the difference between an ordinary assembly line and a mass production one. Meanwhile, Highland Park was laid out for progressive but not fully integrated operation. Wills, who headed all Ford production and machinery procurement after Flanders resigned, left most of the new plant layout in my hands. A room was set aside for my assistants. We set up layout boards on which we worked out the production lines and placement of machines to scale. Numbered brass plates were attached to all machines in the Piquette plant with corresponding tags on the layout boards so that every machine would be set up in its assigned place when the move to Highland Park was made. Edward Gray, the company's construction engineer, whipped these layouts into floor plans and building dimensions. Supplied with this material, Architect Albert

Kahn then made detailed plans and specifications. When Kahn finished, his main building was of striking, revolutionary design. Four stories high, nearly three hundred yards long, it was one of the first industrial structures with glass, saw-tooth roof allowing for an unusual amount of light and air. Machine shop, gas-engine plant, foundry, and office building were soon to follow.

With one-fourth of the plant completed, Piquette was vacated—it is now occupied by the Minnesota Mining and Manufacturing Company, which turns out the familiar Scotch Tape—and production began at Highland Park in January, 1910. This move was followed by tremendous expansion in equipment, for which we now had room.

Until then, our production had been carried on with standard equipment; we had little experience with special machine tools or machinery for multiple operation such as, for instance, a drill capable of boring more than 40 holes at one time and on four sides of a cylinder block. But we soon made up for lost time and knowledge. After moving into Highland Park we began developing special-type machines, multiple-spindled drills, milling machines with multiple heads at different angles. Whenever I approached Mr. Ford on the possibility of new types of machine tools, he never hesitated for a moment. "Don't wait, Charlie," he would say. "Let's get these things right away." He was wonderful in that respect: he never started out being skeptical and then saying "I told you so" when things went wrong. In all my nearly forty years with him, I never had that sort of frustration.

Tool design at Highland Park centered around Carl Emde. We set up studies for special operations. Wills helped in this. He was doing machinery buying, and his staff was on the lookout for multiple-purpose machines, and we would pick up any device that would give us increased production. Now aware that Ford was scrapping old and installing high-production equipment, machine-tool builders flocked around Emde with their latest developments. By 1911, Model T production was two hundred cars a day.

That year we bought an entire pressed-steel plant, moved its equipment from Buffalo to Highland Park, and set it up in a new building. This, as I have recorded, was the John R. Keim plant which supplied steel-stamped coverings for Model T's crankcase and transmission. Because the concern hadn't very strong financial backing, Ford Motor Company agreed to underwrite the new tools and dies necessary for the work. This was common practice with us when suppliers ran into financial trouble when expanding their facilities enough to meet our needs. But in the case of Keim we put up more and more money until I went to Mr. Ford after one of my trips to Buffalo and expressed alarm over our heavy outlay with no protection against loss. We had gone so far that I suggested it would be safer to buy the place outright and run it ourselves. Mr. Ford assented, and we bought out the stockholders for slightly more than $500,000.

The buildings were old, unsanitary, and permeated with smoke and heat. Furnaces needed repair. Altogether it was an unsatisfactory plant, incapable of meeting our expanding needs.

The only way to do this job right, we agreed, was to set up a new plant in Highland Park. We laid out a building that tied in with our main machine shops. It was high with cranes overhead so that everything could clear over the top of the tallest presses and no mechanical parts were buried in pits similar to the one Bill Knudsen had crawled out of when I first met him. We put up this plant in eight months and moved to Detroit the presses and other equipment and key personnel, including John Lee and Knudsen, all of whom turned out to be very useful to the company.

By 1912 we had made tremendous strides. Our yearly output was 75,000 cars but, even though we operated on round-the-clock shifts, production was still far behind demand. Hawkins's sales force was flooding us with orders and pouring imprecations on the heads of manufacturing. Mass consumption was here.

Henry Ford had no ideas on mass production. He wanted to build a lot of autos. He was determined but, like everyone else at that time, he didn't know how. In later years he was glorified as the originator of the mass production idea. Far from it; he just grew into it, like the rest of us. The essential tools and the final assembly line with its many integrated feeders resulted from an organization which was continually experimenting and improvising to get better production.

It became apparent that we should revamp the plant to cut down operation time in the different parts assemblies and speed up deliveries to the big ground-floor room where the cars were put together. It was for this purpose that I installed the first conveyer system.

Radiators were put together on the second floor. Originally tubes and fins came from a supplier, and our people inserted tubes one at a time into the fins. This required the expense and handling effort of keeping a considerable stock on hand. Then we stamped out fins on our own press, conveyed these and other parts on belts past various assembly operations, and sent the finished radiators by conveyer downstairs to car assembly. Things went along nicely until one of those rare occasions when Mr. Couzens went into the plant. On that morning he came inside the manufacturing building and asked George, the doorman, where Mr. Ford was. At the same time he noticed the radiators dangling overhead on their way to the assembly line. Looking up and down, he apparently wasn't too pleased with what he saw. "What's all this?" he asked.

"That is one of Mr. Sorensen's accomplishments," George said.

Later Mr. Ford warned me: "Look out for Couzens. He is on the warpath over the radiator conveyer. When he calls for you, better be prepared, but don't take him too seriously."

I didn't have to wait long for that call. Mr. Couzens went at me hammer and tongs. How could anybody spend money like that without his knowing anything about it? I told him that I had never had a chance to explain what a great saving it was. I described the situation in the past, how great stacks of material piled up in the radiator department awaiting assembly, how all radiators were taken by truck down to the first floor where another large stock accumulated ready to be carried to be bolted to the cars. I gave him cost figures and the hours of labor involved in this cumbersome procedure.

Couzens listened with great interest, then asked what the conveyer had cost. Given that, he figured that the savings in just a few days' operations paid for the conveyer. This experience was similar to many that I had with Mr. Couzens; when convinced that initial expenditures meant long-range economy and more production, he made no trouble. He never found fault after that with similar developments in other parts assemblies, and it wasn't long before I got a nice increase in salary.

This proved beyond question and further opposition the success of the conveyer system. Years later, in *My Life and Work*, a book which was written for him, Mr. Ford said that the conveyer-assembly idea occurred to him after watching the reverse process in packing houses, where hogs and steers were triced up by hind legs on an overhead conveyer and disassembled. This is a rationalization long after the event. Mr. Ford had nothing to do with originating, planning, and carrying out the assembly line. He encouraged the work, his vision to try unorthodox methods was an example to us; and in that there is glory enough for all.

With Mr. Ford's endorsement and Mr. Couzens' approval

of cutting costs by spending more money for speedier production, we extended the conveyer system to other parts assemblies and set our sights at turning out 200,000 cars the next year. That would be at the rate of one car every two minutes during the twenty-four hours of a working day.

As assistant superintendent on the assembly end I had Clarence W. Avery, who came to us a couple of years after we moved to Highland Park. He was raised on a Michigan farm, attended the University of Michigan, then took up teaching and was Edsel's manual training instructor at Detroit University School. The Fords brought him to me one day and asked if I could use him in the plant. Avery said he was through with teaching and wanted to learn factory operation. I put him through a course of training which took him into every production department. Beginning at the bottom in each department, he did all the physical work necessary to understand its operations, then moved on to the next. This training lasted about eight months, then I took him under my wing in my office.

With firsthand familiarity with each step in each parts department, Avery worked out the timing schedules necessary before installation of conveyer assembly systems to motors, fenders, magnetos, and transmissions. One by one these operations were revamped and continuously moving conveyers delivered the assembled parts to the final assembly floor. Savings in labor time were enormous; some parts were put together six times as fast.

By August, 1913, all links in the chain of moving assembly lines were complete except the last and most spectacular one —the one we had first experimented with one Sunday morning just five years before. Again a towrope was hitched to a chassis, this time pulled by a capstan. Each part was attached to the moving chassis in order, from axles at the beginning to bodies at the end of the line. Some parts took longer to attach than others; so, to keep an even pull on the towrope, there must be differently spaced intervals between delivery of the parts along the line. This called for patient timing and rearrangement until the flow of parts and the speed and intervals along the assembly line meshed into a perfectly synchronized operation throughout all stages of production. Before the end of the year a power-driven assembly line was in operation, and New Year's saw three more installed. Ford mass production and a new era in industrial history had begun.

Today historians describe the part the Ford car played in the development of that era and in transforming American life. We see that now. But we didn't see it then; we weren't as smart as we have been credited with being. All that we were trying to do was to develop the Ford car.

The achievement came first. Then came logical expression of its principles and philosophy. Not until 1922 could Henry Ford explain it cogently: "Every piece of work in the shop moves; it may move on hooks on overhead chains going to assembly in the exact order in which the parts are required; it may travel on a moving platform, or it may go by gravity, but the point is that there is no lifting or trucking of anything other than materials."

It has been said that this system has taken skill out of work. The answer is that by putting higher skill into planning, management, and tool building it is possible for skill to be enjoyed by the many who are not skilled. A million men working with their hands could never approximate the daily output of the Ford assembly line. There are not enough men on earth with skill in their hands to produce all the goods that the world needs.

When skill is built into machines and material flows continuously into those machines, two things are done at once. It has been made possible for unskilled workers to earn higher wages, and the products they turn out satisfy human wants that otherwise wouldn't be satisfied at all. Under this system man is not a slave to the machine, he is a slave without it. Machines do not eliminate jobs; they only make them easier —and create new ones.

In January, 1914, this new industrial revolution began. Its start was unnoticed at the time—lost in the sensation caused by an announcement Henry Ford made five days after New Year's.

PART
4

11

The Five-Dollar Day

In March, 1956, the minimum wage became by act of Congress $1 an hour or $8 a day. Back in 1914, Henry Ford raised *his* minimum wage from $2 to $5 a day. The passage of time has dulled the significance and far-reaching results of that action of more than forty years ago. Proportionately, the Ford increase would be equivalent to raising today's $8 day to $20. But establishment of a $20 minimum wage, fantastic though it seems, would scarcely parallel the Ford announcement either in importance or in world-wide sensation.

The $5 day did not come about by any legislative act. It was not the outcome of collective bargaining. It did not result from any labor pressure—in fact, its establishment without union participation would be illegal today, and the man who made it could be haled into court for unfair labor practice. The $5 was merely one man's decision, after seeing some chalked figures on a blackboard in his office, that it would be a good business move. And he was entirely unaware that the consequences of that decision would be a revolution in business outlook and economic thought, and the evolution of what today is the distinctly American productive system of free enterprise.

The Ford Model T was built so that every man could run it. Ford mass production made it available to everyone. Ford wages enabled everyone to afford it. The Ford $5 day rejected the old theory that labor, like other commodities, must be bought in the cheapest market. It recognized that mass producers are also mass consumers, that they cannot consume unless they are able to buy. But, like Ford mass production, the principles of Ford wages were not expressed until years after the event.

In a recent advertisement was a photograph of Memorial Gate at the University of Pennsylvania. Over it was a Latin inscription of which the English translation is, "We shall find a way or we shall make one." That was also the working philosophy of Henry Ford in the days of his greatness and when he arrived at the $5-day plan.

The plan was worked out in his office one Sunday morning in January, 1914. Until this writing, all existing accounts of what went on that morning are, at the nearest, second or third hand. Those stories vary, not necessarily according to the narrator but according to the one who heard the narrator or the one who heard the person who had the story from the narrator. So, a collection of fantastic myths and suppositions has arisen over the origin of the $5 day. It's like the old parlor game in which all present sit in a circle. Occupant of No. 1 seat whispers something in the next person's ear, who whispers what he thinks he hears in the ear of his neighbor, and so on around the circle until what comes back to its originator is nothing like the original message.

It has been said that the idea originated with Mr. Couzens, but he knew nothing about it until Mr. Ford told him. Another account is that it was the brainchild of John R. Lee, who was one of the executives of the Keim Mills which Ford

Motor Company bought and moved to Detroit. At Ford, Lee became employment manager and simplified the company's pay schedules, but instead of endorsing the plan, he denounced it.

Myth also surrounds the participants at that Sunday morning meeting. Couzens, Wills, and Hawkins were said to have been there. They were not. The only ones present were Mr. Ford, Ed Martin, Lee, and I. The events of that day are still very clear in my mind, which is understandable, for this was a milestone in industrial and economic history. I am the only man alive who took part in that meeting; and since none of the others ever set down their accounts, mine is the only first-hand recollection. The $5 day happened this way:

Late in 1912 or early in 1913, Mr. Ford began to think about further expansion. We had been in Highland Park less than two years, we had not solved current production problems, and the parts assembly lines were still experiments. Yet the mind of Henry Ford bridged these gaps to toy with the idea that sometime our immense new plant would be as obsolete as the Piquette Avenue one. He anticipated that ultimately we should smelt our own iron and make our own steel, and he had his eye on the River Rouge-Dearborn area where he had grown up, and where he was then buying up farm property. He took me for a ride over the area and told me his plans for the future.

At his request, I began compiling production estimates for the next few years. I did a lot of night work on this. Model T production had virtually doubled each year—34,000 in 1910–11; in 1911–12, it was 78,000 cars. The prospect for 1912–13 was more than 168,000, and by 1920 it should be one million, or beyond the capacity of Highland Park. At the rate earnings were mounting, it was apparent that they could be funneled into new plant construction. It should be remembered that there was no tax problem then; and for the first time I could see how these estimates of earnings and greater volume fitted perfectly into a pattern.

As I began building production figures and costs with varying increasing columns, what caught Mr. Ford's eye particularly was the ever-decreasing costs as volume increased. Finally he said, "That's enough, Charlie. I have the smell of it now. I don't need any more figures. Just keep them available; I may want them again someday."

I put the figures away in a small safe in my office where they remained until Sunday, January 4, 1914, when Mr. Ford asked me to meet with him and Martin and Lee to discuss wages for the coming year. Ever since it was founded, Ford Motor Company had shared some of its prosperity with its people. Employees who had been with the company for three years or longer received 10 per cent of their annual pay, and efficiency bonus checks were handed to executives and branch managers. The year 1913 had brought a $28,000,000 surplus and dividends of $15,000,000. This extraordinary good fortune came about because of lowered production costs resulting from parts-conveyer systems; and now, with the whole plant geared to final moving assembly lines, our 1914 costs seemed destined to go lower yet.

Mr. Ford said that he wanted new wage scales to be tied more into profits than they had been. Customers were getting the benefits of lower costs. Lower costs, greater production, lower prices, higher wages were his aims. Lee and Martin showed skepticism. "Charlie," said Mr. Ford, "go over to the plant and bring back those figures you prepared on volume and cost."

Then I caught his idea and saw how those estimates of gains and earnings fitted into his plan. Mr. Ford had a blackboard in his office. On it I chalked up figures for materials, overhead, and labor based on expanding production and lowered car prices. As expected, production rose, costs fell, and up

Forty years with Ford. Charles E. Sorensen (*below*) and Henry Ford, his son Edsel, and his grandson Henry II — three generations of Ford presidents. Sorensen, who called the relationship between Edsel and his father "Henry Ford's most tragic failure," resigned shortly after Edsel's death and the return from service of Henry Ford II.

Career. Born in the second-floor apartment in Copenhagen shown above, Sorensen began as a patternmaker's apprentice in the Jewett Stove Works, Buffalo, got his first job as foreman (*right*) in Milwaukee when eighteen, and built the home below in Miami Beach after thirty years as Ford's production genius.

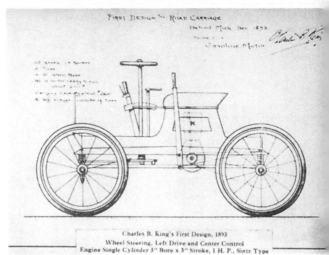

First Design for Road Carriage

Detroit Mich Dec 1893

Gasoline Motor

Charles B. King's First Design, 1893
Wheel Steering, Left Drive and Center Control
Engine Single Cylinder 3" Bore x 3" Stroke, 1 H. P., Sintz Type

ght. These designs by Charles King, released in 1893-1894, inspired Henry Ford's first car in 1896 (*below*).

Below, the world's first body and chassis assembly line. Highland Park, 1914. Bodies tobogganed from second-floor body shop to an overhead sling which plopped them over a chassis fresh from the assembly line.

Forerunners of Model T. *Above left,* First car produced by Ford Motor Company in 1903 — Model A, two cylinders, 8 h.p., chain drive, $750.00 — and Henry Ford's first groping toward an inexpensive car. *Above right,* Model N; visitors at 1908 New York Auto Show noticed the $500 price tag but not the fact that under the hood there was no engine — which was not ready in time for the show.

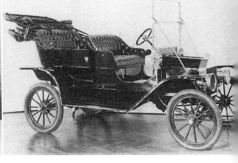

Above left — What Ford Directors wanted: Luxurious Model K of 1906. Price, with few buyers, $2,800. *Above right* — What Henry Ford wanted — and got: Model T, which changed the face of America and built an industrial empire. Price in 1908, $850; price 15,000,000 cars later, in 1926, $295.

Versatile Model T. *Below left,* "Picking Flowers" in a 1914 sylvan setting. *Below right,* mid-1920's urban setting; Tudor sedan with central door and "bath tub" rear window.

Right, Henry Ford's one and only attempt at mass production of seagoing transportation. A top-heavy World War I Eagle Boat on an uneasy trial spin.

Left, America's entrance into World War I brought pacifist Henry Ford into all-out war production. Here is a Ford-built Liberty aircraft engine. Few ever reached the front. Rum runners put them in their boats after the war.

Below — The last of Model T. Born 1908; buried, 1926.

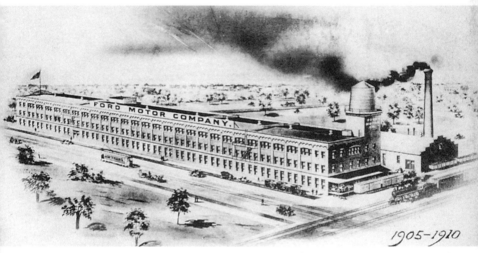

1905–1910

Visible growth of one man's fixed idea. Each of the first three Ford plants was outgrown almost before it was finished. *Above* is the Mack Avenue plant, where it all began. *Below* it is the Piquette Avenue plant, birthplace of Model T. *Below* is Highland Park, birthplace of assembly-line mass production; in terms of man hours, this photograph of 12,000 of its 16,000 employees is one of the most expensive pictures ever taken.

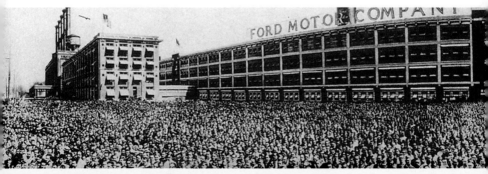

The world's greatest machine shop. The Ford River Rouge plant where iron ore goes in at one end and finished cars come out at the other.

Right, a World War I Bundle for Britain. Henry Ford and Sorensen give send-off to one of first overseas-bound Fordson tractors.

Below, Dagenham plant of the English Ford Company on the Thames. Sorensen laid it out. German bombers laid it waste.

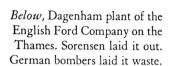

Beginning of a ten-year road to Ford collective bargining. A 1933 picket line at the St. Louis assembly plant. *United Press Photo*

Right, Harry Bennett, Ford's pistol-packing Man Friday, arrived at the scene of some trouble at River Rouge armed with a truce flag and a belief that the workers loved him. His skull was fractured. *United Press Photo*

Sit-down strikes shut down assembly plants. Here 1,200 Ford workers in California sealed the gates from the inside and sat down for 22 hours. *United Press Photo*

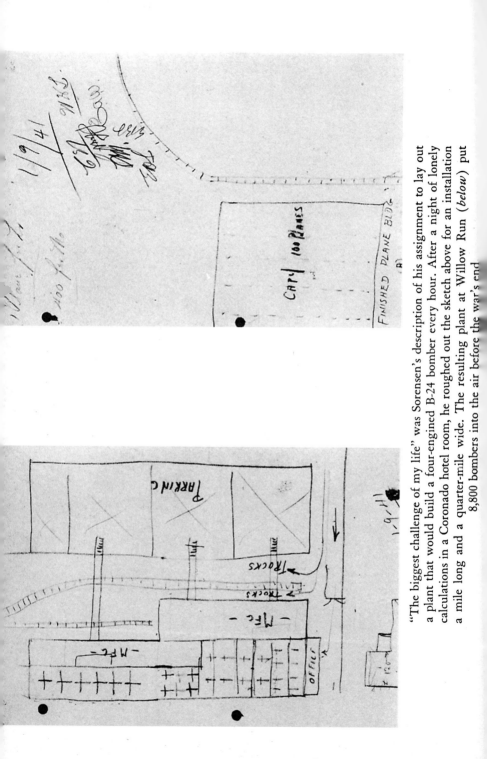

"The biggest challenge of my life" was Sorensen's description of his assignment to lay out a plant that would build a four-engined B-24 bomber every hour. After a night of lonely calculations in a Coronado hotel room, he roughed out the sketch above for an installation a mile long and a quarter-mile wide. The resulting plant at Willow Run (*below*) put 8,800 bombers into the air before the war's end

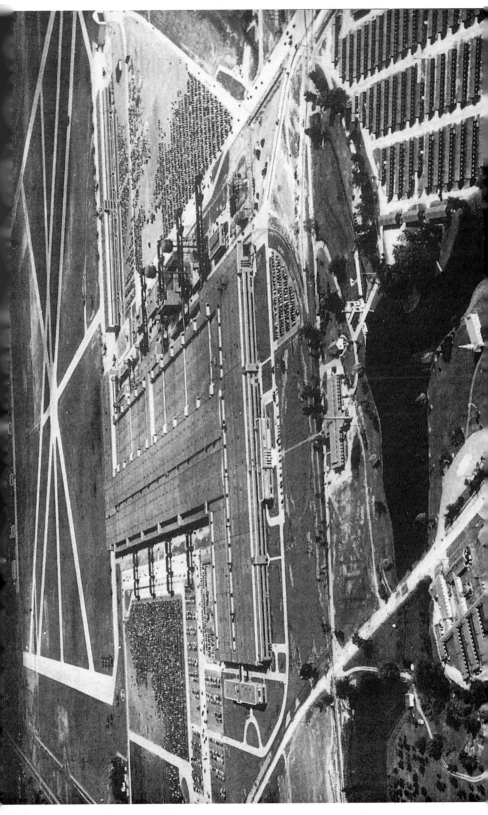

Let Henry Ford Build His Planes!

THE resources, power, willingness to help and patriotism of American industry when it is left perfectly free was never better illustrated than in the statement made by Henry Ford that

"If it became necessary the Ford Company could, with the counsel of Lindbergh and Rickenbacker, under supervision and without meddling ment agencies, swing into the prod thousand airplanes of standard desi

A THOUSAND PLANES A DA six months of preparation, as Mr. F is a titanic conception.

But, this industrial America of been a titan—when i red ta

Above, the photograph of a B-24 on which Sorensen penciled dividing lines for breaking down the entire plane into units for subassembly lines feeding into final assembly. *Left,* in production.

Right, over eight thousand four-engine bombers came out of Willow Run besides knock-down fuselages sent over the roads to other war-plane plants.

Sorensen was in complete charge of all Ford wartime production. In addition to bombers he built, among other things, tanks (*right*) and (*below*) gliders seen on the old Ford airport.

War Production Board chief, Donald Nelson, with Sorensen, Henry Ford, and Great Britain's Oliver Lyttelton on a Willow Run inspection tour, June, 1942.

Father, son, a troublemaker, and the man in the middle. Harry Bennett (*above left*) carried out the orders of the aging Henry Ford (photographed on his seventy-fifth birthday by Sorensen) to harass Edsel. Sorensen did what he could to keep peace.

"Henry Ford wants me to see Edsel and change his attitude on everything in general. Some job!" *Above*, Sorensen's notes on that phone call. Forty-one days later, Edsel was dead.

Sorensen with the two Henry Fords ten days before he announced, "I'm leaving for Florida tomorrow and I'm not coming back."

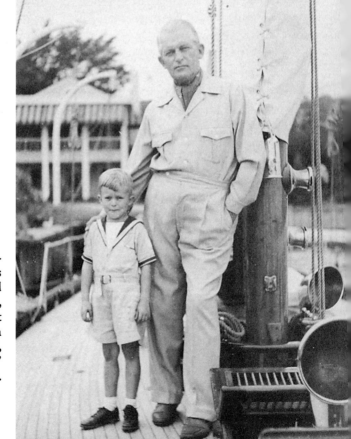

"I guess there's something in life besides work," Henry Ford told Sorensen. Here, on his racing yacht *White Cloud* and with his grandson Charles II, "Cast Iron Charlie" found it.

went figures for profits. Mr. Ford then had me transfer figures from profits column to labor costs—two million, three million, four million dollars. With that daily wage figures rose from minimums of $2 to $2.50 and $3. Ed Martin protested. I began to see how the increases would give greater incentive to our workers and that savings from lower costs and resulting higher production might be sufficient to take care of the major part of the increases. I could envisage more efficient production facilities that would reduce cost, and that there would be further economies from satisfied, willing workers.

While I stood at the blackboard, John Lee commented upon every entry and soon became pretty nasty. It was plain he wasn't trying to understand the idea and thought he might sabotage it by ridiculing it. This didn't sit well with Mr. Ford, who kept telling me to put more figures down—$3.50, $3.75, $4.00, $4.25, and a quarter of a dollar more, then another quarter.

At the end of about four hours, Mr. Ford stepped up to the blackboard. "Stop!" he said. "Stop it, Charlie; it's all settled. Five dollars a day minimum pay and at once."

Mr. Ford took an eraser and cleaned off the board. When we left the office, Lee was furious with me. "This crazy scheme will wreck the company," he said. Before and afterwards, I heard the words many times—not only from Lee but from others. But the company was not wrecked, dire predictions of disaster did not materialize, and most of the headshakers, as did Lee, changed their minds.

When I arrived at the plant on Monday morning I found Mr. Ford waiting for me in the garage. "I've thought about that five-dollar plan all night," he said. "I'll have to tell Couzens about it. I feel he should announce it. He will support it if he makes the announcement and gets the publicity that goes with it."

Knowing how Mr. Couzens could squeeze a penny until it

hurt, I wasn't so sure about his accepting the plan. Mr. Ford had no such doubts. The chief reason for his confidence was Couzens' growing appetite for personal publicity, an appetite Henry Ford would soon acquire, and a heightened interest in public affairs which was drawing him into local politics. I have already mentioned the Couzens tendency to assume the glory for Ford achievements, as illustrated by his press announcement which took credit for designing and producing Model N.

Mr. Ford asked me to accompany him to Couzens' office. "I'll go inside and see him," he said, "while you wait outside his office until I signal you."

Through a glass partition, I could see what was going on. I saw a short conversation between the two men. In less than a minute, Mr. Ford wagged his head at me, and I went in. I was astonished to find Couzens in full accord. The supporting figures I had with me weren't even called for. Mr. Couzens made some remark on how announcement of the plan would benefit him: "I want to be governor of Michigan, and this will help elect me."

The immediate effect of the $5 plan on the Ford worker was electric. The plan not only put $5 a day in his pocket, but the contrast between the Ford wage and wages elsewhere had strong psychological effect upon his attitude toward his job.

I never saw anything before or since which got such world-wide publicity and attention. We got so many inquiries that we had to set up a special department to answer questions and explain details. The $5 day made the name of Henry Ford world-famous—even more familiar than the name of his car. It was hailed as a great humanitarian act and social experiment. It was denounced as "socialism," "economic madness," "industrial suicide," and "undermining business." But it was none of these things. It was just good, sound business. As

Henry Ford said at the time, it was not "charity" but "profit sharing and efficiency engineering."

Other auto makers were particularly critical of what we had done. Alvin Macauley, president of Packard Motor Car Company, got me on the telephone that night at my home. "What are you fellows trying to do?" he demanded. "We got the news about your $5 day while we were having a board meeting. It was so astonishing that we broke up the meeting. We all felt, 'What is the use; we can't compete with an organization like Ford Motor Company.'"

"Of course, Mr. Macauley," I replied, "you don't have to follow our example unless you want to. Perhaps you have an advantage over us if you don't pay as much wages as we do."

"That would be fine," he said, "but how are we going to avoid paying these wages once you start paying them here in Detroit? We are not running a philanthropic business like you."

"There is no philanthropy about it," I answered. "If you will take the time to come and have a look at what we are doing, I'll explain it in a way that you will understand and not assume that it is philanthropy."

To refute those who said the plan was impossible, we had to prove that it could work. Henry Ford told me many times that I was the one who at the start had given him more confidence than anyone else because I had worked it out in simple figures so that he could understand.

The facts that appeared as we went along with the $5 day were startling. There was little social significance in the fact that the buying power of the Ford wage earner was increased. But raising the buying power of Ford workers increased in turn the buying power of other people and so on in a sort of chain reaction. The real significance was that the Ford high-wage policy was just the forerunner and then the example throughout American industry. As a result of it, workers' pay throughout the country increased. Also increased was their purchasing power and this bore out Mr. Ford's idea that every man working for him should be able to afford one of his motorcars. It meant a new era for workers in this country. It was a movement which energized every type of business and spurred awareness that everybody wants more of everything.

Five years later, when the minimum wage had been increased to $6 a day, we knew that our establishment of the $5 minimum for an eight-hour day was one of the best cost-cutting moves we had ever made. Results from the $6 day were further evidence. How far it could go, we did not then know. Over the next few years, as we gradually got into the Rouge operation, the minimum wage was increased until it reached the high of $7, and all other wages were scaled up in proportion. With it all, the company made more cars and greater earnings than ever before. That is why I say there was never any thought of philanthropy about it.

The most progressive period of Ford Motor Company was between 1914 and 1919. The only things we did not do were those we could not think of. Wages were not entirely responsible for that success. They had to be tied in with ability to produce. Higher wages, higher production: that was the formula. And by applying it, the cost of producing an automobile fell before our very eyes.

Not until after World War I did Henry Ford begin to sense what he had accomplished. It was the job of his chief spokesman, William J. Cameron, and of Samuel Crowther, to clothe Mr. Ford's sudden flashes of intuition with reason and to house them in simple, understandable words. I have already quoted one of his familiar sayings: "We go forward without the facts, and we learn the facts as we go along." He might have added, "I have a hunch; and I'll have it put into words if it works out."

Through Cameron, Mr. Ford was saying that one ought to be one's own best customer; that unless an industry keeps wages high and prices low, it limits the number of its customers and destroys itself. By 1926, in collaboration with Samuel Crowther in his book *Today and Tomorrow*, the complete theory was stated: that the wage earner is as important as a consumer as he is as a producer; and that enlarged buying power by paying high wages and selling at low prices is behind the prosperity of this country. Thus it took a dozen years before Mr. Ford saw the full import of his idea.

I still get a thrill when I recall the $5-day plan as I am now doing here, when I can see its significance better than forty years ago. It and the River Rouge plant never would have been possible if Henry Ford had listened to his directors and few stockholders. They would not have accepted the formula —indeed they did not and went to law about it when Mr. Ford tried to apply profits to building at the Rouge. With them, profits came first and set the price accordingly. Ford held that if the price is right the cost will take care of itself. Price first, then cost, was a paradox. It ran counter to prevailing business practice, but Ford made it work.

We first reduced the price to a point where we thought the most sales would result; then we went ahead and tried to meet that price. What use is it to know the cost if it says you cannot manufacture at a price at which the article can be sold? Actually the new price forced costs down; and one way to force costs down was to name a price so low that everybody in the shop would be forced to higher efficiency.

Our sharing profits with the public by lowering the price had a stimulating effect on our business. When prices went lower, we did more business and employed more men. Wages and profits rose and car prices dropped.

To those who could not understand the Ford idea, price reduction was the same as reducing the income of the business.

During World War I, Mr. Ford was contemplating a reduction of $80 a car. Since the company was turning out 500,000 cars a year, it was argued that this would reduce the company's income by $40,000,000. This calculation had nothing to do with the matter. What was entirely overlooked was the fact, as brought out in the $5-day calculations, that the $80 reduction would sell more than 500,000 cars and that the savings from the lower costs of greater production would more than absorb the price cut.

Until then, American business had operated on the principle that prices should be kept at the highest point at which people would buy. That is still the operating principle of much French and British industry. But the foundation of the American industrial system, which today outproduces the world, is the mass production technique worked out at Ford Motor Company coupled with Henry Ford's economic heresies that higher wages and lower prices resulted in more abundant production at lower cost.

With announcement of the $5-a-day plan all employees were notified that Ford Motor Company was setting up a department which would render legal advice to those in need of it. It was anticipated that many Ford workers would buy homes out of their additional income. Most of them were inexperienced in such matters. To protect them from unscrupulous operators, the staff and the new department would examine and advise on deeds, home financing, and building contracts.

This department was the beginning of what ultimately became the sociological department. Its first head was John Lee, who was later succeeded by Dean Samuel S. Marquis of the Detroit Episcopalian Cathedral, which the Fords attended. Dean Marquis carried on for several years, and the sociological department rolled on like a snowball, growing larger and larger. The bigger it grew the more unpopular it became with the workers.

So long as the department and Dean Marquis did not interfere with production, it was none of my business what they did or how much they pried into employees' personal affairs. But when they began calling men away from their work during the day, plant foremen and superintendents responsible for efficient production became so annoyed that I had to call a halt.

It all came to a head one day in the early 1920's when Mr. Ford asked me to come up to his office on the second floor of the Highland Park office building. When I arrived I found Dean Marquis there. I had no more than entered when he sailed into me for "interfering" with him and his staff. It was a surprising accusation, but that did not take me aback half so much as the vigor of his language. I had always treated clergymen with deference. Many times in my life I have been called an s.o.b., but never before or after was I called one by a supposed man of God—in fact, that day I heard from Dean Marquis some words I'd never heard before.

It was plain that he had arranged this session with Mr. Ford, expecting to snow me under. When he started in on me, I wondered whether Mr. Ford was in accord with him or not. I had enough evidence to make clear that he was interfering with the operations of the plant, but the good Dean was in no mood to listen. Then he got as big a surprise as I had. He was astonished to find that Mr. Ford supported me in everything I had said. Before he got through he discovered that both Mr. Ford and I were set on his keeping his nose out of the plant.

Dean Marquis left the office in a huff, and I never saw him again. A few days later he sent in notice that he would not carry on, and a great sigh of relief went through the entire plant. Later on, in press statements and in a book, he treated Mr. Ford in as ungrateful a way as did Harry Bennett, who later headed an even more prying and unpopular department in Ford Motor Company.

Dean Marquis's book was only one of many which appeared after 1914. The world-wide attention accorded Mr. Ford changed him from a modest man content with remaining in the background to one who delighted to bask in the great white light of publicity. If Ford mass production altered the pattern of American industry, it also changed Henry Ford.

The $7 day was installed after the great stock market crash of 1929. Again Mr. Ford said, "Raise wages and cut prices." Unhappily this dramatic contribution to hopes of quick economic recovery had no effect. Other manufacturers were thinking of ways to cut wages, and the man who by example and precept had caused one revolutionary change had little part in the era that began with the New Deal. Both labor and industry owed him an immense debt, and both paid it off in bad coin.

Merely to increase wages was not enough. It did not increase the buying power of Ford workers because almost immediately the Ford plant had to go on short time. Had there been the equivalent of a guaranteed annual wage, the effect might have been different. The New Deal put the unemployed on an unproductive or partially productive dole which enabled them to subsist but not to consume; and we, the people, paid for that in taxes which took more money away from production and consumption.

After the war employment continued high. Up went wages but production man-hours per car in the automobile industry either increased or remained about stationary—much of it because of new gadgets which the prosperous public demanded in even low-priced cars.

In 1955 the automobile industry was virtually kicked into a form of guaranteed annual pay. It had a magnificent opportunity to exercise some industrial statesmanship. Instead, one at a time, each company was forced by Walter Reuther's union to adopt a regularized pay pattern negotiated at Ford. That pattern goes only part of the way to the guaranteed annual wage—all of which means more bickering between management and union leadership; and industrial bickering imperils efficient lower-cost production.

What is not generally realized is the fact that more than half the automobile industry employees were under the regularized employment equivalent of a guaranteed wage before the Reuther negotiations. These include sales and purchasing, office workers, and in the plant itself there was union seniority which ensured full employment for older workers. So far as Ford Motor Company was concerned, its financial statements for 1954 and 1955 show its ability to apply the guaranteed wage to all employees with little or no increase in sales price per car.

In 1954, Ford net earnings were $227,800,000 from $4,062,-300,000 sales on 1,990,000 vehicles—trucks and passenger cars. That averaged $2,041 sales price and $114 earning per vehicle. In 1955 earnings were $437,000,000, sales were $5,594,000,000 on 2,614,000 vehicles. The 1955 average per vehicle was $2,140 sales price and $170 earnings. Setting aside $30 a car would ensure a fund of from $50,000,000 to $70,000,000 for guaranteed wage purposes. And with more stable employment and production, cost might be lowered enough to absorb most if not all of the $30 per car.

To one who sits on the sidelines yet can claim as much acquaintance with the principles of mass production as anyone living, the guaranteed annual wage is an inevitable pattern for all major American industries. The worst thing that can happen is to have men out of work without money; we've got to support our present economy by keeping men on the job.

As I see it, the guaranteed annual wage is a logical step along the path blazed by Henry Ford's $5 day. When Mr. Ford put his low-price, high-production policy into effect he was derided by orthodox industrialists and financiers. They said it would lead to socialism. Instead, it led to the greatest development of productivity the world has ever seen.

The same argument—"socialism"—is raised against the guaranteed annual wage. Actually, it is the reverse. Since World War II we have had a phenomenally high employment rate; and only mass consumption which results from high employment can support the productive economy of the country. Even if the American people pay for it in higher prices—the necessity for which I dispute—that is better than paying for unemployment in high taxes which siphons money away from production.

In other words, the guaranteed annual wage is avoidance of socialism in that it is industry's replacement of the unproductive government-taxed dole. It is, moreover, the necessary accompaniment of the new turn our national economy has taken since the 1930's. Consumer credit is at an all-time high of $34,000,000,000, which is equivalent to about four-fifths of the national income at the depth of the Great Depression. In fifteen years it increased 400 per cent.

Installment buying is now a feature of our economic system. Once it was the exclusive activity of high-percentage loan and finance companies and was scorned by orthodox banking; but now even the biggest banks in the country not only engage in it but aggressively seek pay-by-the-month installment accounts. Consumer credit enables a wage earner to have an automobile or a household appliance at least a year before he finishes payment for it. By just so much time is production of that car or appliance speeded up.

Although consumer credit buying stimulates production, it depends upon regular employment; unemployed creditors are unable to meet their installment payments. And this, to my mind, makes the guaranteed annual wage essential for safe, orderly operation of consumer credit. It is further recognition of Henry Ford's principle that the producer is also the consumer.

CHAPTER

12

We Start the Rouge

IN the late summer of 1915, I was lunching with Henry Ford at Highland Park when he left the table to answer a telephone call from Mrs. Ford. He came back to me and said, "Where is Joe Galamb? I want him to go to the house with me. I want him to do some interpreting for me from a Madame Schwimmer who speaks Hungarian. Joe is Hungarian."

I found Joe and they left at once for Fair Lane, the Ford mansion that had recently been completed. Madame Rosika Schwimmer was clever. She convinced both Henry and Mrs. Ford that a delegation headed by him and sailing to Europe could enlist enough public sentiment to stop the war. Louis P. Lochner, a newspaperman and official of the American Peace Foundation, would organize the group that supposedly could bring about an armistice. Mr. Ford agreed to give it his support and delegated his secretary Liebold to work with Lochner. Soon they had it organized. The Scandinavian-American Liner *Oscar II* was chartered, and Gaston Plantiff, our New York manager, was detailed to manage the expedition. Lochner made deals with the members to take care of their finances for hotels and traveling expenses, going and returning. Plantiff picked up the bills and paid them from a fund which Liebold set up. Henry Ford left for New York with Dean Marquis and Ray Dahlinger and on December 4 sailed with the strangest assortment of living creatures since the voyage of Noah's Ark.

I could understand Mr. Ford's wanting to do such a thing; it was a noble thought. But he lacked knowledge about Madame Schwimmer and the group she had around her. He certainly was out of his element.

It is history now how he failed. He knew it was an impossible situation before the ship reached Norway. He landed and took return passage on the first available ship a few days later, while the pilgrims continued on, at his expense, to Copenhagen and The Hague.

Mrs. Ford and a group of Detroit friends met him in New York and returned in a private car which was switched through to Dearborn. I had word to meet the party at the Dearborn station where Mrs. Ford drove home and Mr. Ford and I walked the short distance down the Michigan Central Railroad tracks to the plant. It was obvious that he was glad to be back in his own environment. He had not a word to say about his adventure, and I never heard him talk about it afterwards.

His answer to the critics was "They gave me the best free advertising I ever got." Mrs. Ford kept silent. All in all, Mr. and Mrs. Ford did not come out too badly in the long run. The cry was that this was a war to end all wars. Eternal peace was the purpose. Did we get it?

One thing the Peace Ship expedition did was to set off a chain reaction which culminated in the great River Rouge plant, a place justly termed "one of the wonders of the modern industrial world." I'll leave out the adjectives and impressive statistics of its 1,045 acres. Its immensity and completeness are now so much a matter of course as to cease being a wonderment. What is overlooked, however, is its basic simplicity: raw materials come in at one side, a complete motorcar comes out at the other. Also frequently overlooked is the essential philosophy behind its building and operation.

Of the raw materials, coal and iron are the backbone of the automobile industry—iron because it is the principal component of the motorcar and coal because it is an essential in the smelting of the iron and in furnishing the power without which there could be no manufacturing. No matter how efficient that manufacturing, coal and iron costs are prime elements in determining the cost of the completed automobile. These fluctuation costs are beyond the control of other auto companies. When Ford built the River Rouge plant he either owned or had lined up enough coal and iron deposits to handle his production. Thus, he controlled sources of his two most important materials.

As a result, Ford Motor Company emerged from World War II to peacetime manufacture of automobiles with five great advantages over its competitors: First, as we have seen, it had its own source of raw materials. Second, it had the world's greatest, most complete industrial manufacturing plant—the biggest machine shop on earth. Third, the Rouge plant, with assets of $1,500,000,000, was owned outright and was built out of profits and not a cent of borrowed money. Fourth, it had a work force and supervision at the foreman level trained in Ford production methods. Fifth, it had its own steel mill and therefore was unaffected by a steel shortage after the war which crippled the operations of many less fortunate companies. True, its postwar top management was new, but given those five incalculable advantages, how could it fail?

The first explosion in the chain reaction set off by Henry Ford's Peace Ship was the resignation of James Couzens as treasurer of Ford Motor Company. That came in October, 1915. The Couzens statement accompanying his resignation made plain that the final spark to his quitting was Mr. Ford's peace views. It also made plain that if it had not been this, it would have been something else, for Mr. Couzens said that, while he was willing to work *with* Mr. Ford, he could no longer work *for* him.

I have already designated the years between 1903 and 1913 as the "Couzens period" of Ford Motor Company. He should be forever blessed by the company for his relentless drive. After his resignation, Henry Ford was in the ascendancy. Before January, 1914, he had been relatively in the background, but the $5 day focused upon him the intense light of personal publicity in which he remained and reveled for thirty-three years—a whole generation, as time is reckoned—until his death beside the flickering light of a kerosene lamp.

In the early days Henry Ford could not have succeeded without James Couzens; now he was no longer needed. Financially, the company was not only above water but was making millions in profits. The chief control of expense was no longer the treasurer's office, but was in the supply and mechanical operations of the company. A million dollars' worth of new machinery might cut a car's production cost by X dollars, permitting its price to be cut by Y dollars, and resulting in added profit of Z. Couzens never blocked expansion, even after he ceased to be treasurer and remained on the company's board of directors—in fact, he was generally yelling for more production so as to keep up with sales. After our little run-in over the radiator assembly line I had installed, Mr. Couzens put no obstacles in the way of spending money to reduce production costs; but his mind was almost blank on anything mechanical, and thus the initiative of cost control passed to production departments.

Couzens resigned October 13, 1915, but remained a director of the company. Edsel Ford succeeded him as secretary-treasurer and also became a director. Two days later, Henry Ford and I moved from Highland Park to Dearborn. This move was a forerunner of his war over profits with the Dodge brothers. At Dearborn, where Ford Motor Company Engineering Laboratories are now, Mr. Ford had been experimenting with a farm tractor, this under a separate, recently organized company of Henry Ford & Son. Before he was ready to put it on the market, he wished me to plan and organize its production as I had done for Model T at Highland Park. I did not return to Ford Motor Company until after World War I. My time was divided between tractor development at Dearborn and in wartime England and Ireland and with plans for further Ford Motor Company plants along the River Rouge three miles away on a big tract of land Mr. Ford had quietly bought up in July, 1915.

Both Mr. and Mrs. Ford were sentimentalists about the Dearborn-River Rouge area. They were born there, grew up there, were married there, and spent the first few months of their married life there. At the first flush of prosperity of Ford Motor Company, Mr. Ford bought a few acres in the neighborhood and built a bungalow for weekend visits. From then on he continued to add to his acreage. By 1913 he had acquired, with the help of Fred Gregory, a real estate operator, some 2,000 acres of farm and woodland on both sides of the Rouge between Michigan and Warren Avenues. He had no more privacy in his Edison Avenue home in Detroit, and both he and his wife pined to return to Dearborn. Accordingly, he built Fair Lane, a mansion of rather dismal gray limestone, and urged me to be his neighbor, buy some farmland and build a home nearby. So, I bought on both sides of the river for a mile north on Warren Avenue On a site fronting on that avenue, I built in 1914 a white, colonial-type home, the rear of which overlooked the River Rouge. Part of my land had once belonged to one of Henry Ford's uncles.

He used to drive sheep from his farm to a little sandy beach where later I often went wading. There he washed his sheep before clipping and young Henry Ford used to help him.

After my wife and I got settled in our new home, Henry and Edsel Ford would ride over on horseback Sunday mornings to call. They tried to get me to ride, but I was not too keen about it. Once they brought along a big gray mare with a groom. "This is a gentle horse," they said. "We want you to try her out."

Horse and Sorensen eyed each other with mutual distrust. I mounted reluctantly, and the big gray mare started down the road full speed. There was a gate at the entrance and it was closed. I was scared stiff. The way the mare was going she would go right over the fence, but when she neared the gate she slid to a stop and I slid off somehow and hung onto her bridle. That was the last time I ever got on a horse, and I was more than ever in favor of the horse being displaced by the automobile on the road and by the tractor on the farm. Henry and Edsel Ford had a real scare out of it themselves, and I don't believe Henry Ford ever rode again, either.

At the same time that he was considering a new home for himself he was also thinking of a new one for Ford Motor Company. Although production was scarcely fully under way at Highland Park, Mr. Ford foresaw the time when that supposed last word in manufacturing magnitude would be outgrown. He had me compile estimates of future production, costs, and profits. Apparently they satisfied him that all expansion to meet these estimates could be paid for out of Ford Motor Company profits, for he had me put them away; and my next use of them, as I have already related, was to prove the feasibility of the $5 day.

It was not sentiment alone that directed his mind to the Rouge area for manufacturing purposes. From firsthand knowledge dating back to his boyhood, he knew it had all the natural requirements for a large plant—level ground, available rail transportation, and a river which might be useful if it could be dredged. He took me for a ride to show me what he was thinking about. I was the first one to cover this area with him and hear his thoughts and plans for the future.

In addition, we studied every tract of land available for industrial purposes around and about Detroit. We went the length of the Detroit River in a motorboat and as far up the Rouge as we could. The only vacant Detroit River water-front land was some 400 acres, which would not be enough at the rate Ford Motor Company was expanding. This left the Rouge as the largest undeveloped area. Dredging it for deep-water shipping offered no unsurmountable problem; a much more difficult accomplishment had taken place at Cleveland, where the Cuyahoga River had been deepened, enabling the largest lake vessels to dock at industrial plants alongside.

Even so, deep water wasn't as important a consideration then as it became later. All that Mr. Ford was thinking about was a plant site which could be a feeder for Highland Park, just as the Piquette Avenue plant was kept for a time as a feeder. The idea of the Rouge as a self-contained manufacturing unit did not at first enter his mind. Meanwhile, mass production by the synchronized moving assembly line had been perfected at Highland Park. The $5 day went into effect amid an avalanche of world-wide publicity. Branch assembly plants were spotted over the country. A European war had broken out, and Britain and her allies looked to American heavy industry to supply them with munitions. That meant more steel, more steel meant more iron, and because of this voracious war appetite, the phenomenally expanding Ford Motor Company would be on short rations.

Early one morning in July, 1915, Mr. Ford, Fred Gregory, Ed Martin, John Lee, and I met on Miller Road near the River Rouge. Gregory had plats of an area bounded on the north by the Michigan Central; on the east by the Pere Marquette, taking in Miller Road; on the south by Dix Avenue and River Rouge; and on the west by the Rouge. It was all level farmland, ideal for plant construction which would be served by two railroads. Mr. Ford knew most of the owners, and he told Gregory to assemble a staff of real estate operators who could get options on the land all in one day. So as not to involve Ford Motor Company in any publicity at the moment, the land was bought in the name of Henry Ford, who was known to have bought large tracts in the Dearborn area. For the Rouge site he paid $700,000—slightly better than $700 an acre.

When the plant site would be used and for what was not then decided—nevertheless, Mr. Ford had a hunch that he would need a waterfront. And so matters stood until October, when Couzens resigned, and Mr. Ford and I moved to Dearborn. When Mr. Ford left seven weeks later on his Peace Ship expedition, he gave me power of attorney to act for him at Henry Ford & Son during his absence. Edsel was the family representative on the board of directors of Ford Motor Company, and that ordeal, plus having to handle two rambunctious stockholders, the Dodge brothers, became an increasingly unpleasant one for this 22-year-old, sensitive young man.

Nineteen-sixteen was a year of decision and crisis. Early that spring I had assembled enough machinery at Dearborn to build our first Fordson tractors. On one of my office walls I hung up Fred Gregory's plats of the Rouge area. Mr. Ford would come in, and we would sit before them and talk about them for hours at a time. Edsel would come to Dearborn occasionally to see his mother at Fair Lane and then to my office with his father. The tractor plant was about three miles away from the River Rouge site. I suggested that Ford Motor Company acquire the land between it and the Rouge. That would make a solid block between old Dearborn and Miller Road, south of Michigan Avenue. In this area today, in addition to the Rouge plant, are the engineering buildings, testing grounds, airport, and Dearborn Inn; also Greenfield Village and homesites in a developed subdivision.

Decision to build blast furnaces and a foundry at the Rouge came out of these discussions in my office—a decision born of necessity. The need for steel and iron castings had become a vital problem. We were competing with other manufacturers for supplies and materials. Edsel and his father realized that we could not stop expanding and that a program of raw materials to finished products was a must.

The more than 1,000 acres of the Rouge site gave opportunity for expansion, and it had been the universal experience that iron- and steelworks thought to be ample at the outset were found to be wholly inadequate in a few years.

The project did involve a two-mile channel up a relatively narrow river. Actual dredging of the channel was a Federal government matter. One problem, however, was how a steamer going up two miles of river could turn around. Backing down a vessel of several thousand tons and 600 feet long for that distance would be impossible. This was ingeniously solved by a turning basin. Ore docks at the Rouge would be along a canal at right angles to the river. Out in the river a circular channel would be dug, leaving a small, round island, and steamers would round it as motorcars round a traffic circle on land. Canal, dock, deep water, and turning basin would be at Ford Motor Company expense.

William B. Mayo, who was in charge of engineering at Highland Park, where he had built the power station, was called in to make preliminary studies for the blast furnaces and coke ovens. We wanted estimates on the area necessary for operation of two blast furnaces of 500-ton daily capacity each. We also needed ore storage, coke ovens, coal storage on the same dock with the ore, dock space for lake ships to unload coal, ore, and limestone, a building to pour iron into pigs, and a slag-disposal operation. The layout and area required would determine the exact location of later foundry and machine shops and then assembly buildings would follow in order.

The problem of handling the work force in and out of the plant was given careful consideration. We had learned our lesson at Highland Park, where traffic had become a major problem, for we had not foreseen that our workers would come to work in their own automobiles. Considering that the Ford dream was "every man a car owner," this was either a glaring oversight or equally glaring lack of faith. Woodward Avenue had the only streetcar lines and all other streets were narrow and we tried to stagger coming and going shifts over a two-hour spread. If for no other reason, we had to move some of our operations to a new location, all of which taught us not to get caught on this again at the Rouge plant. We didn't realize it then, but in some installations at the new plant we would have as many as a thousand men to the acre.

To get in and out we needed bus lines that could enter the plant and unload in departments. Street railway tracks were laid to points where, with bridges over parking areas and Miller Road, no traffic lanes would be crossed.

With the final plan on the blast furnace and its subsidiaries decided on in principle, we then had a shakedown in grouping everything in as small an area as possible and still having room for future expansion. Although plans called for two blast furnaces, we allowed room for a third—which was not built until 1952, more than thirty years later. The blocking in of foundry, machine shop, and motor assembly came about in an orderly way. The capacity to build 10,000 automobiles a day was visualized, although not realized until October 31, 1925.

I set aside a separate room with large tables on which the

Rouge site was laid out to scale. In the same way that I had followed since I first went to work for Mr. Ford, I started in Dearborn to show on layout boards in model form what each building would look like. I showed ship canal, docks, and blast furnaces on a scale of one-eighth of an inch with roads, railroads, highways, bus lines, and streetcars all fitted in to serve present and future. It was the only way that Henry Ford could see the ultimate plan.

These studies were made both before and after the company directors approved the project. Financing appeared to offer little difficulty. There was no occasion for going into debt—a Ford anathema—and borrowing from banks. Ford Motor Company profits for the fiscal year ending June 30 were $60,000,000, more than enough to pay for enlarging Highland Park and branching out at the Rouge. That summer Mr. Ford made two significant announcements: first, Model T prices were reduced; second, the bulk of Ford Motor profits would be reinvested in the business.

Those announcements brought roars from John and Horace Dodge, who even in relaxed moments were good noisemakers. They were no longer represented on the company's directorate, having left to form their own automobile business, but as holders of a considerable amount of Ford Motor Company stock they had their fingers in the cashbox. They knew about the expansion plans and felt that the cost would be at their expense, for Ford dividends had helped and would help to finance their new business. They called in lawyers and threatened to go to court.

Ford Motor Company directors—Couzens, David Gray, Horace Rackham, as well as Edsel Ford and Klingensmith— also were aware of the plans. Mr. Ford was, of course, a director but since going to Dearborn he did not attend meetings. On the last day in October they approved a $1,000,000 contract for fabrication and erection of blast furnaces at the

Rouge; and this action was taken before the directors had even approved acquisition of the River Rouge site.

This omission was rectified three days later. On November 2, in three windy resolutions, the directors approved the expenditure of nearly $23,000,000. Of this, Couzens making the motion and Rackham seconding, some $12,000,000 was for the company's "manufacture of its own iron and the erection of a manufacturing plant on lands to be acquired from Mr. Henry Ford at the River Rouge." The other expenditure was for a Highland Park expansion program—buildings, equipment, jigs, and fixtures. Supply shortages were holding up Model T production, or suppliers would not expand their facilities to keep pace with Ford. Some departments had to be shut down a few days at a time because of suppliers' failure to deliver parts. Something had to be done, and done in a hurry, and Highland Park expansion would enable the company to make some of its own parts.

But here, at one pouring, nearly half a year's profits were being diverted from dividends and drawn off for plant expansion. The Dodge brothers lost no time. The day after the directors' action the Dodges applied in a Wayne County court for an injunction restraining Henry Ford from going forward with certain plant extensions, to order distribution of all future earnings above those needed for emergencies, and to appoint a receiver, if necessary, to manage Ford Motor Company. I never could understand the Dodge attitude except to call it a selfish one. Of course after Ford Motor Company stock was sold to the public early in 1956, there was nothing to prevent a group of stockholders from attempting a similar legal holdup.

Within a month the Dodges got an injunction restraining Ford from diverting profits, and ten days later the court slapped another order at Ford restraining him from proceeding with his plan to smelt iron ore at the Rouge. Had that order stuck, the company would have been hamstrung, but on January 6, 1917, the court relented to the extent of permitting Ford to go ahead with development at the Rouge, provided a $10,000,000 bond was posted to safeguard Dodge interests until the case was tried. There never would have been a Ford Motor Company as it is today if expansion to the Rouge plant had been permanently blocked or if Henry Ford had been less determined.

Just as he had done when the Selden patent suit hung over his head, Mr. Ford went ahead with plans to develop the Rouge. Now that blast furnaces were decided upon, the key to the project was, of course, a deep-water channel for lake shipping to deliver iron ore. The Federal government started to act with remarkable speed. An Army engineer was dispatched to survey the possibilities of deepening the Rouge, and he reported favorably by St. Valentine's Day. Within days the House of Representatives passed an appropriations bill. While the Senate was debating the Armed Ship Bill and the "little group of willful men" was delaying its passage, Senator William Alden Smith of Michigan introduced the River Rouge measure. Under it, Mr. Ford and other riparian owners would provide free of cost all land needed for the improvement if the government at a cost of $490,000 would deepen and maintain the channel. With a war on, the Senate had other things to talk about and did not get around to passing the Rouge appropriation until August. The first lake steamer to navigate the two-mile-deepened Rouge to our ore docks was in 1923—two years after the first blast was blown in the new smelter.

The year 1917 was not one of Henry Ford's happiest. First, we were at war—a war he had vainly and amid much ridicule tried to stop. Second, Edsel was exempted from the draft. I shall develop that episode more fully later; suffice it to say now that Edsel's war service at Ford Motor Company, which

was overloaded with war contracts, was greater than had he
been in uniform. Third, Mr. Ford had an uncomfortable time
on the witness stand during the trial of the Dodge suit. Fourth,
the Dodge brothers won their suit in the lower court; 50 per
cent of profits must be distributed as a stockholder dividend.
The decision was appealed, but it would be fourteen months
before the Michigan State Supreme Court would decide.

My time was spent partially on tractor development and a
wartime trip to England and Ireland, where I arranged for
5,000 tractors to be ready to plow for the 1918 crops. I was
still with Henry Ford & Son, ostensibly having nothing to
do with Ford Motor Company, but my heart was at the
Rouge. Mayo, I knew, would do splendidly in setting up designs for the most efficient, up-to-date—even advanced—iron-
smelting plant. I was intent upon a foundry that should be
the world's finest. So, I returned once more to the activity
that inspired Henry Ford's nickname of me as "Cast-Iron
Charlie."

The need for such a superplant was stressed by our experience at Highland Park, which was based on the best we knew
how but also on some practices that would have been familiar
to Egyptian bronze casters of 2500 B.C. When something new
and different is sought, it is useless to copy; start fresh on a
new idea. This means fresh minds at work. Seeking help on
planning this new foundry, I had to cast aside all precedent,
for there were no engineering groups that could or would
satisfy our demands for something different.

I wanted someone who had worked in a foundry, yet
could do layout work for foundry operations. Harry Hanson
fitted these requirements perfectly. He had been hired back
in 1914 as a molder, but he had taken an engineering course
and could develop new thoughts on paper and make studies.

One of our first innovations was to draw molten iron direct
from the smelters into the foundry furnaces. We wouldn't

wait for the stuff to be poured into pigs, then cool and be conveyed to the foundry melting cupolas. However, iron melting had been a hit-or-miss operation which caused variations in cylinder-casting metal. It just couldn't seem to be controlled, so we developed smaller holding furnaces in which to control the analysis just before pouring into the molds. All this called for an almost entirely different foundry practice in which temperatures of sand and iron both were joined.

I kept Hanson busy on foundry details and studies for multiple-story plans. He worked out a four-story arrangement with molding and pouring done on the top floor. Core rooms were to be on the third floor. Cooling and shaking out castings was to be done on the second floor. Then the castings would be dropped to the machine shop and all sand would be revivified and elevated to the fourth floor.

With this plan before me, I decided on one-floor foundry operations with a machine department adjoining. With a single floor, fewer conveyers and no elevators, with labor losing time going up and down, would be needed. Hanson drew the men he needed from Ford Motor Company drafting departments, and the final layouts were made by the organization he set up. Then Albert Kahn, the architect, took these floor plans and designed the buildings.

I fought the battle of the foundry plans hard. There was no example we could adapt or copy; and there was no one to stop me from installing a superplant. Nothing less would satisfy me.

13

We Finish the Rouge

IN February, 1919, the Michigan Supreme Court handed down its decision in the Dodge case. Ford Motor Company must pay an immediate dividend of $19,000,000 plus 5 per cent interest from date of decision in the lower court. Financially, this was not much of a setback, if any. The Dodges owned only 100 of the 1,000 shares of Ford stock; hence they would be paid $1,900,000. Henry Ford owned 585 shares; he would get $11,000,000 of the enforced dividend, and that covered the initial development at the Rouge authorized by the company directors. But the court held further: Henry Ford's withholding of dividends from stockholders was unlawful and arbitrary, and he was admonished against doing so again. There is no question but that it was this injunction against future "arbitrary" diversion of profits from dividends to expansion which decided Mr. Ford's next move. To give him freedom of action and to protect himself from further interference from stockholders (the Dodges were minority shareholders) he would buy them out and secure complete control of the company.

He had already anticipated the State Supreme Court decree when he resigned as president of Ford Motor Company on January 1, and Edsel succeeded him. Klingensmith took Edsel's place as treasurer. He kept away from Highland Park and let it be known that Henry Ford & Son was considering branching out from the tractor field to build a new car in the same price range as Model T. That either scared or prompted the remaining Ford Motor Company stockholders into selling out. The figures are the most dramatic in American industry. In round numbers they are:

	Original Investment	Selling Price
James Couzens	$ 2,500	$29,308,857.50
Mrs. Rosetta Couzens Hauss	100	262,036.67
Estate of John Gray	10,500	26,250,000.00
Horace & John Dodge	10,000 *	25,000,000.00
John Anderson	5,000	12,500,000.00
Horace Rackham	5,000	12,500,000.00
	(* Not all in cash)	

These stockholders had originally put up $33,100. Sixteen years later they sold out for more than $105,000,000. Also, in those sixteen years, their total dividends were more than $30,000,000. It will be noted that the Couzens selling price is proportionately higher than the rest. There are two reasons for this: First, Mr. Couzens, along with Mr. Ford, bought up holdings of stockholders who had sold out early. Second, Couzens didn't scare easily. He raised his price above the others, for he must have remembered his part in a similar tactic back in 1905 when the Ford Manufacturing Company was formed to drive Alexander Malcomson into selling his stock in Ford Motor Company.

The nearest Ford Motor Company came to being short of money was after Mr. Ford had acquired the stock from his former partners. A loan was negotiated for $60,000,000 in July, 1919. It was a lot of money for Mr. Ford to borrow. It was his first venture in that field, but the assets of the company were ample to qualify the loan.

In 1920 there was a slowdown in business, and rumors flew around that Ford Motor Company was looking for additional loans. Gaston Plantiff, manager of our New York branch, denied this in a statement he made after checking with Henry Ford. But Plantiff only knew what Henry Ford told him, and that was true as far as Mr. Ford was concerned. Without consulting him, Klingensmith, treasurer of the company, had taken it upon himself to discuss the matter of loans with some New York bankers. It was Klingensmith's idea that with falling sales we would need to have a line of credit established in the event of business dropping off further. He forgot to keep Mr. Ford posted on these negotiations, but it got to him in a roundabout way and then there was hell to pay with Klingensmith. It happened this way:

One morning when I arrived in my office Mr. Ford phoned to say he was coming over at once and for me to wait for him. Just as he came in, Joseph Bowers of New York also arrived. I knew Mr. Bowers. He represented a New York bank and had once tried to sell me some bonds for financing the international bridge that crossed the river from Detroit to Windsor.

I was surprised to see him. I did not know why he was there and Mr. Ford did not have time to explain. I was even more surprised when Bowers started off as though Henry Ford was soliciting a loan from his bank and talked to him like a teacher talks to a boy kept after school. Loans of this nature, he explained loftily, required that the bankers have a director on the board and a treasurer in the company that they could dominate. Also certain other things would make it difficult to handle such a loan. For one thing, Mr. Ford was inexperienced in finance—in fact, some prominent Grosse Pointe men, all bankers, with whom he had talked did not advise making loans to Henry Ford. They deemed him erratic and irresponsible. Throughout this insulting lecture Mr. Ford sat without saying a word. It was the boldest, nastiest thing I ever saw done to Henry Ford. I could not understand it, and I began measuring this rough type of banker up and down with my eye.

Mr. Ford could see I was boiling. Finally he told Bowers he did not need him and at the same time he gave me a nod that I understood. I got up and gathered up Bowers's briefcase, handed it to him with a short but not sweet "Here are your papers, you run along and peddle them. Goodbye!"

By this time Mr. Ford had stepped into an adjoining office. Bowers could see that he had better forget about any more high pressure around there. We never heard from him again.

As soon as Bowers and his briefcase left, I sent for Klingensmith. I believe he knew Bowers was there, for he came over in a hurry. He was surprised to find Mr. Ford with me. I asked him why Bowers had come, and then we learned how Kling had been talking with bankers in New York. Before Henry Ford finished with him on that matter, he knew his days were numbered. As soon as the deflated Klingensmith left, I asked Mr. Ford why we did not slow down and liquidate the large inventory we had if the company really needed money. I told him that I felt we could even squeeze out enough to pay off the loans we had at the moment. Certainly we did not need the very large inventory we had; it was wise to get that down anyhow.

The queer thing to me was that a financier like Klingensmith did not sense such a solution. I suppose it is banker instinct to make loans, and Klingensmith felt this was the wise thing to do. Having a banker's mind, Kling could not see our real resources beyond a financial statement sheet. I got our sales department, service parts department, and branches together. I talked to every branch manager about our agents taking on more parts, and when I explained the reason for it they all seemed enthusiastic about the plan. Many of these

Ford agents all over the country are still around. They will remember how we allotted parts to them through our branches; and perhaps they may remember it more kindly now than they thought of it then. The managers set up their schedules. We started shipping carload lots. Banks began getting sight drafts for parts shipped to Ford agents, and in many cases the parts were paid for before the carload arrived. Our money rolled in. Meanwhile I cleaned out excess tools and paints and tires, and the like at the plant. We got a clean slate on inventory, and as a result we had more than enough money to wipe out our loans. Klingensmith resigned in 1921, and we never had any more squeezes on finances.

In 1920, Mr. Ford and I returned to Ford Motor Company. Henry Ford & Son had served one of its purposes in scaring Ford Motor Company stockholders into selling their holdings; and thereafter, Fordson tractors would be made at the River Rouge plant. At the same time the Engineering Laboratory was laid out at Dearborn. Until then engineering had been scattered between the Rouge, Highland Park, and Dearborn. Now it was brought under one head, and Mr. Ford remained at Dearborn, where he could initiate or follow up ideas and experimentation. He held no titular position with the company, Edsel was president of Ford Motor Company; but, according to Ralph Waldo Emerson, one of Mr. Ford's favorite authors, "Wherever Macdonald sits, there is the head of the table."

From Dearborn I went to the Rouge, where I continued production planning and development; and there was plenty of it. Ed Martin, who was plant superintendent, and I practically lived at the Rouge. My day would start there as early as seven o'clock; luncheon was at Dearborn. I would then be back in the plant until about three o'clock, when I would go into production planning or tool design. At 5:30 I would return to my office for another hour. Several nights in the week I would come back after dinner at home for more office work.

The first production structure ready by the end of the war was the mammoth *B* Building. It was laid out to build Eagle boats for the government. It was high enough, with cranes the full length, to assemble the complete ship under its roof. It was designed so that we could add three floors the full width and use it for a manufacturing and final assembly after we finished the ill-starred Eagle boats. The building was laid in to fit the ultimate plan.

By 1923 our blast furnaces were in full operation, Great Lakes steamers were unloading iron ore to feed them; and coal and limestone came both by rail and by water. The Ford conveyer system, which is responsible in great part for Ford quantity production, was developing in every direction. One could see with one's own eyes raw material being transformed into parts, parts into units, and units to the assembly lines for the finished product. Solid carloads—even trainloads—of engines, front and rear axles, transmissions, radiators, and stampings for bodies, fenders, hoods, and magnetos rolled out of the Rouge railroad yards to branch assemblies in other cities.

Shortly after we moved to Highland Park, I laid out the first branch assembly plant in Detroit at East Grand Boulevard and Woodward Avenue. This was a sort of pilot plant for similar assemblies elsewhere, and after we took over the Keim Mills in Buffalo, I put Bill Knudsen to work locating and duplicating these plants in other cities. These branches were situated near railroad yards so that cars could be spotted, then unloaded with cranes and special slings for various units and headed for their special places at the assembly line.

By 1920 these assembly branches began to fit into our more than one million cars-per-year schedules. By 1929, eight years after Knudsen left Ford for General Motors, we had thirty-two strategically located branches in the United States, fitting into our average yearly production of 1,700,000 cars—some years in the middle 1920's we hit a 2,000,000-car production. All this was a fine bit of planning, handled and controlled in an office next to mine by Max Wiesmyer, a young man I had the good fortune to pick for the job.

Were I to name every associate who deserves well in the roster of Ford Motor Company achievement, or every ingenious process of manufacture, this narrative would be transformed into a combination biographical dictionary and engineers' and mechanics' handbook, as well as a burden to shelfroom. All that these reminiscences can conveniently handle, with some consideration for the reader, are some of the basic elements which, as I both saw and had a considerable part in shaping, were responsible for the progress of Henry Ford, his company, and his motorcars. Consequently, a detailed account of the River Rouge plant belongs elsewhere, even though during the two dozen years between 1920 and 1944 those details concerned me virtually every waking moment. (I heard of complaints that when sailing my topsail schooner in the Gulf Stream off Miami, I used the ship-to-shore radio telephone even more freely than the Ford Motor Company interoffice switchboard when I was at the Rouge.)

Accordingly, two elements I'd like to illustrate here are why we had to do so much of so many things at the Rouge, and how, blessed with this plant, the Ford organization originated and developed new ideas, new processes, and new models.

Even after it brought out Model T, Henry Ford's motor company expanded like a snowball rolling downhill. The bigger its production got the harder it became to find suppliers who could keep pace. And when a supplier couldn't keep up with our needs for parts or materials, the alternatives were either to cut production or shut down until supplies caught up, or make the things ourselves. Whether production was cut or suspended, not only car deliveries and sales were affected but so were 80,000 to 100,000 Ford employees. So, we were driven into gigantic do-it-yourself programs. As we undertook these new arts, instead of hurting the industries, which we kept hearing at the time, we not only simplified existing processes but in many cases did a lion's share in expanding the industrial output of the country. Take glass and steel, for example.

When we first bought plate glass, the price was around 30 cents a square foot. This kept climbing until it was $1.50 a square foot and still not enough plant expansion to meet our needs. We decided, much against our wishes, to get into the glass business. At Glassmere, Pennsylvania, we bought an old plant which had a capacity of 7,000,000 square feet a year. After we cleaned it up and added more machinery, it was still far from taking care of our needs but it gave us a foundation for expanding glass production.

We decided we must have our own plate glass as soon as possible and install a new modern plant at the Rouge. It was scheduled for 10,000,000 square feet. This revolutionized plate-glass manufacturing. A smelting furnace with mechanical charging of the silica sand so that it could produce a continuous ribbon of the glass was built.

Plate glass was cast in an endless unbroken strip, something the experts of the glass industry declared impossible. Then grinding and polishing was done on a continuous process. We designed and built this machinery. It was an immediate success. Instead of costing from 30 cents to $1.50, our glass was made for 20 cents a square foot. We also added another unit of 3,000,000 square feet at St. Paul, Minnesota, where we had both water power and silica sand on the same site. This way we added 20,000,000 square feet to the over-all production in the United States, and American glassmakers began improving their facilities—all because we were driven into a field about which we knew absolutely nothing but refused to adopt prevailing practices.

The story repeats itself in steel. Between 1919 and 1929 the demand exceeded the supply. We were tearing our hair. Purchasing steel and following up orders and deliveries produced headaches in many of our manufacturing divisions. Shortages meant holdups and layoffs in production. The profit motive seemed to interest steelmakers more than increasing facilities. Somewhere there had to be an increase in steel output. An increasing demand was apparent to anyone—all-steel auto bodies, furniture, refrigerators, stoves, freight cars, home utensils; someone had to cut loose and put up more steel mills. If others would not provide enough steel for our needs, then we would. It was just as simple as that.

Also, no other installation would add so much stability to our Rouge plant as a steel mill. By themselves, our blast furnaces were an unbalanced operation because they produced more iron than we needed for normal foundry purposes. Our scrap, an essential charging material for steelmaking, we were almost giving away to dealers.

This so-called scrap consisted of machine-shop borings and turnings, sheet-metal trimmings from the press shop—all baled into sizes for furnace charges. It sold as scrap for $8 a ton, as much as basic pig iron when sent direct to open hearth. A lot of money was involved in our scrap piles. A steel mill of our own would eliminate all this handling and piling for storage and reloading for shipment, a sizable but not in itself a deciding consideration.

When I showed Edsel and Henry Ford a plan of a steel mill that United Engineering laid out for us and told them it would cost $35,000,000, there was not the slightest hesitation on their part. Mr. Ford's answer was "What are you waiting for?"

I had to overcome the prejudices of follow-up and purchasing departments in our own organization. They feared that our steel suppliers would drop us before we could get our production underway. Strangely enough, I never ran into any objections from the steelmakers.

The mill would embrace every operation of steel manufacture from open hearth to blooming mill and rolling mills for sheets, bars, and rods. We already had blast furnaces with 1,000 tons a day capacity. We would run one on basic iron for our steel and the other on foundry iron for casting. It proved to be a big operating economy all around. We added to our coke-oven capacity, which in turn gave us more gas and waste products that we could use in our powerhouse, which was then able to take on the power load of the steel mill.

Besides assuring a dependable supply, the most noteworthy accomplishment of the steel mill was to shorten the production cycle. The elapsed time between the receipt of raw materials and the finished products in the hands of dealers had its effect on cost. Before we moved into the Rouge, the production cycle was twenty-one days. This came down gradually to fourteen, but after the Rouge steel mill was in operation this cycle was down to four days.

After we were in the steel business I was approached by several big steel men like Charlie Schwab of Bethlehem Steel and Bill Irwin of United States Steel. They wanted to buy our mill and give us our full requirement. They would guarantee volume and prices. Schwab was most persistent about this. "You can have it," I said, "if you're prepared to buy all of Ford Motor Company with it." And that closed the book on that.

During the Great Depression period we took on a spectacular job of handling used cars. Local agents had now run into increasingly difficult problems of disposing of old cars that were turned in when they sold customers new Fords. We did two things: One was to set up rebuilding lines in the Rouge and some branches and put flat prices on various types of overhaul jobs. The other was to give the agents a flat price for any type of "junkers" they took in. These junked cars were shipped to the Rouge and a sort of disassembly line was set up in the open-hearth plant. As a car moved down the line, tires, radiators, glass, and cloth in the bodies were removed. The remaining steel bodies and chassis were dropped at the end of the conveyer into the largest baler ever built.

The baler had three hydraulic rams. One ram pushed straight ahead until the bulk was compressed to thirty inches. Then a vertical ram pushed down to thirty inches and a side horizontal ram moved to where a pressure control stopped. This made a bundle thirty inches square by about forty inches high which was then used for cold scrap charges in one of our 100-ton open hearths. In costs, we did not come out ahead on this somewhat cannibalistic but spectacular operation but indirectly it helped us sell more cars.

I see no reason why this process should not be repeated. Before the mid-1950's the secondhand car became a bigger problem than ever. So many used cars were for sale or still on the road that new car production was cut back.

The postwar situation from 1946 on confirmed the good judgment of the mid-1930's in building the Rouge steel plant. Despite its tremendous expansion through the war years and into the 1950's, the steel industry was deafened by the continued cry for more steel. Immediately after the war, gray markets and controls sent prices skyrocketing. Scrap was being sold to the mills at prices comparable to those for steel in 1935. In the face of rising postwar prices, Ford Motor Company had the advantage of an assured supply of steel and of controlling its cost. Without that mill it is a question whether it could have brought out a postwar car as quickly as it did.

From 1920 until all civilian motor automotive production stopped in the World War II year of 1942, there had been produced at the Rouge plant Model T, Model A, a V-8 Ford, a V-8 Mercury, a Ford 6, numbers of truck models, and several varieties of tractors. All these required not only initial designs and tooling up but changes and adjustments in component parts. How was the Ford organization set up for development and make-ready for production? How were new projects created and put into operation? This was the procedure:

Basic ideas on new products centered around Henry Ford and the Dearborn Engineering, which we labeled the "Henry Ford job." Projects in the development stage centered around a few individual engineers. They were usually labeled secret and were carefully guarded so as not to let the idea be tossed around among all the members of that staff.

There was a complete experimental staff in the Dearborn Engineering Building, which contained a pattern shop, a machine shop, a tool department, sheet-metal department, department for clay models, an electrical department, and an office staff that handled its own payroll and purchasing requirements.

There was also a fine kitchen and dining room with a private room with a roundtable at which Henry Ford lunched daily. There were a few regulars at this table. Edsel, Ed Martin, Cameron, Wibel, and I were there every day. The table would hold twelve, and we occasionally brought a guest or some member of the organization. There was a rule that no business be discussed during luncheon.

After lunch was the time for a look around at any new project that might be coming along. Henry Ford would go with me and some of the engineers to see the progress on some live job. Edsel would drop in at the body and styling division.

The tractor, car, or truck went through this stage of making small-scale models; then, when one was finally decided upon, a full-scale model would be made. While this was going on, I would drop in with Edsel and discuss the mechanics of the model.

Henry Ford spent little time on that. Edsel had proved himself a good stylist and his father would let nothing leave Dearborn until Edsel had passed on it.

Henry Ford and I would boil down the engine, transmission, and axles. Eventually we would agree "This is it," when we would pull in Sheldrick and his Rouge production engineering group and cut loose the developed design for him to make-ready for the production lines. First we had to determine the number of men Sheldrick would put to work. This depended upon a work schedule necessary to meet the deadline I set for production to start.

In a plant like the Rouge, where this division had been growing for years, this type of work could be scheduled like a production job. Engineers were specialists. A specialist on crankshaft design could estimate his time on a new crank. His work involved metallurgy, the material to be used, also a breakdown test to check experimental castings or forgings of the crankshaft. The test would be made on a dynamometer at all speeds and loads. Records would be kept of the performances of these experimental cranks until the designer satisfied Sheldrick that he had one suitable for production.

When crankshaft development approached the final stage, the superintendent of the division that would manufacture it would come in with his foremen. Then with the plant planning group and William Pioch, head of tool design, an operation sheet would be written up showing every operation, machining and heat treat and their sequence. The planning group would study the machines required and draw up specifications and purchasing requisitions.

These groups which I have outlined were all located in the

same building where I had my office. Each day Ed Martin and I would meet with these division heads and pass on tools and equipment. Since time was the essence of these projects, we had prepared charts showing bottlenecks, and follow-up crews were put on these spots. Men in outside tool- and machine-manufacturing plants gave us daily progress reports on the items that were behind on promises. All this meant an organization that could coordinate. Discord would show up and spoil effort. That was where I came in—looking for the weak spots, and I would live with them night and day until they cleared up.

The skill in manufacturing the finished article was reflected in the planning. Casual visitors looking at parts being made would be astonished to see how simple it was to make a crank-shaft. What they did not see was the time and experience involved in designing and in the organization that was responsible for it.

When an experimental job was cleared and Henry Ford released it for production, no complication arose because Edsel, Ed Martin, and I had been watching the progress in the experimental stage. Actually I might be pulling the jobs through. I followed them closer than Mr. Ford did. He would never get down to fine details, but depended upon me to finish up the development work. I would keep Edsel posted and pull Martin into the manufacturing details.

I don't include Edsel, Martin, or myself in the experimental staff because we were primarily interested in clearing ideas with Henry Ford. He would not assume any responsibility for any failures that showed up in the finished cars.

After we passed the experimental stage, it was taken over by the Rouge manufacturing organization, headed by plant superintendents for machine departments, assembly, small parts, foundry, engine assembly, press shops, steel mill, blast furnaces, and so on.

These superintendents and their assistants were not of the sitdown type. I did not permit the top men to hold down a chair in an office. My formula for them was "You've got to get around." In addition to watching work progress, I insisted that they keep their plants clean. I insisted upon spotlessness and kept an ever-watchful eye on conveniences and facilities that would lighten men's work loads.

CHAPTER

14

Mr. Ford Buys a Railroad

Of all the many fantastic things the Ford Motor Company tackled, I put the Detroit, Toledo & Ironton Railroad at the top of the list. The idea of buying this worn-down-to-the-flanges, 380-mile line was fantastic. Equally fantastic was the achievement of nonrailroad men in making the road pay and in selling out at a 250 per cent profit. Behind it, then a cloud no bigger than a man's hand, was the threat of Federal regulation and compulsion that was to plague Henry Ford so much in later years.

We automobile men didn't want to run a railroad, but we were driven to it because this appeared the best solution to a vexing problem. By 1920, Ford was producing a million cars a year—more than the railroads could swiftly deliver. The bottleneck was freight shipments. The country had emerged from a world war with a badly run-down railroad system just then being turned back to private ownership after government operation. Especially in the Detroit area, where the automobile industry was concentrated, service and available rolling stock were at their worst. With motor transport on the increase and threatening their revenues, railways had little incentive to help auto manufacturers.

Still worse was the delay in getting shipments through to our branches over the country. The lockup of goods in transit piled up, and the money tied up by these delays was far above our experience and then current estimates. The greater the delay in shipment of materials the more we had to enlarge our inventories. This in turn necessitated ordering more materials and added further to freight delays. To break this vicious circle and keep our supplies moving, our traffic department had men stationed at every interchange where one rail line met or crossed another. Our branches had traffic men haunting freight marshaling yards in their territory. And as soon as spotters located cars with "Ford Motor Company" on their destination labels, they went after the railroad people with blood in their eyes and fire on their tongues.

Irregular delivery of parts to our branch assembly plants raised operation costs and wrecked schedules of delivery to dealers. Superhighways and haulaway cars with half a dozen new autos riding them piggyback were then hardly known. Even so, throngs of dealers came to Detroit for delivery of cars at the factory and drove away over the road to their agencies. This irregular demand knocked orderly operation of our Highland Park and Rouge assembly lines galley-west, and there was much biting of nails and shattering of the Third Commandment over this tangled problem.

The solution came by accident and in a way that had never occurred to the many agile minds pondering the situation. Construction of the River Rouge plant depended upon widening and dredging the river, which was authorized by an act of Congress. But before shipping could move up the Rouge, several stationary highway and railway bridges had to be replaced by new bascule bridges of a type wherein the roadway across the stream was weighted at one end and so delicately balanced that it lifted like a box lid to allow the vessel to pass through the channel.

Among the railway crossings to be removed and replaced was one which took tracks of the Detroit, Toledo & Ironton Railroad over River Rouge to Zug Island. This road was a rattletrap freight route connecting Detroit and Toledo with the Ohio River. Its president, Frederick Osborn, met Frank Klingensmith, our treasurer, in New York.

"The project to widen and dredge the River Rouge," he said, "has caused a crisis for us. Our road lost money during the war, my father paid its deficits out of his own pocket for two years and has decided he won't do so any more. A new bridge will cost $400,000 and no banking house will take our bonds for that amount."

Since Ford Motor Company had initiated the River Rouge improvement, Osborn suggested that it buy the necessary $400,000 of bonds. Klingensmith realized that any more delay would hold up the river widening; that if the D. T. & I. couldn't raise the money there'd be no drawbridge.

"Come on out to Dearborn," he said to Osborn, "and explain this matter to Mr. Ford."

When Osborn went to Dearborn, Klingensmith took him to Liebold's office, where Henry Ford and I met him. I'll never forget my surprise when he unwound from his chair, for he kept unwinding until he stood his full six feet ten inches tall. The young giant—he was then thirty-one—was as fascinating as his height. He was a Princeton graduate who had studied at Trinity College at England's Cambridge University. His distinguished New York lawyer father, William Church Osborn, had acquired the Detroit & Ironton through a receivership and had placed his son first as the road's treasurer and traffic manager and finally with doubtful promotion to president. Too tall for the Army in World War I, Frederick Osborn became a major general in World War II in charge of the army's welfare and educational program. He died in 1949.

Young Osborn outlined his problem as president of one of the sickest railroads in the United States. It is a monstrous exaggeration to term his financial statement a balance sheet, for liabilities were far out of balance with assets. Six times the road had been in receivership, and the last two years had been the worst ever. It was also plain that equipment was in bad shape, for the outlay for upkeep was almost microscopic. Mr. Ford and I had been quite successful in picking up and mending broken-down manufacturing enterprises, but we'd never considered or even encountered such a run-down plant as this.

Still, if we didn't do something, there'd be no new bridge and River Rouge shipping would be blocked. The railroad couldn't do it, and the $400,000 in bonds Osborn suggested that the Ford Motor Company buy would be nearly worthless. We asked a few more questions about the road, for it never had received any of our business. From Zug Island, we were told, the D.T. & I. ran south through Trenton and Flat Rock, Michigan. A spur ran into Toledo while the main line meandered 380 miles across the state of Ohio to Ironton, a small city on the Ohio River between Portsmouth and Wheeling. At different points the road crossed the New York Central, Pennsylvania, Erie, Wabash, Nickel Plate, and Big Four.

While the others in the room were talking, I took Mr. Ford aside.

"Here's a chance," I said, "to pick up a railroad that will break our freight shipment bottleneck. This road on its route south cuts across every main line going east and west north of the Ohio River. If we buy it, we can run it into the Rouge plant and handle all our outgoing and incoming materials. By improving the interchanges at the main lines it crosses, we can throw our assembly units into the Chicago, St. Louis, Kansas City, Cincinnati, Pittsburgh, and New York areas. And at the

Ironton terminus on the Ohio we can also take advantage of river shipments into the Mississippi."

There were other advantages. The road could bring Ohio and West Virginia coal direct to the Rouge blast furnaces, and limestone deposits, also needed in the process, were only a spur track's distance away at Trenton.

"Tell that tall young fellow to stick around a few days," said Ford, "while we look into the matter further."

A quick look-see more than confirmed my suggestion. It would be possible to buy the road in one transaction, for the Osborn family controlled the majority of the common stock and young Osborn was sure he could get options on most of the rest. The biggest obstacle at the moment was in the Ford organization, some members of which behaved like frightened chickens. Loudest squawks came from the traffic department, which would be the chief beneficiary of the scheme. Its people knew the railroad's weak points: it was broke; its equipment had long cheated the scrap heap; the road didn't go anywhere; and anyone knowing railroads would term Mr. Ford a sucker for buying it. Each of these objections, considered by itself, was true, but together they didn't add up to anything. Here was another instance, so often encountered since early days of Ford Motor Company, in which experts were dead set upon being dead wrong.

Anyway, Mr. Ford decided to buy the railroad. Osborn had most of the common stock sewed up, Liebold had studied the inventory, and a $7,500,000 price was agreed upon. Ford paid 60 cents on the dollar for the income bonds, $4 a share for preferred and $2 a share for common stock. A new company, the Detroit & Ironton, was formed. Ownership consisted of Mr. and Mrs. Ford, Edsel, and Ford Motor Company.

President of the new railroad company was J. Gordon of the old D. T. & I., and he moved general offices up from Springfield, Ohio, to Dearborn and into an old schoolhouse on Miller Road, opposite my office. Osborn remained a director of the new company. Division superintendent was Kenneth Chorley, a young Englishman in his late twenties, whose first job had been as a trackwalker. He is now head of the Rockefeller-restored old Williamsburg in Virginia, a project about as far removed from a broken-down railroad as can be imagined.

Before the Detroit & Ironton could take over the Detroit, Toledo & Ironton, two minority stockholders named Tannenbaum and Strauss sued to prevent transfer. The case dragged through the courts during the summer of 1920, until the Appellate bench upheld lower court refusals to grant an injunction. Then we went to work.

This was the year after Ford's million-dollar suit against the Chicago *Tribune* for having called him an anarchist. Public comment upon that affair was dying down; and now came new gags and wisecracks. So Henry Ford had bought a railroad! Would its motive power be Model T's? Would the D. T. & I. become the T. L. RR., the Tin Lizzie Railroad? Veteran railroaders either sneered or held their sides with laughter.

Now that we had bought the railroad we made an inspection trip to determine what to do with it, and how. Our special train included the D. T. & I.'s official car, a venerable affair, plus diner and sleeping cars hired from the Pullman Company. That trip was memorable for me both for what went on inside the special train and for what we saw along the road's 380-mile length. It was a marvel for anyone with mechanical training and working with measurements to see how young Osborn adjusted his six feet ten inches to a six-foot railway berth. And for anyone concerned with the law of averages there was a remarkable demonstration, engineered by Henry Ford, of the pastime sometimes referred to as "African Golf."

The train had stopped for the night; Ford and D. T. & I. officials met in the private car for discussion of the road's problems and what the new owners might do about them. Gradually, the group melted, leaving only three or four of us with Henry Ford. As we passed through the dining car on the way to bed, the cause of the disappearance was apparent. An active crap game was in progress on one of the tables, with Edsel Ford one of the participants. There was a sudden silence as the older Ford walked through apparently not noticing what was going on.

The next morning, however, he sent ahead for some preserve jars and $40 or $50 in small change. Then he assembled the colored porters, dealt them out the change and told them to get busy with the dice. With almost camp-meeting fervor the porters got to work, Ford looking on as enigmatic as a sphinx. The game continued until all porters but one were cleaned out. Then the rest of the party got back to railroading. Whatever was Henry Ford's purpose, whether it was a rebuke for Edsel or whether he wished to see the game played by its traditional experts, I don't know. But the story got around, and no one ever heard of any more crap shooting among the Ford organization until World War II days when a "quickie" strike resulted after six employees were fired for shooting dice on company time.

From what we saw along the right of way during this inspection trip, it was a question whether we had bought a railroad or a junk pile. There were several miles of abandoned equipment. Rusted rails lay all over the place. Wooden gondolas had been idle on sidings for so long that trees as thick as my arm had grown up through the car bottoms. The rails were ordered to be shipped to shears at the Rouge where they were cut and melted. We sent cranes to lift and stack the wooden bodies from the gondola cars. After the wreckage had been burned, big electric magnets drew old bolts and

straps from the ashes, and all scrap was hauled away to our
foundry to become charging metal for our melting furnaces.

For two years salvage of scrap was the most profitable
operation on the Detroit & Ironton. It went a long way toward
paying for the railroad. The first year's deficit of more than a
half million was met by another bond issue to the Fords. By
1923 we had thrown away the red-ink bottle and continued to
make a profit while other railroads screamed to high heaven
that they couldn't make both ends meet.

The D. T. & I. had never had the kind of service we gave it.
The roadbed was in terrible shape. Rails were a hodgepodge
of various sizes, some of them so light that they almost might
have been barbed-wire fencing torn down and strung along
for track. When we decided to standardize the main line with
90-pound rails, we found that almost every road in the country had a new rail program. Rolling mills were months behind in delivery and no immediate rails were in sight. We
found some in Cuba, where they had been shipped before the
demand stepped up, and we bought these at under the U.S.
market price. We also bought some Belgian rails for $31 a
ton, a price likewise under our market. But this was not
enough. Then we learned that the Baltimore and Ohio was
replacing its 90-pound rails with 120-pound ones. We got
these discards at almost scrap-metal price by taking them as
soon as they were lifted from the track and by hauling them
off without stopping to grade them.

To nail rails to wooden crossties set in crushed stone seemed
to Henry Ford a flimsy method of road building. Ever the
innovator, he asked, "Why not lay the rails on steel ties em-
bedded in concrete? You'd have a permanent roadbed and
small maintenance cost."

"It isn't practical," he was told. "There must be a give to
the track as the train passes over it. Otherwise the cars would
jump the track."

"Has it ever been tried?" Ford asked.

"No."

"Why not try it?"

So, a section of track was laid in cement. A train passed over the rigid roadbed, was nearly derailed, and almost shook to pieces.

"Well, we know now," said Ford. "Rip up the track."

But when it came to locomotives, the Model T man showed the railroad people a thing or two. Before he tinkered with gasoline motors and brought out his first car he was an expert steam-engine man. He had repaired steam tractors at Westinghouse thirty years before, and at Detroit Edison he was chief engineer of the steam plant. Accordingly, when it was proposed to replace the D. T. & I. leaky teapots with new locomotives at $60,000 each, Ford demurred.

"Let's overhaul the old ones at the Rouge," he said.

We had an ideal plant for that purpose in the blast furnace repair shops. The building was high, with cranes capable of lifting locomotives. Here, after stripping the boilers from the driving gear, we set up a boiler overhaul section and installed wheel- and axle-turning lathes and a big hydraulic press. The place became a special pet of Henry Ford, who stayed there for hours at a time. I studied all such overhaul jobs as cylinders, crossheads, and valves and set up equipment to handle each job mechanically. Joe Galamb designed a new steel cab which was made in the same department. And instead of paying $60,000 apiece for new locomotives, we turned out old ones as good as new for about $35,000 apiece.

Meanwhile, at Henry Ford & Son, we had built a gasoline-engine-driven passenger car which figured in the only political row ever to engulf me and my sole public altercation with James Couzens, who had become mayor of Detroit after selling out his Ford stock. The local transit system was a mess. The Detroit United Railway was on the rocks financially and

was no better operations-wise than the Detroit & Ironton before Ford took hold of it. Detroit was expanding. Thousands
of mechanics from other cities flocked there each month to
work in the automobile plants, and D.U.R. couldn't handle
this extra traffic. Getting to and from work was a nightmare
for the many who did not then own autos.

Couzens held that the solution was for the city to take over
the D.U.R. I held that municipal operation of an antiquated
transit system was no solution at all, that the real solution was
efficient, economical, up-to-date service. Even then, in the
early 1920's, it was plain that electric street railways were on
the way out. To tear up the tracks and replace streetcars with
buses would have been too drastic and extravagant a change.
Consequently, I advocated abandonment of costly overhead
trolleys, substitution of gasoline-driven streetcars running on
the existing rails, and addition of buses as feeders on cross
streets.

To prove my contention I built the type of streetcar I had
in mind. Like the old-fashioned trolley, it had an aisle between wicker seats, but it drove like an automobile. Of course,
steering was unnecessary; the operator sat in a front corner
and changed gears and stepped on the gas in automobile
fashion.

Couzens ridiculed my position. I lashed back in public
statements and found myself in the midst of a violent political
Donnybrook. Couzens put the question of municipal ownership of D.U.R. on the ballot. I opposed the purchase because
the price was too high and the system itself out of date. During the campaign I was pretty thoroughly kicked around.
Couzens won the referendum. The city took over a pile of
junk which is still a financial headache, and I was left with my
gasoline-driven streetcar.

After we acquired the Detroit & Ironton we used the car
for inspection trips. It proved so easy to operate that Edsel

once took over in the driver's seat. Spinning along at a mile a minute, he neared the road's intersection with a Pennsylvania line and zipped past a warning signal to stop before reaching the crosstracks. This signal set a derailing device which Edsel saw too late. He jammed the brakes down hard, the car struck the derailer and bumped over the ties, shaking the passengers like dice in that crap game on an earlier inspection journey.

Henry Ford preferred to ride in the locomotive cab, a fondness which probably inspired the ridiculously tall yarns which had him perched on the coal pile of the tender tootling a harmonica in time to the clicks of the rails. These locomotive rides, however, may have influenced his decision to raise engineers' pay to equal that of conductors. "But, Mr. Ford," he was told, "the conductor is boss of the train."

"Yes," he replied, "but the engineer runs it. All the conductor does it to punch tickets and at station stops wave to the engineer to start."

As a result, Detroit & Ironton wages were rescaled. Engineers and conductors got as much as $100 a month more than on other roads, and even trackwalkers got up to $300 a year more for less time. Ford also installed a profit-sharing system, but not without vain legal moves by minority stockholders and a long wait for the Interstate Commerce Commission to approve the scheme. This was the first time Ford encountered governmental regulation of his business. Nor was it the last time, but he fretted considerably over having to secure permission from Washington before he could give more liberal benefits to his employees. I wondered, too, whether the $5 day would have come about had we had to get governmental approval.

Meanwhile, the road was operating at a profit. Virtually the whole of its right of way had been rebuilt. Thirteen miles of track had been laid from Flat Rock through Ford-owned farmlands directly into the River Rouge plant. The traffic bottleneck was broken. With the speed-up in distribution came a dramatic reduction of volume of parts in transit. The inventory en route was reduced by more than half, a saving sufficient to pay the purchase price of the railroad. In addition, coal, iron, and limestone were transported direct from mines and quarries to the Rouge's blast furnaces. All and more than we had expected from taking over the D. T. & I. was being realized. What had not been anticipated, because Henry Ford hadn't encountered it before, was the hampering hand of government.

Despite some $15,000,000, mostly out of profits, having been sunk into the Detroit & Ironton, the Interstate Commerce Commission figured the road's value on a depreciation basis as $11,000,000. Ford figured it at book value of $23,000,-000—cost price plus the millions sunk into improving the property—and the final selling price three years later makes that figure conservative.

The success of Model T was based upon Henry Ford's then revolutionary assumption that greater production resulting from highly paid labor lowers prices to customers. But after Ford raised the pay of his railroad workers, securing greater efficiency, and sought to lower freight rates of the Detroit & Ironton, he met with a solid "No" from the Interstate Commerce Commission.

Mr. Ford told me to notify the railroad officials to cut freight rates regardless of the ICC. I argued long with him that this would be illegal, only to meet stubborn insistence. Finally Ford decided to get out of a business that he could not run as he wished. The road, he said, was taking too much time of Ford officials which could be better spent elsewhere. Finally, in 1929, he sold the line to the Pennsylvania for $36,000,000.

This was a few months before the Great Depression. Henry Ford got out just in time. In nine years he had completely rebuilt a railroad which contributed to successful operation of our branches and reduced our investment in material in transit and branch stocks. It improved all our shipping and freight-receiving problems.

The Detroit & Ironton sold for a profit of $26,000,000. No other railroad then—or even now—was being sold at a profit. But the indirect gains were at least three times the profit. We felt this wasn't bad for a bunch of amateurs operating a railroad.

15

Russian Adventure

DURING his publicity-appreciation days, Henry Ford delighted in enigmatic remarks. Some were dutifully clarified and embellished by his collaborator, Samuel Crowther, and by his radio and editorial representative, William J. Cameron. Others were tossed off at interviewers and reporters, who set them down literally; and, because the meaning was obscure, the words were accepted as profound and oracular. Such an observation was one which Mr. Ford made in 1928 to a magazine writer, "I never made a mistake, and neither did you."

That was the year I had dealings with some Russian visitors, and a few months later I was in Russia to plan Ford production there. While I do not subscribe to the Ford claim to infallibility, I cannot wholly endorse the almost equally sweeping boast of former New York Mayor Fiorello LaGuardia, "When I make a mistake, it's a beaut." My Russian trip was probably a mixture of achievement and error. I believe no other American industrial firm ever did so much business with Communist Russia as Ford Motor Company. Between 1929 and 1936, Ford transactions with Russia amounted to more than $40,000,000; and I may say that, although I found the

Russians evasive or unreliable in many other things, they were scrupulous in their financial dealings with us.

Early in 1928 a Soviet government commission visited the Rouge plant to arrange for building Ford-design autos in Russia. I handled the negotiations and found the group very difficult to deal with. None of its six members could speak English. All discussions were through interpreters.

I offered a plan similar to procedure in our foreign branches. They would have all the rights for selling and distributing our products in Russia. Ford Motor Company would plan the layout of an auto manufacturing plant in Russia. We would give them all the necessary engineering data, and after the plant got into operation we would be paid a royalty and engineering fees. This took more than a little bit of explaining. For not only words had to be translated, but working principles of private enterprise had to be explained to uncomprehending Communists. I might just as well have been talking to a delegation from Mars. Our visitors either didn't understand this plan or they were stalling because they lacked authority to go ahead. After two months of tiresome discussion, they left without having agreed to anything. Not all of them returned to Russia, for the head of the delegation decided for reasons of his own to remain in Berlin. We never heard from him again, and I suppose that final report of the negotiation never reached higher authority in Moscow.

Much to my surprise, another Soviet commission came over in the latter part of 1928. This group was entirely different from the earlier delegation. Two of its four members spoke English very well, and the other two could understand it. Head of the delegation was Valery I. Meschlauk, who, for a time at least, became chief of the Soviets' Supreme Economic Control. Meschlauk was a very able and pleasant man to work with. Of German descent, he was a trained mechanical engineer and during World War I was an officer in the Czarist

Army. I introduced him to Henry Ford and Edsel and all other members of our staff, and he became very popular throughout the organization.

With Meschlauk we were able to construct a rounded-out program which was about the same that we had with most of our European branches. To begin with, we would ship knock-down autos for a complete unit, together with a specified amount of parts. Then, when they got into production, delivery of units from the U.S.A. would cease.

We agreed to train some Russians in our Rouge operations, and at the same time send over members of our staff to help start production of Ford units in Russia. After we had completed all these preliminary arrangements, Meschlauk requested that I go as early as possible to Russia to discuss and advise upon the plan of building Ford cars there. This I agreed to do on my next trip to Europe. In the early summer of 1929, again on my annual swing around all our European branches, my last stop was at Berlin, after looking over possibilities of a new plant on the Rhine at Cologne. Fred Rockelman, then our manager of sales, and Lord Perry, head of the British Ford Motor Company, were with me, and Carlson, who was then the manager of our German operations, joined us in Berlin.

We stopped off at Warsaw, where Perry talked with the authorities about putting a warehouse in Gdynia, the Polish seaport. Our stay was enlivened by our Fordson Polish distributor, Count Mirski, who had made numerous visits to Dearborn and had a well-established place in Warsaw. My pleasant memories of that short stay are saddened by the thought of what happened to Poland ten years later, when Hitler overran the country only to be run out later by the Russians, and it is a question under whom the Poles suffered most. Today the Detroit neighborhood and its automobile factories shelter more free Poles than any other place on earth.

They are a fine people, and the American automobile industry owes this vigorous people a deep debt of gratitude for manning its machine tools and assembly lines.

An overnight train ride from Warsaw took us to the Soviet border, where we were met by Meschlauk and a numerous delegation whose names, like the names of the hundreds of others I met in Russia, had a threefold challenge: first, to pronounce them; second, to spell them; third, to remember them. At any rate, my diary records a few names of those who met us at the border. They were Messrs. Osinsky, Piolunkovsky, Lehr, Ivanoff, and Turbine, or names to that general effect. The other names I could not unwind from Russian to Western alphabet to write in my diary. Here we four Ford officials were led into a magnificent private railroad car. It was, I was told, in the service of one of the top generals of the Red Army. It had a wonderful kitchen with a chef, also had a steward and a valet. The car was at our disposal for railway travel during our entire stay in Russia.

Only two members of this commission dined with us. I don't know why the others were left out. As soon as we'd had our meals the two commission members left for their own car. This was an adjoining Pullman with bunks in tiers of three high into which Messrs. Osinsky, Piolunkovsky, Lehr, Ivanoff, Turbine, and the rest disappeared like spare parts into the bins of a Ford agency stockroom.

At Moscow we were taken direct to the Europaski Hotel, where the police took up our passports to hold until we were ready to leave the country. I suspect this was the normal treatment given to all visitors in Russia. However, we had no trouble in identifying ourselves at all times. Meschlauk or Osinsky, Piolunkovsky, *et al.*, were with us constantly.

Among the industrial plants around Moscow that Meschlauk showed us during the first few days of our stay was one which turned out motor trucks. Originally, it had assembled parts they had bought in the United States. A variety of American-made engines were adapted to Russian-designed and built chassis with axles purchased in the U.S.

With this as a start, they had gradually begun to make their own engines and axles. In my judgment it was a very badly run plant. I saw no control of the machine operators, and there was more visiting than working.

I would have liked to see the plant in full operation with everyone on his job, but our visit seemed to be a good excuse for a holiday. Everybody stopped work to have a look at us, and much to my surprise I heard shouts of, "Charlie, how are you?" and "Hello, Charlie."

I discovered that some of the men had worked in Detroit at our Highland Park plant. None of them had been more than bench workers, but the Russians had recruited them as "experts" to help them set up their motor-truck plant.

At lunchtime we were invited to eat in a big dining room where all the workers were served a meal. I don't remember exactly what we had to eat, but there was a lot of it and everyone had all he wanted. We sat at a large table with other workers who came strolling in. Somebody was always walking past and slapping me on the back. It was apparent that all knew who I was and why I was there.

After these plant visits we spent three solid days in conference with Meschlauk and his group. All our meetings were held in the Kremlin. Joining us in these sessions were two commissars. One was A. I. Mikoyan, the able Armenian with a shoebrush mustache who is now deputy premier. Then he was the Commissar for Internal Trade. The other member was A. F. Tolokontzev, who was the jovial head of the United Heavy Machinery Industry.

Occasionally other members of the top Soviet hierarchy would look in on us to see what we were doing. I remember particularly Stalin who would pass our table with the greeting

I heard almost everywhere I went in Russia, " 'Allo, Sharley."
None of these august visitors took part in our discussion, however. Of the eight Soviet top-rankers, then, only two, Molotov
and Mikoyan, are alive today.

In the midst of these conferences Mikoyan got up on several occasions and motioned for me to come along with him.
Each time he showed me a different part of the Kremlin, and
he certainly showed me as only one in his position could do.
Each commissar had an office as well as an apartment within
the Kremlin itself. All were heavily guarded. One had to go
through two doors with an area between where there were
always several guards. The living quarters were very dreary
and more like cells. The offices were well furnished and well
lighted and the meeting rooms for large gatherings were
splendid with large windows looking up and down the Oka
River, which runs through Moscow. It was very hot and nude
bathers crowded the beaches.

At the Kremlin meetings Meschlauk unfolded his plan. We
had discussed it in advance, so I knew what was on his mind.
He wanted to build the Model A in Russia. I tried to sell him
on the V-8 which we were designing but the group that he
had with him in Detroit decided that that was just too complicated for them to start with. The Model A was considered
a more simplified operation which would meet all their requirements.

This was to fit in with a Soviet Five-Year Plan which
Meschlauk and the Soviet Supreme Economic Council was
preparing and which he announced more than a year later.
The main plant was to be at the Volga River port of Nijni
Novgorod. One of the first two assembly plants would be
there, the other one at Moscow. Later there would be others
elsewhere.

The next item on the agenda was inspection of the site of
the proposed plant at Nijni Novgorod. That took a lot of

doing for it was some time before we were allowed to get down to what we had come there for. As soon as we got off the train we were whisked to a dock on the River Volga and a smart-looking yacht and an equally smart-looking uniformed crew—and a sort of voyage to nowhere and back.

The life of the party was Tolokontzev, the Soviet's top heavy machineries man. He was a very jovial person. He spoke only Russian, but it was plain that all hands enjoyed his company.

He had a splendid voice and loved to sing. I tried in vain to think of any high American official with a similar gift, but I couldn't. Twenty years later we did have a president who played the piano, but that was far in the future; Mr. Truman then never dreamed of being president, and none of us had ever heard of Mr. Truman. Every little while Tolokontzev and the group around him burst into song. When we docked at noon, while a monumental lunch was being prepared, Tolokontzev shucked his clothes and went in swimming. Below the yacht on the riverbank there were a lot of other swimmers. Men and women, they were all naked.

Lunch was always preceded by a round of drinks, vodka being the favorite. I had a hard time persuading Tolokontzev that I was a teetotaler. It was a tremendous luncheon.

Back at Nijni Novgorod, there was a reception in the city hall with some speechmaking. It was evident that all orators enjoyed making speeches and regretted that they were limited to a mere two hours. Nijni Novgorod was famous over the years as a market place. People from lands to the east and southeast of it brought their products there, some arriving on camelback.

After we returned to Moscow I spent another two days with Meschlauk. I tried to find out what the material resources were—iron, copper, aluminum, lead, tin, and zinc. He had people studying such Russian economic requirements.

I asked Meschlauk where the coal and the iron ore and the limestone were coming from for Nijni Novgorod. I particularly wanted to know where the center of this type of operation would be. Some Chicago engineers specializing in building blast furnaces were staying at the same hotel. They, too, wondered about the raw materials.

They got the same answers I did: records on material resources were in Leningrad. I pressed Meschlauk for this information, and he agreed that on my way home he would accompany me to Leningrad where we would meet with the State Institute of Metallurgy and Design.

During my last two days in Moscow we discussed a contract. Meschlauk and I worked out a complete understanding, and I had his assurance that the contract would be signed and forwarded to Detroit at once. We left on our sumptuous private car for our last trip through Leningrad.

All the people that we had associated with in Moscow came to the railroad station to say goodbye. Every one of them had been kind and helpful and this gave me the final opportunity to thank them for their continued interest in Ford Motor Company. They loaded down our car with all types of rich food, big cans of caviar, cigarettes, cigars, fine wines, and candies.

"This," Meschlauk explained, "is the Russian way of extending thanks to departing friends."

We got the usual Russian reception, headed by the mayor, when we arrived in Leningrad. They took us to a fine big turbine and boiler plant in Leningrad. This plant was very well equipped with the best type of machinery for making large turbine water wheels as well as steam-power turbines. Next we inspected the Putilov Steel Works, one of Leningrad's famous and oldest companies, with a great history behind it.

I had heard of it, but had never expected to see it. The

minute we got inside I saw the oldest types of building that I had ever seen in use for any manufacturing purposes. They apparently had been built with the idea of protection against the cold Russian winters.

There were few windows. The walls were all stone. The roofs were all flat-tops with a little angle on them and were of wood construction. They had no modern equipment such as open hearths or Bessemer plants. The melting was all done in crucible furnaces that were all underground. The ingots likewise were all under the floor when they were cast.

The rolling mills would have been fine specimens for a museum. I was amazed at the manual labor carried on in these operations. Meschlauk realized as I did that this was an antique way of making steel, for when we were alone for a moment he said he would appreciate it if I would express myself publicly on what I thought of what I saw.

Later on in the little group he asked me, "What do you think of our steel plant, Mr. Sorensen?"

My reply was not diplomatic, but I think it made the point that Meschlauk hoped for. I said, "Tell you what to do, Meschlauk. Get me a barrel of dynamite."

He said, "A barrel of dynamite? What do you mean?"

"Well, I would put this right in the middle of this plant, get you fellows all out of the way, and blow it up. It is the most ancient, out-of-date plant that I have seen. Before you start putting in a lot of up-to-date plants, you had better get this one straightened around first."

While we were walking through the plant I asked the same question I had in Moscow and had gone to Leningrad for the answer, "Where are the raw materials coming from that go into the products here?" Again, no answer, but Meschlauk assured me that as soon as we visited the State Institute of Metallurgy all would be put before me so that I could understand it.

The Putilov plant also had a manufacturing division that we finally got into. We came right on into the assembly room, and I stopped in astonishment. There on the floor lines they were building the Fordson tractor.

I turned to Meschlauk. "Where did you get hold of the design for this tractor?"

"We have been working at this now for about three years," he replied. "We engaged some of the engineers that had worked in your tractor plant."

I could not imagine at first whom he meant by "engineers," but I soon found out. As I walked by a bench, one of the mechanics turned around and waved his hand at me and shouted, "Hello, Charlie." I got the same now-familiar greeting from a dozen others scattered around the department. When I stopped to talk to these men I learned that they had been employed at Highland Park as well as in the tractor plant. I asked Meschlauk if these were the "engineers" he had referred to. "Yes," he said.

What the Russians had done was to dismantle one of our tractors in the Putilov works, and their own people made drawings of all the disassembled parts. I visited a department where the rear axle and the final drive were being assembled. The moment I appeared I heard "Hello, Charlie," and a foreman walked up to me with a broad smile. Sure enough, he was one of our old employees.

He asked me to look over the final worm drive, which was giving them a lot of trouble. It would not stand up long when the tractor was put to work in the fields.

It was plain what the trouble was. In Detroit the making of the worm started with a steel forging which was turned to size, then put on a hobbing machine which cut the thread accurately but left a little material for finishing by grinding after the forging hardened. Next the worm was put into furnaces and packed in carbon material and left there until it was carbonized to a definite depth. When removed from this treatment, it was reheated, then quenched in an acid solution. This made a very hard surface. The worm was then put on a grinder, the angle and the pitch were ground to great accuracy, and then finally onto a polishing machine, which put a high glazed finish on it.

Contrasted with this, the worm that was being made at the Putilov works looked as rough as a bastard file. I doubt that this foreman had ever seen the actual production in our tractor plant. I sensed the whole trouble in a few minutes and offered to straighten it out if my instructions would be followed to the letter. It was apparent that, while the Russians had stolen the Fordson tractor design, they did not have any of our specifications for the material that entered into the various parts. And you can't find that out merely by pulling the machine apart and studying the pieces.

Meschlauk got the Putilov works control heads together, and I gave them a thorough going over. I really heaped coals of fire on their heads over the poor quality work they were doing.

In spite of the fact that they had stolen everything they could of the tractor, I offered to help them clear up the whole matter by sending them one of our experts from Dearborn. They showed some signs of being overcome by my generosity, but I really couldn't take that too seriously.

Anything that meant mass production seemed to have the Russians stumped. I saw similar evidences in an airplane factory and a motor-truck plant in Moscow. In the higher field of engineering, like turbine building, they did a pretty good job in the plant that I saw while I was in Leningrad. But ever since that day I never felt particular concern about the Russian competition in the Ford product field.

The State Institute for Metallurgy and Design was in a building inherited from the czarist regime. As the walls of rooms we were in would indicate, all planning for new ventures the Communists entertained were planned and settled in the institute. I spent an entire morning in the drafting rooms where these different projects were laid out. There were big power sites to develop on the rivers in Central Russia. Also on the plans were blast furnaces and steel plants.

Again I asked for the location of needed raw materials. They finally brought in a man who was a prince under the Czar but threw his lot in with the Communists and was now one of the institute's staff members. From him I learned that the iron ore came from the Ural Mountains in an area that was frozen much of the year and a long way from Nijni Novgorod.

I tried to learn, but couldn't, the specifications of the ore bodies. The coal that they proposed to use in reducing this ore was just as far off in the opposite direction from Nijni Novgorod, and their limestone was in the same areas as the iron ore. Other required materials like copper, lead, and manganese were likewise widely scattered. I could not learn what the grades of ore were. He showed what maps and records were available, and I asked who had made them. He replied that they were done by an American, Herbert Hoover. The czarist government had a survey made by an English corporation and Mr. Hoover was one of their engineers.

The prince made it clear to me that if I really wanted full details as to location and grades of ore I should be able to get them from Mr. Hoover. There I was, away off in Russia trying to help plan a big industrial operation and told by a Communist prince that I would have to go back to America to see Mr. Hoover to get this information about needed raw materials!

My time was up and I was ready to leave. Our friends in Leningrad came to the station to see us off and give us good-bye presents. Among them was Meschlauk, who handed me a very nicely wrapped package which I did not open until I reached Stockholm. It was a beautifully hand-wrought silver box with a card explaining that it had been a jewel box used by Empress Catherine the Great. It certainly was a beautiful present. I still have it.

Back in the United States, I had V-8 production problems on my hands and did not follow the Communist prince's suggestion that I get in touch with Mr. Hoover regarding Russian mineral deposits. It was late in 1929, a time of bitter memory to many Americans who had put their trust in securities, and Mr. Hoover was a pretty busy man. After he left the White House in 1933 we did talk about Russia. My wife and I were on a houseboat cruise through the Florida Keys and decided to dock at Craig dock, where we tied up behind another houseboat. The steward from the neighboring boat brought over this pencil-written note on a piece of memo pad paper:

Dear Mr. Sorensen:
If you are in the "port" over noon would Mrs. Sorensen and yourself lunch with us at one o'clock?

Herbert Hoover

I had met Mr. Hoover previously in Florida and had fished with him once or twice off Long Key, so we were not strangers. At the luncheon table were the Hoovers, the Sorensens, and the Hoover newspaper columnist friend, Mark Sullivan. I found that Mr. Hoover knew I had been in Russia and that he wanted my reactions. After a rather hurried sketch of my trip, I brought up the materials program and how impossible the situation looked to me. We talked for several hours on this point, and found ourselves in accord. Russia lacks easy bulk transport from her steelmaking raw materials. She has no such ideal setups as we have in the United States with iron from the Minnesota deposits brought down by

10,000- and 20,000-ton ships to Great Lakes ports like Cleveland and Ashtabula to join up with the coal from the Ohio and Virginia fields. And today tidewater steel plants get rich iron direct at dockside from Labrador and South America.

I remember well the close of our talk. Mr. Hoover said, "Do you know where the greatest ore fields, together with coal and limestone, lie practically untouched in this world today? They are up the Yangtze River in China. When I get back north I will send you some information that you can use for calling for records that are on file in Washington. It will give you the over-all picture of what these resources are."

Later I got all this information together and studied it thoroughly. More than a quarter century has passed since I made that trip into Russia; and now that I see how the Russians and the Chinese are cooperating with each other, an obvious conclusion is that Russia has her eyes on these resources.

Upon my return from Russia I got our plant engineers working on a plan for the Nijni Novgorod project. Albert Kahn, who had been in Russia at the same time, was to be architect for the buildings and plant requirements. Before I left Russia I had agreed with Mr. Meschlauk on a tentative plan to fit in with their Five-Year Plan. I liked it because it did not call for putting on too much of a rush for any of their requirements. I plotted out the plan that we would work on with our own plant engineers. The accepted one was that ultimately they would build 30,000 cars a year.

The first year only complete knockdown cars would be shipped from Dearborn. By April, 1930, Ford Motor Company announced the plan for the construction of the factory in Nijni Novgorod. Actually it was January, 1932, before the plant got under way.

The first items in production were to be bodies, fenders, hoods, and all sheet-metal parts. In the third year the engine production would be under way. In production by the fourth year would be rear and front axles, and in the fifth year all the instruments, batteries, and electrical equipment.

In this plan no tires would be made in Russia but would be purchased from the outside. And even that deficiency, as I shall relate, was made up, but in vain, by Ford Motor Company. While the plant was being erected and machinery set up, we sent over several groups of mechanics. At the same time the Russians sent their technicians to the Rouge plant, where we put them to work in all production divisions.

Under such arrangements the Russians had full access to all that we were doing. Some members of our staff criticized me for being so generous in helping them. It was thought that in so doing we were building up competition with our own branches and subsidiaries in Europe. But I wasn't a bit worried about their possible competition in world markets. After their plants started production I expected to find some Russian cars drifting into Southern European areas. The only ones I heard of were a few that got into Turkey. I had one of our Turkish representatives pick up one of these cars and ship it to Dearborn for study of its construction.

It was a pretty poor reproduction of Model A. I was doubly sure then that it would be a long time before they could make enough cars to meet their own requirements; and this still holds true even with, as I understand it, only a few thousand miles of paved roads. I have not yet heard of any Russian cars in other areas.

As time went on, we got fewer and fewer reports about Nijni Novgorod production. After the first year that the plant was in operation, no more Ford employees worked there, and only an occasional Russian drifted into Detroit with some vague report. Our only and meager information came to us on request from Amtorg, the Soviet trading operation in New York.

During our contractual relations with the Russians we did a large turnover in parts. After we finished production of Model A, a lot of machine tools used in its production were stored in warehouses and crates in our yards. I sold them all this machinery and many old dies which they adapted for their Model A cars. Despite all this, the Russian Model A was inferior to ours.

Inferior though Model A was, Meschlauk was right in rejecting my suggestion to tool up for our forthcoming V-8. He was satisfied to begin at the beginning, just as Henry Ford had, with a simpler car. After our contract went into effect and all details were covered, I never saw Meschlauk or heard from him again. I wrote him a number of times, but all my letters remained unanswered.

Some years later, returning to the United States on the *Europa*, I met William C. Bullitt, who was coming home after serving as our ambassador to the U.S.S.R. I asked him about the Nijni Novgorod Ford plant. He said he knew it was there but had been unable to get any details about its operation. As for Meschlauk, he knew him and saw him occasionally in Moscow. Mr. Bullitt said he wasn't surprised that I hadn't heard from my friend because all Soviet officials had been proscribed from direct business dealing; all such transactions were carried on through Amtorg. My inquiries there about Meschlauk were futile. If I could know where he is now, if he is still living, and how to reach him, I would certainly like to pay my respects. Meschlauk was the outstanding man in Russia to carry on the developments we prepared for him.

I would have liked to go back later to follow through and see how the Russians were operating all that we had laid out for them. But the only way to get back there was by invitation, or as a self-appointed "refugee from American capitalism and tyranny of the ruling classes," a designation for which I was not eligible. That situation seems to prevail today. When I told Mr. Ford about my curiosity to go back to Russia to see what Ford Motor Company had initiated, he said, "Charlie, don't you do it! They need a man like you. If you went over there, you would never come out again. Don't take that chance!"

I was inclined to agree with him. Later on, when we got into World War II, a real opportunity presented itself to go over on a government mission. Possibly I might have been useful; but my trip was blocked because one official was feuding with another. Which, now that I reflect upon it, is a pretty good illustration of the difference between business and government administration. And this is the story:

I resigned from Ford Motor Company, March 1, 1944. The middle of May I was back in Detroit and Donald Nelson, then head of the War Production Board, telephoned me at my home. Come to Washington, he said.

Before this I had had a few hints from some of my Washington friends that President Roosevelt was considering sending a commission to Russia and that he wanted me to head it. Donald Nelson's telephone call confirmed what I had previously heard: the President had spoken to him about this commission and for me to head it up.

A few days later when I went to Washington to talk over the matter with him, Nelson told me about a trip he had just made to Moscow. He met many of the men with whom I had dealt and found that I had made many staunch friends. He was so impressed that when he returned to Washington he reported at the White House.

President Roosevelt wanted good relations with Russia continued, and that was why I was called to Washington. As soon as I arrived Nelson asked me to see Averell Harriman, our ambassador to Moscow, who was then in town.

I wrote in my diary of that day: "Arrived in Washington

at nine a.m. Went to the Mayflower Hotel. George Ritter met me and I went to his room in the hotel and stayed with him. Called on Averell Harriman in the State Department. Talked on going to Russia. Then to Nelson's office. Visited with him and Batt. Discussed the Russian trip. I'd like it."

Nelson and I had a long talk about the purposes of the trip and how to make it. A four-engine bomber would be put at our service for the trip across the Atlantic to England. From there the British would take us through and guard our flight into Russia.

The purpose of the trip was primarily to keep up the contacts that I had made and learn everything we could about technical requirements for the Russians' war program. It was Nelson's suggestion that the commission comprise the four to six members agreed upon by Batt and me.

After an afternoon of talk with Nelson and Batt, I declared that I was interested but wanted some time to think the matter over. As I left Nelson's office I ran into Charles E. Wilson, the General Electric Company chief who was in the War Production Board as Nelson's assistant.

"Come back with me to my office," he said. "I want to talk with you."

When Wilson joined the war production program, I dealt with him directly on all matters pertaining to our Willow Run B-24 bomber program. He would come out to Willow Run and I would also meet him at Washington. So we saw quite a lot of each other. My resignation from Ford Motor Company was apparently both a surprise and a shock to him, and I had many telephone calls from him while I was at my home in Florida.

After I left Nelson and met Wilson in his office, it was soon evident there was discord between him and Nelson. Wilson did not want me to go to Russia. He had something in mind which he felt was much more important.

I told him frankly that I hadn't decided what I was going to do and certainly wanted time to think things over. He pressed me not to take too much time. He hinted that I might even be drafted for what he wanted me to do. That I will reveal in my last chapter. At any rate, one result of my talk was that I notified Donald Nelson, after a decent interval, that I had decided against heading a commission to Russia.

From this distance of years I am not sure what that trip would have accomplished—and I'm not sure that it would have done any harm.

Another wartime adventure we of Ford Motor Company had with the Russians dates back for its beginning to shutdowns and sitdown strikes in the Akron Rubber Company plants in the mid-1930's. As a result, we had to set up a plant of our own to make rubber tires. This, of course, was not by choice, because we had always had good relations with the rubber companies, but we were driven into it. Shutdowns, sitdowns, and slowdowns made it impossible for such tiremakers as Firestone, Goodrich, and Goodyear, our chief suppliers, to deliver regularly enough to meet our demands. We were sitting on a powder keg—sitting, looking, waiting, and hoping for a solution of that problem.

I suggested to Henry and Edsel Ford that I go to Akron and learn firsthand whether there was prospect of a complete stoppage or whether the tiremakers could see where their problem would clear up. Mr. Ford telephoned Harvey Firestone, Sr., who seemed reluctant to have outsiders enter the picture, but it was agreed I would go to his home inconspicuously so that no one in Akron would know I was there. I was there early next morning. By that time Mr. Firestone had had time to think things over; now he wanted me to go with him to his plant and look over the entire operation. He also arranged for me to visit the tire plants of his competitors. He now wanted everybody, plant owners and workers, to know I was around. "That is exactly what I want to do, too," I said. The more rubber workers and employees who saw me the better, for we wanted them to know that Ford Motor Company was very much concerned about the situation and was going to do something about this.

I walked and talked a lot for two days. I particularly wanted to see the working conditions and find out the grievances of the workers.

When I was satisfied that I had covered the problem and understood it, I went to Mr. Firestone's office and announced that I would suggest that Ford build at River Rouge a tire plant, the most efficient plant we could conceive and capable of meeting about 50 per cent of our requirements. We would develop some details that I felt were necessary in handling materials and mechanize many heavy lifting operations. I said I could see room for improvement in all the operations. Mr. Firestone, whom I knew very well, interposed no objection.

I am sure it was a difficult decision for him to make, for he must have hated to see us go into the tire business. Then I eased his mind by explaining, "When we get the plant running, if it is a success, you can take over. We don't want to make tires. All we want is assurance of a continuous supply."

I suggested he lend us a good man who knew all operations, time, and cost. I wanted him in the Rouge plant to lay out plans, then stay with us and erect and operate the plant. I asked Mr. Firestone to go back with me to Dearborn so that we could confirm the entire matter with Henry and Edsel Ford.

Mr. Firestone drove me to Cleveland, where we took the night boat to Detroit. Next morning we met with Henry Ford in Dearborn and everything was settled. The Firestone people sent us E. F. Wait, one of their experts. We brought in the United Engineering Company and with their engineers laid out a new progressive plant. Every operation was mechanized, with the units feeding into a final tire assembly—a typical Ford assembly line.

Shortly before Christmas, 1937, the plant began operations and did exactly what had been predicted. It lightened the heavy, laborious work and turned out more tires per man. We could train men for each operation. We had variable wage rates and no piecework, which was the real problem on labor relations in Akron. With this installation our worries about the tire supply vanished. This is perhaps the best illustration of why we had to take on so many supply problems. It was never understood by the public, perhaps because we did not try to explain our reasons. We did not want to be our own suppliers, but picture 80,000 men out of work if even one supply failed.

Within a couple of years things changed, Akron got over her early labor problems, and we finally stopped making tires. Thus we made good on our promise to Mr. Firestone that we would get out of the tire business as soon as we felt suppliers could handle our requirements safely.

In the fall of 1942, a month after President and Mrs. Roosevelt visited our great Willow Run bomber plant, I received a letter from William M. Jeffers, the Union Pacific Railway president who was in charge of our wartime rubber program.

Dear Mr. Sorensen,

The Government of the United States is committed to supply the Soviet Government with the equipment for a large and up-to-date tire factory.

A thorough study of the best and quickest way to secure this equipment for the U.S.S.R. has been made, and it is clear that a certain substantial portion of it should be obtained from existing plants in the United States.

We have made a survey of the existing machinery and after careful consideration have decided to ask you if you can spare the pieces of equipment listed on the attached sheet.

I will appreciate it, therefore, if you will indicate to me your willingness to make this equipment available to the Government on reasonable terms and if you are willing so to do, advise me of the official of your company with whom the Procurement Division of the United States Treasury, acting as the government purchasing agency, can conclude the details of the purchase.

If you feel that you cannot make this equipment available, I hope you will describe the situation back of your conclusion in some little detail.

The same afternoon I shot back this letter to Mr. Jeffers:

It is our desire to be cooperative and in every way help to carry out the commitments of the Government of the United States.

We are enclosing herewith three sheets out of our inventory list, showing you the number of machines on hand. We have shown in a circle the number that you are asking for. . . .

We will go further and say that if you want a complete tire plant, with molds, vulcanizers, and all the other machinery for making complete tires, here is probably the one that you could pick up easiest, load in ships right alongside the plant, and ship to Russia. We are enclosing a blueprint showing the full layout of this plant. As you know, it is considered one of the best in the world today. When you take machines and do not take the motor drives and other things that go with them, you leave us in a situation where we have dead equipment that never can be used unless the machines are replaced.

If you are interested in the above suggestion, we would be pleased to hear further from you. You can send a representative direct to my office any time and we will discuss the matter with him.

Let's give Russia some first-class service. She deserves it.

There was not merely a bit of equipment here and a bit there, but a complete plant was available. The President ordered Jeffers to pick it up and get it to Russia at once. Jeffers and I agreed on a price. I never did understand how the Russians would get the rubber needed to run the plant, but ours not to reason why. Our people began to dismantle the plant and make layouts that showed how to set up the equipment in its new site. Every machine had a number on its crate and a number plate on the machine itself. A Russian crew stood by until all was loaded aboard ship at the Rouge plant docks. The shipment was very hush-hush. I tried to learn from Jeffers whether the shipment arrived in Russia safely. He said he knew nothing about it. Anyway, the Russians got some first-class service, typical of how the United States helped them in the crisis they were in.

After the war, when I was on the Congressional aviation policy committee in Washington, Secretary of the Navy Forrestal, who was on this committee, asked me if I knew what had happened to our tire plant. "The last I saw or heard of it was when the ships left the Rouge and swung down the Detroit River to Lake Erie," I said. He then told us he had just learned that the entire plant, the most up-to-date in the world, was lying in Russia still in its original crates.

To sum up my Russian adventure—here and in U.S.S.R.: The industrial deficiencies I saw in Russia back in 1929 existed only a dozen years after the Bolsheviks seized power. More than a quarter century has passed since that visit. Even in their most advanced industries, the Russians then were at least a quarter of a century behind the United States. How long does it take one people to catch up with another? I doubt that anyone knows the answer. But I do know that in the intervening quarter century our American technology has not been idle. This means that if our professional and amateur viewers-with-alarm are right in their insistence that Russian technology surpasses ours, then the Russians have performed two sensational miracles. Not only did they catch up with where we stood industrially twenty-five years ago, but they also passed ahead of our almost incredible progress since then. This taxes credulity beyond any measurement of stress and strain of which I know.

It was Edmund Burke who said he did not know how to

indict a nation. By the same reason all genius and industry cannot be ascribed to one country and its people. To that extent, our viewers-with-alarm are useful, even necessary. They spur us to continued alertness and to greater effort. They combat oversmugness, excessive vanity, and fatuous boasting of our ability, power, and genius. But the Russians lacked then, and from all accounts do not have now, the free economic climate in which Henry Ford and his motor company brought about a new concept of industrial production and changed our way of life. It is true that Henry Ford succeeded over the opposition of his financial backers, despite the trend of the automobile industry and in the face of the forebodings of the supposed "best minds" in the field of finance. But no bureaucracy laid down plans and quotas for him to adhere to; his dream of a car for the masses would never have got off the ground under such conditions. I said then and I say now, "The Ford system, and that of other large industries in this country, is barren ground in which the seed of the Communist system cannot flourish." I said then to a Congressional committee and I say again, "if our industries are as sound as they are advertised to be, the country has little to fear from the Reds."

If ever the Russians should foster freedom to work where and at what one chooses, if they should encourage individualism and the voluntary teamwork of individuals, then I would fear lest, with such release of their boundless energy and vast undeveloped resources, they might overtake us. The mere fact that they are trying to catch up with us is, I believe, a helpful thing. This means competition. Competition is part of the American way of life, and the more we have the better our chances of success—and survival.

CHAPTER

16

Farewell to Model T

BETWEEN October, 1908, and May 26, 1927, we had turned out 15,000,000 Model T's. I was sick of looking at them—sicker, in fact, than the public was.

The people for whom Model T was made had outgrown the sturdy little vehicle that emancipated them from the horse, made the farm a suburb of the town, and put the automobile within the financial reach of practically everyone. Henry Ford had made a car for the common man, and now the common man was getting some uncommon ideas. He was becoming style conscious and was turning his back on Model T for the very thing that enabled him to buy it: its sameness and cheapness. The people for whom it was made had become prosperous. Mr. Ford's remark to me back in 1912, "Give them any color they want so long as it is black," epitomized the reasons for Model T's success and its ultimate decline.

My distaste was stronger than the public's because I had more reasons for it. One reason was the effect the Model T was having on the Ford organization. The worst thing that can be done to an organization is to kill its initiative; eighteen years is a fairly long time to run under full steam on the same track; for the first time, Ford Motor Company seemed on the point of losing its ability for dynamic expansion. Model T was notorious for its lack of glamour. It was a practical car in every sense, and it dominated its field. Attempt after attempt had failed to bring out a car which could compete with it in price and utility. But with the advent of good roads, larger cars and higher speeds were in demand. Now we had competition, not from a cheaper car, or a better-made one, but from a better-looking car—the Chevrolet. Although twice as many Fords as Chevrolets were being sold in 1926, the proportion two years before had been six to one. The used-car market, a post-World War I development, also affected the situation. For less than rock-bottom price for a new Model T one might buy a not-too-elderly secondhand car like a Buick and have such conveniences as a self-starter, demountable rims, and a smoother ride on the road. Finally, I was in the middle between those who were clamoring for a change and Mr. Ford, who had the last word on the subject.

Edsel Ford also was in the middle. He was between his immovable father and Ford salesmen. Model T production was nearing 10,000 cars a day, but Model T sales were falling off, and unwanted Fords were piling up in the branches and agencies and backing up in the Highland Park and River Rouge lots.

Until then sales had always been on top of production, and the Model T formula had been "Sell it as it is." Instead of yelling for more production, Ford salesmen were now calling for a new product. To all this, Henry Ford paid no attention. "The only trouble with the Ford car," he said, "is that we can't make it fast enough." Of course, the real trouble was that the dealers couldn't sell it fast enough. Eighteen years is a long time to carry on with any one product.

It was not necessary to approve Henry Ford's position to understand it. Recall how, against all opposition from his financial backers, in the face of the trend of the automobile industry and the higher economic status of those who were automobile purchasers, he had held stubbornly to his idea of a car for the masses, a car which required no more intelligence to drive and care for than it did to keep the horse it supplanted. And he won out. Remember that in doing so he not only fostered a new system of production, which in turn as it was imitated and adapted raised the scale of American living.

As a single-purpose man, he could not abandon the biggest single purpose of his life. That achievement had brought him world-wide renown which he enjoyed to the fullest. Vanity alone would keep him from acknowledging that Model T was outdated. For three years Henry Ford was in no mood to abandon it. None of us was sure that he would ever do so.

Normally, a change of model can be planned with a minimum of shutdown time. Stopping Model T did not come suddenly. It was first a slowdown. Mr. Ford wanted first of all to learn what the true situation was with Model T. Sales department people hardly had the temerity to tell him that they could not sell his product; they told Edsel, Edsel told his father, and for the first time a real break between father and son was apparent.

Finally, on May 26, 1927, Model T assembly lines at Highland Park and the Rouge shut down. No new cars came from the branches, and the only business done for nine more months was the sale of parts for survivors of the 15,000,000 Ford cars still on the road. Henry Ford is supposed to have taken a year to create Model A. That is not quite correct. He would not even think of tackling a new car until the last Model T came off the line. I knew instinctively that when he said "Shut down" he wanted to do some serious thinking. Actually when Mr. Ford finally decided to replace Model T, clearing the design and getting Model A into production took only ninety days. But it was six months before Henry Ford would go to work.

For the supervisory staff, this was twilight time. The ability to produce a new car was there, but what was it to be? I sat in with our domestic and foreign service and parts departments demanding as heavy a parts replacement schedule as could be set up—enough to carry them for several years. Estimates coming in from the branches gave us enough for a healthy run, and I was thus able to keep the ablest of the supervisory staff together for the duration of the nine months' shutdown.

As can be imagined, it was difficult for me to keep my balance in this situation. As production manager then chiefly concerned with development—new machines, plant rearrangement, and setting up foreign branches—I was between Edsel, president of Ford Motor Company, and Henry Ford, who though holding no official title in the company owned it.

During those nine months I had my first and only disagreements with Edsel and my long-time associate and friend Ed Martin. They felt I was not doing all I could to bring on another car, because I would not battle it out with Mr. Ford on what they wanted. I believed that Henry Ford had built Ford Motor Company around his idea of a motorcar. He had shown by past performance that he could meet a critical situation, and I felt he would come up with something to meet this one.

To bring out his Model T he overcame the prejudices of his partners, then moved in and took full control and from then on saw his dream develop into the wonder plant of the world. When his son and those he could gather around him started screaming at him, much like his partners used to do, I just could not join in. As I had done in the Dodge and Couzens days, I remained neutral, confident that Mr. Ford probably had another new idea and we'd better let it develop. Henry Ford knew how Edsel, Ernest Kanzler, his wife's brother-in-law, and Ed Martin were high-pressuring me. I was with him one morning in the Dearborn drafting room, where Farkas was working on the layout of an engine which became Model A. After we had discussed details for about one hour, he stepped aside and said, "Now, Charlie, if they are annoying you too much down there at the Rouge, why don't you move over here for a while until we get matters all settled?"

I did not even comment on his friendly gesture, I just laughed it off. In a way, I enjoyed the heat, for I was sure a better all-around understanding would come from all this turmoil. I could plainly see the course for me to follow and I did.

I stayed with Henry Ford until I found out what he wanted. This was a repetition of my first days in Ford Motor Company. Mr. Ford did his work by intuition. Every day I would see and talk with him. I never pressed him. I felt he must have a new idea. Any hint of what it might be would be something for me to grab and do something about, but until I could see it I would let nothing bother me. At that same time he told me something that astonished me. I had been telling him that with his new venture he might control or dominate the motorcar business. We had 50 per cent of it in 1924. His reply to control was "Charlie, I don't want all the business. Twenty-five per cent will satisfy me."

Of course, to me that looked like coasting along, but it gave me a hint of why he was not in a hurry to start up; he could get all the business he wanted. When people told him he was slipping with a closed-down plant, that he was losing $100,000,000 and possibly $200,000,000 by not having a new model ready as soon as we quit making Model T, he laughed at them. "Slipping? How?" he asked. "What in the world do we want of that money? Just to keep it in the banks?"

When he was reminded that other automakers boasted that during the shutdown they had hired the best Ford salesmen, leaving only the ones they didn't want, he was unconcerned. "I know some people think that salesmen make a car. We believe that a car, if it is good enough, will make salesmen."

That line of reasoning at that particular time only increased the impatience of Edsel and his friends.

Edsel set out to line up his idea of a car. When he tried to get me to go along with him, I asked him if he was sure this wouldn't involve both of us in trouble with his father. I offered to go with him to see his father. I knew Edsel had a designer working on a new car. I wanted his father to know it, too, but Edsel didn't. He must avoid Henry Ford. It was this struggle between father and son that was the chief reason for the delay in bringing out Model A.

Relations between Henry and Edsel Ford once reached such a serious state that Mr. Ford told me to tell his son to clear out, go to California, and stay there until ordered to come back. I held off from delivering that message, and after a couple of days good feeling returned, an episode which belongs more fully in my chapter dealing with the elder Ford's treatment of his son.

My own feeling during all this pulling and hauling was that Henry Ford would come up again with the right product, and that it was better to wait for it. I was not going to fall into a trap by avoiding him and his ideas, so I decided to wait for the storm to blow over.

I suppose this must be treated as lost time, but it was no waste of time to Henry Ford. To him, it was the ideal time to give the organization a good shaking up, to trim out all unnecessary overhead. He made it clear to me that he would wait until this was all done before he would begin any new venture. Here again Edsel and his father had differences of opinion. Edsel was the kindest man I ever knew. I never saw him discharge any man. Cutting staff just never happened around him.

Whenever matters reached a point where Henry Ford lost patience with his son, I would have the job of seeing Edsel and convey a message from his father. I never had any real difficulty with Edsel in these talks. I felt that he trusted me and understood my position and that he was glad to talk about his disagreements with his father. With the coming of Model A, Edsel became more of a factor in policy matters. He was willing to step out on his own. He now wanted Model A to meet the popular features of competitors' cars. He wanted a shifting-gear transmission, and there was more trouble with his father on that.

The Model T planetary was the elder Ford's idea for the future car. He called the shifting gear a "crunch gear." He said the transmission would never stand up because the gears would clash when changing speeds. He discussed an automatic planetary transmission with me. I realized there would be a lot of development work to do before that could be ready for production. Model A's sliding-gear transmission was the result of a compromise between Edsel and his father.

There was never any real acceptance of this by Henry Ford. As he put it, "We are imitating others." Although he could not see how to make his planetary transmission automatic then, look where it is today. Hydromatic transmissions are the planetary type with automatic clutches actuated by hydraulic pressure.

Had Mr. Ford understood a torque converter that is used in hydromatic transmissions today, I am sure he would have had his way on the Model A transmission. It would not have been a sliding-gear type.

When Model A was ready for production, another argument started over brakes. Edsel was promoting the use of new-type brakes. Our competitors were playing up their advantages over our Model T brakes. We checked up on service on our brakes in several of our branches, and there was evidence of some failure.

In all the years with Model T no one worried or bothered Mr. Ford with design changes, and it was hard to be told that he should adopt something else for Model A. Reports that I made to him on brakes did have effect.

Lawrence P. Sheldrick prepared the brake specifications for the first Model A's. At this time safety authorities in Washington were strongly criticizing Model T brakes, saying they were unsafe. Some state safety boards even threatened to stop the use of Model T on the road. Regulations were now being set up for inspection of brakes, lights, and tires.

The German government issued orders to stop the use of Ford cars because brakes on Model T did not meet its requirements. Our competitors in Germany wanted to stop import of all cars, and the brake question was convenient for that purpose. Our agents in Germany got around that by installing brake cables instead of rods.

We developed the Model A brakes with balanced pressure on all four wheels. We had provided ample brake surface. It proved very satisfactory and the safety commissions in all the states gave full approval. I felt this was a sound policy; public safety required it.

Henry Ford did not want to be told by anyone how he should build a car. The order to regulate brakes he treated as the cunning work of some politicians. They were influenced by agents and auto manufacturers. He felt that if he had to accept their regulations, real development would be stymied. Here was still another reason for delaying Model A. Mr. Ford believed shutting down the plant for a while would shunt aside all protests on brake regulations.

There came a great change in father-son relations with the advent of Model A. The shutdown and mystery talk heightened popular interest. In 1928 we produced 633,594 Model A's. In 1929 we produced 1,507,132, and in 1930 we produced 1,155,162. In 1931 we produced 541,615. By April 14 of that year, we had produced a grand total of 20,000,000 motorcars. But 1930 was the beginning of the Great Depression, and our 1931 production was more than 50 per cent less. Our energy to create and produce was never fully released until World War II, ten years later. Meanwhile, we were designing an entirely new car.

The V-8 came out in 1932, the third year of the depression. This was the elder Ford's last mechanical triumph. As it developed year by year to meet competition, Edsel was now the styler. Fewer ideas came from his father and more from the organization, subject, of course, to his approval. The old philosophy of the car making the salesman was kicked out the window. Edsel was now bent on getting suggestions from the sales department on color schemes and accessories. "Get cooperation from our agents" was his attitude—a pattern being set by competitors in the medium-price field.

We at Ford were first to develop an eight-cylinder engine economical enough for the low-price field. It was not just an eight-cylinder engine, but a V-type eight-cylinder engine. Before Ford Motor Company brought it to the low-price field, the V-8 engine was found only in the world's most costly cars. By simplifying construction and successfully casting the V-8 cylinder blocks, crankcase, and exhaust passages in a simple integral unit, and by eliminating many parts, we made automotive history.

The Ford V-8 became a brilliant performer. It won road races and hill-climbing contests all over the country. Now, with a product that gave all the assurance that one could ask for, our aim was to stabilize it for a long run.

Strangely enough, our V-8 went on the market just twenty days after we were shown another newcomer to the low-price field. On March 10, 1932, I noted this in my diary: "Walter Chrysler called today. Showed us a new Plymouth."

I had known Chrysler from the beginning of his career in the Buick Company in Flint. We were fellow members of the Bloomfield Hills Country Club and the Detroit Athletic Club. We were about the same age and with the same mechanical experience, although I started earlier than he in the automobile business. We had been close friends from the time we met. Later, when he organized his Chrysler Corporation, he asked me to join him, but he found my flag pinned on Henry Ford.

Because of his friendship with me he brought his Plymouth car to Mr. Ford and me and asked for our opinion of it. The most radical feature of his car was the novel suspension of its six-cylinder engine so as to cut down vibration. The engine was supported on three points and rested on rubber mounts. Noise and vibration were much less. There was still a lot of movement of the engine when idling, but under a load it settled down. Although it was a great success in the Plymouth, Henry Ford did not like it. For no given reason, he just didn't like it, and that was that. I told Walter that I felt it was a step in the right direction, that it would smooth out all noises and would adapt itself to axles and springs and steering-gear mounts, which would stop the transfer of road noises into the body. Today rubber mounts are used on all cars. They are also found on electric-motor mounts, in refrigerators, radios, television sets—wherever mechanical noises are apparent, rubber is used to eliminate them. We can thank Walter Chrysler for a quieter way of life.

Mr. Ford could have installed this new mount at once in the V-8, but he missed the value of it. Later Edsel and I persuaded him. Rubber mounts are now found also in doors, hinges, windshields, fenders, spring hangers, shackles, and lamps—all with the idea of eliminating squeaks and rattles.

The V-8 was a stimulant for the organization. It brought new problems. With the first hint of building a V-8 engine, I sensed that many prior operating notions would have to be set aside. New methods with closer tolerance on dimensions would demand new tools and machines.

The first major problem was a unit casting. All previous V-8's had been cast in more than one piece. What we proposed to do was to cast whole a V-8 in a single solid, rigid block.

So I went back to my old trade of patternmaking. I had to get out of the designer, Joe Galamb, a layout that I could adapt to our Rouge foundries. With the study of the casting I tied the plant layout group under Hanson.

We studied every move in the molding operation and mechanized its handling. The sand for each mold was shot into flasks from overhead chutes. Pattern and mold were then vibrated with a raise-and-drop movement which packed the prepared sand. This did away with all the sand handling by shovel, and heavy pounding of the sand by hand was eliminated.

A mechanical lifting device raised the finished molds from machine to a conveyer which took them to a point where the cores, fresh from vertical tower ovens, were brought by conveyer and set in place. At a steady pace of 100 molds an hour, the assembled mold was conveyed to an iron-pouring line.

Pouring iron into a moving mold was a spectacular affair as well as a new and original method. A pouring furnace containing two tons of melted iron moved alongside the conveyer at the same speed. Its pouring spout was tilted into the mold, and the iron ran in and filled the mold. The moving furnace was fed from a nearby 20-ton electrical furnace in which the iron analysis could be controlled by alloy additions. This furnace was fed in turn by cupola melt from our own blast furnaces.

Achievement of a continuous moving operation of this foundry work eliminated all the backbreaking toil from the molding and pouring and handling of the casting as it came out of the mold. It was a revolutionary method, developed entirely within the Ford organization. There was nothing like it anywhere else on a large scale.

Cooling of the casting after pouring was important in order to control hardness and cracking. These controls produced a casting that went through the machine operations with added life to the cutters in the milling machines, drills, and reamers. The speed of all operations was stepped up. This, of course, showed us the need of new machinery to meet this casting development.

Improved cutting steels that could handle higher speeds added to the new development. The solid, rigid, single V-8 casting could now stand any load that machines could put on it.

None of this could be visualized on the drafting board, and I enjoyed the battles I had with some of the designers in Dearborn. When they found me making changes in design so as to fit the foundry and machine needs, they actually believed I would ruin the engine. But I knew the engine as well as they did because I had lived with it just as closely. They knew nothing about the technique that we were developing in the plant, and I deliberately kept them away from that until we built some engines.

It was a grand feeling to get into something new with such great possibilities. Mr. Ford would come to my office for his daily contact. I kept him up to date and always primed him on how the organization was adapting itself to this V-8. All his doubts were cleared up. I showed him that to revamp the plant we would spend $50,000,000 in the next two years.

Instinctively I knew that would not concern him, but I was amused at one of his remarks about spending money for this new engine.

"Charlie," he said, "we have too much money in the bank. That doesn't do that bunch in the front office any good. When they look at it they become self-satisfied, and I know they are getting lazy. Let's you and me pull that down. You do that until it hurts. I know this new car will bring in more money than ever, but don't tell them I said so."

Well, I never did tell until now. I understood his philosophy, that money is spent properly only when you can see how to get it back. To spend a million dollars and spend it right is more of a task than most people can understand. I don't see any indications of that kind of thinking in our government spending today. Money spent right always returns and then is ready for recirculation. Henry Ford became uneasy when he saw funds accumulating. "We have too much money, Charlie," he would say. "Let's you and me get it working."

The V-8 engine showed the way to spend and get it back. It stayed in production longer than Model T's nineteen years. It lasted with no major change for twenty-one years, and it took that long before it was adopted as a standard type by our closest competitors. The present-day V-8 engine has adapted overhead valves, but the principle of a unit block remains the same.

So far as Ford Motor Company was concerned, the casting of a unit block was the real factor in the engine's success. We produced the finished machined block for less per pound than our previous cost. One real factor was the loss in foundry practice. Our loss was under 2 per cent. Machine-shop losses and foundry rejects were less than 1 per cent. Foundry practice had run 10 per cent loss.

Complete revamping of the foundry gave us new fields to

work in. Steel castings were not used in motorcars. They were too high in cost, and machine work was expensive. A five-pound finished casting would weigh on the average 7½ pounds in the rough. The cost was double that of gray iron, on which much less finish was allowed and which had to be removed by cutters and drills.

The V-8 crankshaft started as a forging. H. McCarroll and I searched for a steel that could be cast and still meet the physical requirements of a crankshaft. We started casting round bars, two inches in diameter and twelve inches long. We poured them at various temperatures, then removed them from the sand molds at temperatures ranging from close to molten down to normal room temperature in order to see what changes occurred in structure and shrinking in these different phases.

Next we doubled the length of the test bars and decreased their thickness. We put acceptable bars through cutting tests at various speeds and carefully charted all for comparison. Out of this came the discovery that our cast steel was better crankshaft material than any suitable forging bar.

Again I went to work in the pattern shop, where we developed a vertical hard-sand mold which enabled us to cast four cranks at a time with one pot of molten steel. It proved to be a better crank than we had anticipated, and I had the entire practice covered with patents. All physical characteristics were improved, and the finished crank cost us $1 less than the forged crank. This took us into casting stronger and lighter steel pistons. The crankshaft foundry was equipped with special conveyers to send the machine-made treated-sand cores through vertical ovens, and then for pouring alongside a special electrical melting furnace.

Heat treatment was started with some of the initial heat remaining from the casting steel. The entire heat-treat operation, through heating and cooling and reheating, was all mechanically controlled and the castings were handled and delivered to the machine shop and into an engine without ever touching the floor.

The effect of this foundry was felt in every corner of our plant. The type of handling equipment that was adapted there was a model for all handling of materials. That is why I term the V-8 period the highest progressive mechanical work in the automotive industry.

High costs of labor and material are danger signals. To see cost climbing and not do anything about it does not make sense. To meet cost by adding it to the price of the product has its limitations. Few people realize what the expense of handling materials means. With the V-8 and the Rouge plant Ford Motor Company again became the example to the industry of the United States on how to reduce the handling of materials.

All materials entering the Ford plant went into operation and stayed there. They never came to rest until they had become part of a unit like an engine, an axle, or a body. Then they moved on to final assembly or into a freight car for branch assembly, and finally to the customer. It was a glorious period; a production man's dream come true.

On February 10, 1942, two months after Pearl Harbor, all automobile production for civilian use ceased. Since 1905, I had taken part in the building of 30,000,000 motor cars.

CHAPTER

17

Tractor Troubles

NOTHING should be simpler than putting a seed in the ground, then wait three or four months and reap the product. But around this supposedly simple seed-to-harvest progress has arisen the Farm Problem, a vexatious complication which affects national elections. Ford Motor Company had its Farm Problem, centering around tractors and a $341,000,000 lawsuit simply because Henry Ford did not believe in written contracts so long as two men gave each other their word.

One thing which impelled the youthful Henry Ford into Detroit and a mechanic's job was his dislike of farm drudgery. The steam engines, like city steam rollers but with smaller wheels, which hauled threshing machines from farm to farm and then furnished the power to operate them, fascinated him; and he is supposed to have repaired one. He saw no reason why, ultimately, machine power should not supplant the horse on the farm. Whether at work or not, a horse had to be fed. But not a machine; it needed to be fed fuel only when working. The frugal Ford boy never forgot that contrast.

The fall of 1905, the year I went to work for him, Henry Ford began talking about making a farm tractor but did not want this to conflict with what we were doing at the Piquette

Avenue works. Early one morning I went with him about three blocks from the plant to a house on Woodward Avenue. There was a big horse and carriage barn in the rear with a large overhead loft. We decided that this was a suitable place for putting in a few draftsmen and developing a new unit, and it was rented on the spot. The place got a thorough housecleaning and a little organization moved in with Joe Galamb as its head.

Joe made many studies, but it was 1907 before a tractor was built. We used a copper, water-jacketed, four-cylinder engine that we had taken out of Model B.

The contraption was sent out to the Ford farm, where it helped to mow hay, harvest oats and wheat, and power other tools on the farm.

All told, we built three of these vehicles and kept them in service plowing throughout the fall, and manure spreading during the winter. The manufacturing of this tractor had to be delayed, obviously because we had more than we could do designing and building motorcars. However, Mr. Ford applied for patents in 1910. When Ford Motor Company expanded to Highland Park he tried to tie tractor operations in with the company but could not sell this idea to the directors. Accordingly, in 1915 he left Ford Motor Company, organized Henry Ford & Son, and moved with me to Dearborn, a short distance from Fair Lane, his new home, to begin manufacture of tractors.

The plant on the south side of the Michigan Central Railroad had been a former brickyard. Adjoining it Mr. Ford had two good-sized farms which we could use for experimental work on the new tractor. There were still a lot of bricks stored in some sheds. We decided that we would use these for putting up a 180 by 60 building suitable for engineering and some light machine operation work.

Starting with me on the job were Gene Farkas, Seyburn Livingston, and Marvin Bryant. At this time several manufacturers produced tractors, and Mr. Ford had acquired just about every available make and tried them out on his farm. We put them in one corner of a building so that we could study them. All of them impressed us as too heavy and very much underpowered, so that became our first problem to solve. We also found that most of these vehicles had either chain or some outside form of drive open to the dirt that was thrown up in farming operations. So, we decided that our tractor's drive would be inside a housing just like that on a motorcar. Our next decision was for a worm and a worm-wheel drive to the rear wheels. Although this might not be the most efficient type of drive, it was evident that with a little additional horsepower it would enable us to have a thoroughly closed-in mechanism with no outside wearing parts.

With this important detail settled, the next problems were an axle and a drive, an engine for the drive, and a front end for controlling direction. Our solution was what we termed the "three-unit system." We designed a transmission that went from the rear end of the engine into a housing which also contained the worm, the worm wheel, and the differential housing. The two outside shafts to the wheel drive were then enclosed in the housing that made the rear unit. All outer housings were of cast iron.

The center unit was the engine with a flywheel and a clutch, and the front unit had a cover to which we fastened the axle and a steering device. Our three units were so designed that they could be thrown on a set of rails which would bring them together on a conveyer where the tractor would be put together.

We prepared the design in ninety days, and then I put orders for fifty tractors into the shop. I had been setting in some milling machines, boring mills, and a general line of drill presses, gear cutters, and the like. We opened an employment and time office. Among those I hired off the street were Mead Bricker, a machinist, and John Crawford, both of whom later became Ford executives. The timekeeper was Frank Mead, a brother of Dr. Mead, the Highland Park plant physician.

This did not stop Henry Ford or me from circulating in Highland Park. We took lunch occasionally in the office basement dining room. This bothered a few like Knudsen, Lee, and Wills. They thought we were in Dearborn, out of their way, and it annoyed Wills to find we were not using the vanadium steel he had developed.

Fred Griffith, of Central Steel in Ohio, was the metallurgist who made the vanadium steel for forgings and gears in Model T. He came to see me with a straight chrome carbon steel that he claimed had higher physical strength than we were using in Model T. I had him make some heats, and the young metallurgist who came along with Fred to prove his steel was Ben Fairless, later chairman of the board of United States Steel Corporation.

It was a terrible blow to Wills and Lee when they discovered that we had decided to adopt this new steel for the tractor. Wills met with Henry Ford to tell him that I was in trouble with this type of steel and Henry Ford, like a good comrade, referred him to me. That is what made me so fond of Henry Ford. Wills was financially interested in vanadium, and I was upsetting his gold mine. Wills tried to hammer me down, but when I pointed out with charges to prove that we had something better, he also learned that I knew he was exploiting vanadium. After I made this clear, he decided I was too hot to handle. Ultimately we dropped the use of vanadium in Ford Motor Company.

We built the first fifty tractors with chrome carbon steel. We could oil-harden the gears, and it did away with the carbonizing operations. We had better gears at less cost.

In the tractor plant I could do anything I wanted. Henry Ford would not bother with details. I was able to get enough machinery set up so that early in 1916 we had built our first experimental Fordson. Throughout the season of 1916, from spring until late fall, we kept these tractors in continuous operation. They did all the power work on Mr. Ford's farm. There was a good deal to learn about the tractors themselves. The design, however, was good. From our experience with them we were able to clean up the bugs in good shape before the season was over. The work we were doing was receiving a great deal of publicity in newspapers and magazines, and soon we had visitors from all over the world.

Among them was Lord Northcliffe, the dynamic English publisher who was later head of the British War Mission to the United States. He spent several days on the tractor, driving it himself, looking at the ones that we had torn down for examination. He was much impressed with it and went away convinced that wartime Britain should as soon as possible get into farm tractor production. Because of German submarines, the British faced a serious food problem. As soon as Northcliffe returned to England, he had a talk with Lord Perry, head of the British Ford Motor Company, who cabled immediately for us to ship him a tractor to England.

We sent him one in January, 1917. The shipping of this tractor had high priority, so it was soon in Perry's hands in England. Northcliffe had arranged for some demonstrations of the various types of tractors that they had available. Perry put our tractor into this test, and it had immediate results. On April 7, the day after the United States entered the war, Perry cabled us:

"The need for food production in England is imperative and large quantity of tractors must be available at earliest possible date for purpose of breaking up existing grass land and plowing for fall wheat. Am requested by high authorities to appeal to Mr. Ford for help. Would you be willing to send Sorensen and others with drawings of everything necessary loaning them to British Government so that parts can be manufactured over here and assembled in Government Factories under Sorensen's guidance. Can assure you positively the suggestion is made in national interest and if carried out will be done by the Government for the people with no manufacturing or capitalist interest invested and no profit being made by any interests whatever. The matter is very urgent. Impossible to ship anything from America because many thousand tractors must be provided. Ford Tractor considered best and only suitable design. Consequently National necessity entirely dependent Mr. Ford's design."

Mr. Ford replied that he would immediately dispatch Sorensen with blueprints, patterns, and that he would lend every aid possible to getting this tractor into production in England. We also asked Perry to arrange for priority for all the equipment that we wanted to bring over as well as for transportation for me and the staff that I would bring with me. All these requests were cleared immediately.

I filled an express car with tractor parts as well as patterns and farming implements to go with it, and on April 25 we took a train for Halifax. Henry Ford and Gordon McGregor, of our Canadian plant, went along to see us off. I also had in my party Mead Bricker, John Crawford, Breedo Berghoff and Arthur Dugrey and William Jackson, all members of our Dearborn staff. We arrived in Halifax, April 28, and sailed on May 3 on the troopship *Justicia*. The *Justicia*, a 40,000-ton three-stacker was half-finished for the Holland-American Line when war broke out and the British commandeered her. She was sunk in 1918 by a submarine whose people reported that they had sunk the *Leviathan*, the biggest ship then afloat.

Arriving in England eleven days later, Perry took me to meetings with S. F. Edge of the Ministry of Agriculture and with committees of British manufacturers who might make tractor parts. We combed England and the Scottish lowlands pretty thoroughly for possible suppliers, to whom we gave blueprints and specifications. By the end of June things were lined up for early production of parts, and I was back in London. One forenoon an air-raid alert was sounded. I was told this was unusual because the Zeppelins which occasionally dropped bombs on the city always came at night. This raid, however, was a daylight one not by dirigibles but by German planes which bombed London's Fleet Street and financial district and caused considerable damage. We watched the raid from a rooftop.

This incident changed our picture completely. Early the next morning Perry called me to say he had been asked by Christopher Addison, who was Minister of Munitions, to get me and come to his office as quickly as possible. When Perry and I rushed over, we found, in addition to Addison, Lord Alfred Milner, Edge, Percy Martin and, several other high officials.

As soon as Perry and I entered, Milner, who was apparently running this meeting, told us that the German airplane attack the day before had completely changed their plans. They decided overnight that England had to go all out for making more planes, and all the facilities that we had gathered together would have to be used for airplane production.

Finally, Lord Milner said to me, "We've got to have tractors. Now what can we do? Can we get them from you out of the United States?"

I explained that, although our manufacturing program was not yet set up, I was satisfied that if the British would handle the shipping end, we could get into production in Dearborn much more quickly than we could in England.

"Well," said Milner, "that is what we will have to do. We will find a way to get them shipped."

I asked him how many tractors he would like to have us make. "What can you do?" he replied. I expressed my confidence that we could get up to fifty a day within ninety days and from there on could increase rapidly beyond that if necessary.

"Splendid," said Milner, "how about 5,000 tractors, and at what price?" I had my cost figures pretty well worked out before I left Dearborn, and I told him we would make these first 5,000 at cost plus $50 per unit, subject, of course, to Mr. Ford's approval. A quick cable to Dearborn brought this typical reply:

"Charlie, go ahead and complete your arrangement with the English government. I am satisfied."

On July 11 I was back in Dearborn and at work. We got a lot of tools and equipment out of Highland Park, lined up plenty of suppliers to help us, and made deliveries in advance of dates on our English contract. Our first shipment was in October, well under the estimated ninety days for tooling up.

When the tractors arrived in England, Perry followed them through with his agents to their farm destinations. In so doing, his agents were broken in on servicing and all operations that the government had set for them to do. Altogether, they made quite a reputation for themselves—so much so that the English company later took on the manufacture of this early Fordson tractor and has continued it up to this writing. It made a fine business for Ford Motor Company, Limited.

In the United States, Fordson tractor production was tied in with wartime food programs in various states as well as with a country-wide Henry Ford & Son distributing organization. By 1920 we had turned out 200,000 Fordsons which were sent all over the world.

By this time Mr. Ford had bought out the remaining Ford Motor Company stockholders and thus removed one of the chief motives for the existence of Henry Ford & Son. In late December, 1919, Ford Motor Company took over supervision of all tractor sales and, next May, Henry Ford & Son was dissolved with all family holdings transferred to Ford Motor Company. I returned to the company, moved to the Rouge, and took charge once again of all production programs. Tractor production was moved to the Rouge in October, 1920, just after Dearborn had achieved a month's record of 10,248 tractors, or 399 a day.

After a promising start, sales—or perhaps the handling of sales—proved disappointing. There was confusion among Ford agents; having specialized in selling motorcars, they were unfamiliar with tractors. Also during the 1920's, while the rest of the American economy was temporarily riding high, wide, and handsome, the farmers were being shaken out of their World War I inflation and many of them were too far in the red to go further into debt for tractors.

Tractors began piling up on Ford agents—so high that we finally had to slow down. Eventually there was a complete shutdown. The decision had to be made whether Ford agents should carry the load of motorcars as well as tractors. It was finally decided that the combination was too much, and that we should favor carrying motorcars only and let the tractor operations stand still for a while.

This decision did not please Henry Ford. He was always keen on keeping in line with his tractors, almost in preference to his motorcar. He felt that there was a great need to help the farmer in every way that he possibly could. However, the decision was made, and we did not build any tractors for quite a while, but experimentation and tryouts continued at Dearborn throughout all the production hiatus.

Lord Perry was in the United States on one of his annual trips when we shut down tractor operations and, wanting them very much in England and on the Continent, asked me if it would be possible for him to take over the machinery and have it erected in England where he could run and supply the demands over there.

I talked with Mr. Ford about this. He was very much pleased and said, "Let Perry have the equipment right away, and let's get it running. They can't have it standing still here. A little later on we will do something else."

Mr. Ford was very much annoyed with the sales department at that time. He never missed an opportunity to show his disapproval of the way the department had been managed, and that is what led to his unfortunate selling arrangement with Harry Ferguson in 1938, which in turn led to a lawsuit ten years later.

While in England I met Ferguson, then a young machinery salesman. Had I been able to foresee the consequence of that meeting I would have avoided it.

As early as 1912, Henry Ford conceived the idea of a tractor and plow as a single unit. Like many simple things, it apparently had not been thought of before. The horse and the plow had been separate, and so, in the reasoning of the day, the tractor that supplanted the horse should be hitched to the plow. The unit tractor-plow was part of our plan when we organized to build the Fordson in 1915. In 1917, in England, I told Ferguson that we proposed to combine the two. He took up the idea and in a few weeks came back with some models. After I left England he kept me advised from time to time as to his progress, which I in turn reported to Mr. Ford.

In 1920, Ferguson came over from Ireland, and I introduced him to Mr. Ford, who looked over what had been accomplished. Realizing that Ferguson was limited in ability to design or to finance, but finding him a good demonstrator and salesman, Mr. Ford suggested that he come to work for Ford Motor Company. When asking me to hire Ferguson, Mr. Ford said he would be a useful man to demonstrate our tractors and added, "With this plow we can use him in our organization."

When I talked with Ferguson about the matter I found that he did not wish to come to the United States; he wanted to be on his own and build a plant in Ireland. He did very much want Mr. Ford's and my cooperation in the design of his plow, but I broke off with him when I could not induce him to go to work for us.

The plow that he showed us did not require any mechanical force to raise or lower it, and he proposed to build and sell it as an accessory to the Fordson tractor. When he found that we were not interested in the form he had developed unless he would go to work for us directly and clean up the engineering on it, Ferguson saw most of this country's implement makers in an unsuccessful effort to get them to take on the plow.

Next he made a deal with Eber Sherman, who was selling tractors in South America for Ford Motor Company, to promote the sale of his plow as well as to find a manufacturer for it. Sherman finally found an Indiana manufacturer who would take it.

After this first session with us, Ferguson came over again several times until 1938, when he demonstrated to Mr. Henry Ford his tractor, on the order of the Fordson, and plow with a power lift. At that time he claimed that between 1936 and 1938 the implements had been tested and proved to be a technical and commercial success. He had made an agreement with an English manufacturer to build his designed tractor and plow. He claimed that during that period about 1,250 tractors were built embodying his system for manufacturers abroad. Ford Motor Company, Ltd., built and sold more than 200,000 Fordsons in England.

When Ferguson appeared in 1938, we were ready with a new tractor, and his plow with a hydraulic lifting device appealed to Mr. Ford, who remembered that the same principle had applied in the big steam tractors of his boyhood. We wanted to adapt a plow to our tractor. We did not need him to show us how to build tractors—he needed us. We did want him to come with us because we knew we would make a suc-

cess of his plow if we could adapt it. Ferguson had no formal
understanding with Ford Motor Company. He had rights to
the plow, Ford had rights to the tractor, and Ferguson was to
sell both. On this flimsy structure of agreement between Mr.
Ford and Ferguson, sales of tractors continued with the Ferguson Company until 1947.

The plow that Ferguson brought over and which he says he
had perfected was a handmade implement from materials at
hand, such as bars of steel, plate, and angles. It was not designed for volume production, and it was not acceptable to
Mr. Ford.

While the implement could give a demonstration for a short
time, as it did for Mr. Ford, it was evident to us on close study
that it would not give the service required on rough, stony,
heavy soils in this country.

Without waiting to notify Ferguson, who was then back in
Ireland, and not wanting any further delay, Mr. Ford and I
decided to develop a plow with the proper design for production and assembly. This design was made by our own engineers,
assisted by McCarroll, our metallurgist and foundryman.

When Ferguson returned to Dearborn and discovered what
we had done, he went up in the air to think we had dared
to change anything on his plow without consulting him. His
surprise was complete when he found his own organization
in full accord with what we were doing. Later, when he understood the improvement, he commended me highly and got
to know me as "Cast-Iron Charlie."

Ferguson was not in on this engineering work. Mr. Ford and
I lived with it daily. The question of the engine, its type and
rating, had to be determined. The design was made and the
initial engine was built, tested, and checked out in Dearborn.
With the major details out of the way, it was released to the
Rouge plant engineering to go ahead on the complete tractor
production.

After our new tractor got into production about 1938, Ferguson induced Mr. Ford to put his name "Ferguson" on this tractor jointly with Mr. Henry Ford's. The use of the term "Ferguson system" came in when we finished the tractor for production. Ferguson wanted to use his name somewhere in the new tractor. He did a lot of talking about it.

Nobody in our field or sales organization knew him. Mr. Ford and I had the reputation in the United States of building the Fordson. As far as the Ford organization was concerned, they did not want his name on the tractor. Edsel was against any name other than Ford. John Crawford had something to do with the name plate. He handled all the Ford patent records and pacified Ferguson on his demands for recognition. The sales field created the term "Ferguson system." That gesture Ferguson made the most of later.

For extra aid in making his plow, Ferguson lined up an Ohio outfit, the Empire Plow Company, from which he enticed a young ball of fire named Roger Kyes. Within months Kyes became vice-president and general manager, and in 1943 president of Ferguson's American company. Kyes will be remembered as the General Motors executive taken by Secretary of Defense C. E. Wilson into government for a short while to do the needful cutting down of expenses.

When the United States got into World War II, production and sales of the Ford tractor-Ferguson plow attachment was killed by wartime priorities for materials.

For the duration of the war, at least, Ford tractors plus Ferguson plows were out. But not in Britain. Unable to get release of tractor production in the United States, Ferguson and Kyes sought to get our new model introduced into the Dagenham plant of Ford Motor Company, Limited. Having already secured priorities for making the Fordson tractor, Lord Perry of the English Ford company opposed a change.

There was an almost daily row between Henry Ford and

me. Ferguson was building the fire under Perry and Mr. Ford seemed in full accord, for he would not pay any attention to Perry's reports. When A. R. Smith, Perry's deputy, came over to see us, Mr. Ford spent a whole day demonstrating the new tractor. "I want you to go back and throw out the Fordson," he told Smith, "and start making this new tractor at once. Forget about Perry. He can't stop me any longer. *I'm* telling you to run that business. I don't care what Perry or anyone else thinks about this. I'm running things now."

Smith tried to explain that he could not remove Perry. Mr. Ford said, "I don't care. I'm looking to you to do as I say." He walked out and left Smith and me sitting there. Smith was flabbergasted. "I can't do a thing like that," he said to me.

Meanwhile British government officials asked Perry to find out from us what Ferguson's standing was with Ford Motor Company of Dearborn.

I replied that he had no official capacity, that he was the head of a sales company and, in so far as development of the new Ford tractor was concerned, stood by as a consultant. I could not put it any other way. I sent Ferguson a copy of this, and he kept it for many days before I heard complaint about it.

The letter got into the hands of Campsall, Mr. Ford's secretary, via Ferguson. After we read it over together, Campsall agreed that the letter was correct.

Then Ferguson came to see me with a long story about how he would lose face with British government officials if they saw this letter saying he had been a mere stand-by consultant. He asked if I realized how hard he had worked to get our tractor into England. I replied with a review of his progress, which was nothing.

I blamed him for the confusion that existed in Ford Motor Company, Limited. I told him how Perry had stood for all his bad display of manners, how his letters had lost him the respect of everybody in Ford Motor Company, Limited, as well as of government officials. And would he please stay out of the picture altogether, so that Perry and I could and would work out this problem together. Ferguson seemed to take this talk very well, but the next day I learned from Campsall that he had gone to Mr. Henry Ford and blamed me for the trouble he was having with Perry, and charged that Perry and I had joined in an effort to embarrass him.

Campsall said Mr. Ford was convinced that Perry and I were against Ferguson and his efforts to introduce this new tractor in England. Over the years I had with Mr. Ford an understanding which he put this way: "Charlie, if there is anything wrong anywhere, I will tell you about it." But now I was not quite so sure.

Campsall asked me to write another letter altering the statement that Ferguson was standing by as a consultant. I told Campsall to write the letter, then Mr. Ford would be in on it, for Campsall would have to clear it with him.

The result was a letter which Campsall composed under date of June 7, 1943, bidding Perry in the name of Ford Motor Company to resign from the English company. He said that Mr. Ford had seen the letter and told him, "Charlie can sign that and clear up the mixup." There was nothing in this letter that reflected statements I had made. Moreover, the new letter had no binding effect. Lord Perry was head of a joint-stock company, whose shares could be purchased by the public, and only the board of directors of Ford Motor Company, Limited, could force him to resign.

I told Mr. Ford this when I tangled with him on the Perry matter. I also told him he was misinformed and that the facts could not substantiate his stand. Mr. Ford replied that he was satisfied that Ferguson had kept him fully informed, that he was thoroughly dissatisfied with Perry and his conduct and was through with him, and for me to be sure I understood it.

This was the first time in thirty-eight years that we had had a complete disagreement, I told him, and if he felt the same about me as he did about Perry I was prepared to step out at once. Mr. Ford did not push the matter any further, and I let it pass. I then took the letter to my office, signed it, and sent it along.

So far as Henry Ford was concerned, that was the finish of Perry and the end of a close friendship that had existed ever since 1906, when young Percival Lea Dewhurst Perry, a motor-car enthusiast, had visited Detroit to get the English agency for Ford cars.

Now, in his disordered mind, Mr. Ford had turned against his old friend.

The letter demanding his resignation arrived when Perry was a very sick man. It was referred to the board of directors, who filed it away without taking action, and it was months before he heard about it.

I did not see Lord Perry again until 1949. I had no correspondence with him, for I felt sure he would understand that I was not responsible for the letter. I called on him in Nassau. He was partly paralyzed from a stroke and had resigned from Ford Motor Company, Limited. He told me about a visit he had in Ways, Georgia, with Henry Ford in 1948. Mr. Ford did not recognize him. Perry heard him ask Mrs. Ford, "Who is that man?" Perry tried to talk about the letter of resignation. Henry Ford said that he did not know anything about it, and so another one of the Ford greats disappeared.

In 1947, three years after I resigned from the company, Ford Motor Company canceled its selling arrangement with Ferguson's company. I am not wholly aware of the reasons, but I am familiar enough with the circumstances under which that arrangement was made to know that the company had a perfect right to take that course if it chose to do so. This annulment, however, knocked Ferguson's American company's operations into a cocked hat, and I understand that it was unable to persuade any other motor or implement manufacturer to take over production.

On October 17, 1947, according to my diary, I met Roger Kyes at the Detroit Athletic Club. Kyes asked me to come to his room, and there I met two lawyers for Ferguson. They discussed with Kyes the likelihood of a suit against Ford Motor Company for canceling Ferguson's sales agreement. I gathered from the talk that Kyes was not in accord with them. He had broken with Ferguson and wanted to be free of his contract. The lawyers wanted Kyes to cooperate with them and they pressed him for information about Henry Ford which they could use in suit against Ford Motor Company. They inferred that Henry Ford was mentally unbalanced and had been so for several years. Between questionings of Kyes, who gave them no satisfaction, they asked me similar questions. I parried them with questions of my own. Had Ferguson ever indicated, I asked, that Henry Ford had raised him from a poor man looking for a job to a successful businessman with Ford Motor Company? No matter what happened, I felt that Ferguson was ungrateful. Was it possible he was repudiating Mr. Ford? Henry Ford was not with us any more to protect himself but, I said, I was still here and could speak for him and what he had done for Ferguson, and I would do so if the case was ever brought to trial. Then I walked out.

Later Ferguson filed suit against Ford Motor Company in the United States District Court for Southern New York. He charged violation of a "gentleman's agreement" with Henry Ford which was never reduced to writing regarding sales arrangements, infringement of patent rights, expropriation of his inventive ideas, and so forth and so on. He threw the book at Ford Motor Company in his allegations and demanded damages of $341,600,000.

Among the many items in his complaint, one was of particular interest to me. That was his allegation that he had final control as to engineering development of the new Ford tractor. As I said in my draft of a letter to Perry, Ferguson was a "stand-by consultant." He was not an engineer, he was not a metallurgist, he had no production experience worthy of the name. If despite these limitations he designed tools and machinery for the new Ford tractor, then he was taking over my job—something that no one ever did in the nearly forty years I was with Ford Motor Company. So I got in touch with William Gossett, the Ford attorney, and offered to donate my services in fighting the Ferguson suit. Gossett and a number of other company executives flew down to Miami Beach to see me and map out the case.

When I returned to Detroit I saw Henry Ford II. The complaint filed by Ferguson was so inconsistent that I wanted to protect Henry Ford and myself against the man's ingratitude. I wanted to know whether it was decided to go all out in court to protect Ford Motor Company; otherwise, I did not care to be involved. If a compromise was considered, I would prefer to stay out. I was assured there would be no compromise.

The complaint was filed January 8, 1948, and came to trial on March 29, 1951. I was involved in the case continuously, in its preparation and depositions. In the middle of the trial Henry Ford II took it upon himself to go to England and try to reach an agreement with Ferguson. That meeting got a lot of publicity and young Henry got nowhere. It did act as a stimulant to the Ford lawyers, who had no desire to compromise, but the trial drew heavily on Henry II, Ernie Breech, William Gossett, and their staff as well as myself. A motion was made to move the case to Detroit so that the Ford officials would not be entirely away from their business. In denying the motion, the trial judge expressed a hope that the case would be settled out of court.

I realize now that Henry II was carrying the responsibility of a case that resulted from bad business judgment by his grandfather. A simple understanding in writing—a very easy thing to do in the absence of a contract—would have avoided the gentleman's agreement that Ferguson claimed. But at the time of the Ferguson demonstration, in the fall of 1938, Henry Ford had just recovered from a stroke. His mind did not grasp things as readily as it used to. I had many sessions with him on tractor design; we would agree on something one day, and a few days later he did not register at all. Dr. McClure kept cautioning him to relax. Mrs. Ford was almost distracted about the situation and tried in vain to keep him out of the plant.

Consequently, I was aware how annoying the Ferguson suit was to Henry Ford II, and I can understand why he followed the trial judge's wish for an out-of-court settlement. On April 9, 1952, Ford Motor Company paid $9,250,000 to Ferguson, who then withdrew his $341,000,000 suit. To settle out of court meant that the cost of settlement plus lawyers' fees were tax-deductible items, so one could say that the government was paying a major part of the bill, while the rest of the payment was probably worth the money to dispose of an annoyance. As for Ferguson, perhaps the most revealing commentary upon the justice of his cause is the fact that he was willing to accept one-thirty-seventh of his original multimillion-dollar demand.

PART
5

18

Ford and the New Deal

THE year 1930 and the beginning of the Big Depression had revolutionary political and social consequences. During the twenty ensuing years relations between the people and the government changed drastically. The welfare of the people became a direct responsibility of government, whereas before then government was the responsibility of the people. American thought and outlook were altered. Large segments of our people were willing to exchange personal freedom for a sense of social security.

During its twenty-nine years before advent of the New Deal, Ford Motor Company had never been closed down by a strike. Henry Ford was looked up to as the best example of a generous employer. Working hours and pay were beyond criticism. Minimum rates had gradually increased from $5 to $7 for an eight-hour day. And although Ford refused to deal with unions, Ford Motor Company officials sometimes suggested unionization to parts suppliers vexed by strikes.

Ford could justify mass production because he had developed it. Mass production had progressively decreased the cost of automobiles, as well as of other things. But to gain that result, management had to control costs, which, in turn, involved wage rates and production methods.

According to Ford's philosophy, the benefits of mass production are intended for the consumer group, which includes labor, since all wage earners are consumers. The consumer is more important than the producer—in fact, he is indispensable, for it is he who buys the products of the machine. But when labor has the power to dictate wages and what it will give for the wage received, it claims for itself the first benefits of mass production. The consumer is forgotten, and thus the economic ends of mass production are defeated. All that is left is a method of producing autos; the purpose of mass production as Ford developed it is absent.

Powerful voices of the New Deal demanded that production be controlled so that only as much would be turned out as people could afford to buy at a fair price. The delusion was that production had caused the depression, that too much had been produced for people to consume. And thereby came about the absurd paradox of want in the midst of plenty.

No man believed less in this than Henry Ford. But the opportunity of running to Washington with one's troubles tempted far too many men in business. If only Washington would help them they were willing to limit production, fix prices, and kill competition.

Ford rejected this idea completely. He became obsessed with the idea that his competitors welcomed government control and union recognition so that he could be kept in line. What he did not foresee was that he would ultimately be engulfed, with his health and mind affected and a tragic breach with his only son, Edsel.

The year 1932 brought a multitude of Communist-inspired big city demonstrations of unemployed. There had been a number of such manifestations in Detroit and some in front of our plant. With few exceptions there was no violence, and it was assumed that in case of any trouble the Dearborn police could handle it.

In March, ten days after our first V-8 came off the production line, a crowd of about five thousand formed ranks in Detroit. To this day, I am convinced there were no Ford employees among them. They were led by a group of open Communists. Mayor Frank Murphy granted them a parade permit and gave the marchers a police motorcycle escort to Detroit city limits.

That noon, while I was with Henry Ford at lunch at the roundtable at Dearborn Laboratories, I had a telephone call from my office. I was told there had been a riot near one of the gates, and Harry Bennett was so badly hurt that he was in the plant hospital. When I returned to the table I hesitated to tell Mr. Ford the news in front of his guests, so I scribbled a note on a pad and passed it to Edsel. He read it and looked at me, then passed it to his father. The elder Ford excused himself, and Edsel and I followed him.

I drove father and son to the Rouge plant. A gate watchman told us there had been some shooting, a lot of people were hurt, and our hospital on the second floor of the B Building was filled with them. We found Bennett in the hospital, where he had recovered consciousness from a deep cut on the head and some internal injuries.

It seems that when the marchers reached the Dearborn city limits they were halted by a police line. When told they had no parade permit and were forbidden to go farther, they pushed forward. The Dearborn police pumped tear shells into their midst, but the wind changed abruptly and blew the gas back at the officers.

By the time the demonstrators reached the Rouge plant area on Miller Road, Bennett heard of the affair and drove up to the head of the line; he believed he could persuade the leaders

to disband their followers. When he got out of his car, someone gave the order to get him. There was a tussle, and Bennett
went down from a blow on the head. The police rushed in and
began shooting, with the result that four men were killed and
fifty went to the hospital.

Bennett certainly did not lack courage in trying, single-
handed, to stop a riot, and he was lucky not to lose his life. In
fact, if I had to enumerate his outstanding qualities I believe
I'd put fearless personal courage first.

One of the many myths about Henry Ford is his relationship with Harry Bennett and the supposed hold this ex-sailor
and former prize fighter had over him. Taken on as a plant
guard during World War I, he was quick of tongue as well as
with his fists and got to be head of the Rouge police. Equally
good as troublemaker and trouble-shooter, he came to the attention of Henry Ford, who installed him in a basement office
near the main entrance to the Rouge plant and camouflaged
his activities under the title of "director of personnel." He
was a flamboyant character who delighted in being spectacu-
larly mysterious, and his cops-and-robbers activities fascinated
the older Ford.

Bennett always carried a gun and had a pistol range in his
office. Here he and Henry Ford used to have target practice.
I mentioned this one day to Mrs. Ford, who demanded indig-
nantly, "Who is this man Bennett who has so much control
over my husband and is ruining my son's health?"

This question startled me. Mrs. Ford had already demonstrated in many ways that she alone had control over her husband. I left her in tears. I couldn't answer the question. I
couldn't tell her that Bennett did not control Henry Ford but
that the reverse was true.

Bennett had nothing to do with making automobiles. He
knew nothing about production methods. And when he or

his supporting cast got to behaving as though they were the
Ford Motor Company they soon discovered they weren't. His
ballyhoo fooled a lot of people. He had a strange collection
of broken bruisers, ex-baseball players, one-time football stars,
and recently freed jailbirds. They never looked or acted like
Ford men, and Edsel and I were continually apologizing for
their bad manners. I was more unconcerned about Bennett
than were Edsel and many others. His ways were not my ways.
His job was not my job, and so long as he didn't interfere with
what I was doing I could walk away from Bennett and completely forget about him.

Bennett never had any real power other than that delegated
to him by Henry Ford. He was a yes man who did as he was
told, and promptly. His job was an unenviable one. He was
greatly reviled and possibly even libeled. After Edsel's son,
Young Henry, discharged him, Bennett wrote a book; and
what he said about himself and his activities revealed him as
no knight in shining armor. It also indicates that if fearless
personal courage was one of his outstanding qualities, shame-
less ingratitude may have been another.

And that's the story of Harry Bennett. It is a story repeated
over and over again with men hired and fired by Ford ever
since early days in the little plant on Mack Avenue. Some were
great, some were good. And they lasted as long as they fitted
Henry Ford's mood.

There was no question but what the talebearing of Bennett
and his people widened the breach between Henry and Edsel
Ford. Nor was there much doubt that Henry Ford expected
these.

As late as October, 1942, Edsel and I had a hot session with
Harry Bennett. Bennett had been telling Henry Ford how his
grandsons Henry II and Benson were in danger of being kid-
naped. He wanted to surround them and Edsel's house with
his servicemen. Edsel blew up. He told Bennett to stop such

talk and let his boys alone. He didn't want protection for
either himself or his sons; and as for the kidnap story, he
didn't believe it and was sure that it had been played up to
Henry Ford.

Whereupon Bennett put on his act. He jumped from his
chair, tore off his coat, and threatened Edsel. I got up and motioned for Edsel to leave, which we did.

It is difficult to imagine such a scene, but it shows what Edsel
was up against. Mr. Ford could have put an end to it. Instead,
he encouraged Bennett to keep at Edsel. Constant turmoil
was Henry Ford's idea of harmony. By keeping things stirred
up, no one else could swell with importance.

The year 1933 ushered in the New Deal and Franklin Roosevelt as president. It also brought the National Industrial Recovery Act, with hard-boiled, gravel-voiced General Hugh
Johnson as administrator. Under NRA's weird-looking "Blue
Eagle" emblem, freedom of enterprise was brushed aside. Each
industry had a code of operations which regulated wages and
hours and required posting of signs that workers were free to
organize for collective bargaining.

Henry Ford would have nothing to do with either Blue
Eagle or the automobile industry's code. He balked at the
code's collective bargaining provisions and said that under the
Blue Eagle he would have to share business and production
secrets with his competitors. The Roosevelt Administration
put every possible pressure on him to sign the auto code. Government contracts for Ford cars and trucks were canceled.
Johnson suggested a boycott of Ford and turned in his Lincoln car. Threats came out of Washington that Ford would
be closed down and the government would take over his plant.
His reply was pure defiance.

General Johnson flew out to Detroit to see Mr. Ford. The
rough and tough old soldier got nowhere with the man whose

stubbornness had put the world on wheels. "Old Ironpants" boarded his plane and returned to Washington.

NRA coasted along without Ford but with Ford working conditions either conforming to the auto code or exceeding it. In 1936 the Supreme Court of the United States declared it unconstitutional. Meanwhile, Congress passed the Wagner Labor Relations Act, which made union-management collective bargaining mandatory.

With the Wagner Act behind them, though with its constitutionality challenged and yet to be thrashed out in the courts, unions redoubled their organizing activities. In Detroit they began an intensive radio campaign against Ford. Henry Ford, Edsel, and I were their main targets. UAW spellbinders claimed we didn't know how to run a plant. The union, they said, could do a better job, but not one man in the union group had ever had plant management experience. Then they would take another tack and attempt to alienate Edsel from his father by praising him. Next they sought to drive a wedge between the Fords and me.

They even played me up as a union man, asserting that I still carried my Patternmakers' Union card, which I didn't. In all my nearly forty years with Ford Motor Company I never dealt with any labor problems, nor did I ever seek to. Yet, unlike some other executives, I moved around the plant as much as ever and was never molested or booed.

After the union organizing campaign began, there never was a happy moment in it for either Ford. Edsel favored bargaining with the union. He felt that bad public relations wrought by the radio campaign was hurting the company, and he believed it possible to arrive at a fair working arrangement.

Henry Ford thought otherwise. He felt that a closed or union shop would be unfair to Ford employees. "It will fail," he said of the organizing agitation, "because our workers won't stand for it, I won't stand for it, and the public won't stand for it."

Father and son had long, heated wrangles. I found it best to avoid my visits when they were together, but I could not do so entirely and would finally walk out with the rather pointed excuse, "I'm going back to work; somebody's got to work around here."

In 1937 the Supreme Court upheld the Wagner Act. Compliance could no longer be withheld on grounds of its unconstitutionality. The law compelled management to bargain collectively with organized labor, but it could not compel agreement. One day after lunch Edsel and I were called to Henry Ford's office. The elder Ford outlined how he would deal with the problem. He would meet with no union official, and he emphatically told Edsel and me not to do so, not to discuss labor matters with anyone, and to avoid all press interviews.

"If things get too warm for any of us," he went on, "we should take a trip and get away from the plant. I've picked someone to talk with the unions. I want a strong, aggressive man who can take care of himself in an argument, and I've got him. He has my full confidence and I want to be sure that you, Edsel, and you, Charlie, will support him. He's waiting in Charlie's office at the Rouge now, so let's go down there and see him."

I drove father and son to my office, and whom should we find there but Harry Bennett! I wasn't too surprised, because Henry Ford had Bennett with him when he talked to the reporters who trailed him daily. But I saw Edsel tighten up. I'm sure he didn't expect to see Bennett.

There wasn't much to say while we four were together, except that Bennett bubbled over with enthusiasm. He was on friendly terms with Homer Martin, who held uneasy sway as the then president of the faction-ridden United Auto Workers. Bennett assured Mr. Ford that he could handle the unions —if necessary, take them over. His main job, however, was to stave off union demands and not come to any working arrangement.

Thus began his curious role as Henry Ford's pseudo peacemaker. From then on he got a build-up which Detroiters don't understand to this day. I hold no brief for Bennett. But he had an unenviable job of being Henry Ford's man Friday. He was ready and willing to do anything Henry Ford wanted. Every talk he had with union officials was reported to Henry Ford, who knew that Bennett couldn't qualify as a peacemaker. He wanted to be sure that the mob that had moved into Detroit would not find in the plant anyone receptive to their bargaining. Everything Henry Ford and I had done to build up that plant and its organization would be jeopardized if we allowed the unions to have a voice in management. I knew better than Bennett what this meant.

At first Edsel did not handle himself wisely. He got word to union leaders that as president of Ford Motor Company he would never accept any agreement in which Bennett was involved. He thus laid himself open for trouble from both sides, and he certainly walked into it.

A feud between father and son was now on in earnest. Bennett added fuel to the flame. He went gunning for anyone who was in accord with Edsel. When I found I was being checked up I had a showdown with Bennett. I told him that I was for his sitting in with Edsel. If he kept Edsel posted on what he was doing, I said, we would at least have peace in the family. Bennett declined to do so, saying he was following orders.

"Were you instructed not to discuss matters with Edsel?" I asked.

"No," he replied, "that is up to me. No one is going to tell me what to do."

That wasn't quite so. One man and only one man told Bennett what to do. That was Henry Ford.

But merely being sure that Bennett would not try to be a peacemaker was not enough. I made it clear to Mr. Ford that someone we could trust should keep an eye on Bennett. For the men who would be dealing with Bennett would not be our own workers. A few Ford employees might sit in, but the ones doing the talking would be complete strangers to us. It was bound to be a high-pressure group, surrounded by smart lawyers.

Bennett had full support from Mr. Ford to keep Edsel out of labor matters. When Edsel tried to talk with his father about the situation, all he got was "You stay away. Let Bennett handle it."

Once Edsel came to me and said he was going to resign as president of Ford Motor Company. He disliked Bennett and would not trust him. We had a long, frank talk, at the end of which I had his agreement to let Bennett have a try at the union negotiations. And I assured him that Bennett was being watched by one of his own men to see that no agreements of any kind would be drawn up; that Henry Ford had that covered.

I was in Bennett's office one morning when a group of union leaders walked in on him. I started to leave in a hurry, but Bennett asked me to meet the group. I was introduced to about six of them, then got out as quickly as I could. I wanted them to know that Bennett would handle their problems.

I went straight to Edsel's office and reported the incident and added some advice. "Please stay away and don't ever deal with the problem," I urged Edsel. "It will be the end of you if you do."

Edsel promised to do so but repeated that he was not in accord with Bennett's handling union negotiations. "Do you believe your father agrees with you?" I asked. That was a touchy spot, and I didn't see Edsel for a week or so.

Edsel finally let Bennett alone on union negotiations. I could assure him that no concessions were being made and that the unions were struggling to find a formula acceptable to us as well as themselves. One of their claims was that a union shop would be more efficient and that the company would benefit in quality work with lower costs. Part of their attack was against the company's foremen and supervisors who, they said, had too many friends and relatives working for them.

The union's big boast that it could show us how to reduce costs and have closer control over foremen was never reduced to any kind of formula. I sought such a formula through Bennett. It would have been a big feather in his cap had he secured that mysterious production secret of how union control would have reduced costs. He never got it, nor would he have understood it if he had. Nor has that secret been revealed since then.

Bennett went along day and night getting nowhere, which apparently was what was wanted. He was evidently enjoying his sessions with union leaders. The labor people were having their own troubles in establishing control of their different locals. New locals with new leaders for each sprang up like mushrooms. When Bennett found one leader reasonable, the others tried to put the skids under him. Reasonableness was not what top leadership wanted.

It wasn't what Henry Ford wanted, either. He knew that Bennett never could handle such matters. That was why he was safe—for Henry Ford. Bennett carried on in this fashion until 1941, when the rug was pulled out from under him and he was instructed to arrange a semiclosed shop with the union.

Because of union troubles, we had to set up our own body plant, but not without another Bennett-Edsel Ford flare-up. A series of strikes at the Briggs Body plant in Highland Park threatened Ford production lines. When there seemed to be no prospect of peace, Bennett expressed the belief that if he sat in on negotiations he might help to bring about a settlement. I asked Walter Briggs to try this. He refused. I reminded him that he was going to shut us down, and did that interest him at all? He reminded me that he was going to run his business his way. I told him I would see to it that Bennett would be in on his next meeting with the union. Bennett was with me when I talked to Briggs, and I did not have to tell him what to do. Evidently he talked with his friend Homer Martin of UAW, for the next move came from the union. Martin told Briggs, "No meetings unless Bennett sits in."

Bennett reported that the real trouble at Briggs lay in labor management. The work was not planned so that materials flowed in regularly, and with every delay in materials men were laid off. In some cases men came in every day for a week to get an hour or two of work and were not paid while remaining idle on the work lines.

I visited the Briggs plant and had a hard day's session with the management. I pressed the Briggs people hard. "Don't start up," I told them, "until you have cleaned up the entire plant. Be sure to wash the windows to let in some daylight. Put in ventilating fans. Clean up! Clean up!"

And so I hammered away all day. Meanwhile I learned that Henry Ford had driven to Highland Park. He knew I was there, so he went to find me. But he ran up against the picket lines, where he stopped and mingled and talked with the strikers. He listened patiently and told them I was in the plant investigating their complaints which were being broadcast on radio and in the newspapers. "We'll help to straighten out this trouble," he said.

It took courage to go into that picket line and hobnob with its members. After this I suggested to Walter Briggs that Bennett sit in with the negotiations that Briggs was carrying on. I couldn't understand Briggs's refusal until I recalled that the

Briggs treasurer was Howard Bonbright, who was a personal friend of Edsel Ford.

Bonbright, a promoter with Wall Street contacts, had financed the Briggs company when it was launched. He prepared a prospectus and handled the transaction for Walter Briggs.

Walter Briggs put it up to Bonbright to see Edsel and stop Bennett from interfering in his affairs. Briggs could have come to me. It would have been a reasonable thing to do because I had been in close touch with him on all his business with us and I considered him a close personal friend. He could easily have sat down with me after my session with Fred Hoffman, but he avoided me and then called on Bonbright to see Edsel Ford. He could not have done worse.

Edsel was hopping mad when he came to see me. He blamed Bennett for the whole trouble in Briggs. He tried to butter me up saying, "Walter Briggs did not find any fault with you. He wanted Bennett to stay away."

Edsel did not know how I had handled the union negotiations and had sought to have Bennett sit in with them. I was furious to think that Briggs and Bonbright would try to throw all this into Edsel's lap. Edsel took the matter to his father, and I was sent for in a hurry. When I arrived there were signs of discord. I soon learned that Edsel had told Henry Ford what Walter Briggs wanted: "Keep Bennett away."

Henry Ford also learned that Bonbright was the one who had put that up to Edsel. Well, it was a bad moment for Edsel. He learned that Henry Ford and I had been in the Briggs plant and he was shocked to think his father had faced that mob on Manchester Avenue. He felt that Henry Ford was lucky some radical had not attacked him.

I took all the blame for what Bennett had done. This was news to Edsel, but he would not agree that Bennett should enter into matters outside of Ford Motor Company.

Henry Ford pulled me aside with a flick of the eyes that I understood. He said, "Charlie, pull that body work out of Briggs. Do it as quick as you can. You can handle it; let no one stop you."

Edsel did not hear that, but late that day he came to my office. He was still worked up about the Briggs affair. He wanted me to do something about Bennett. My answer to that was: "You won't have any trouble with Bennett in Briggs. I am going to take the body work away from them. I can put most of the trim work in the branches. I am now laying out a stamping plant in the Rouge to join up with our sheet mills. I am going to make a better body and save you a lot of money."

Nine years of depression, five years of the New Deal, and month after month of labor problems finally took their physical toll of Henry Ford. In 1938, shortly after observing his seventy-fifth birthday, he had a stroke.

This fact was hushed up. I believe I was the only one outside the immediate family and the medical people to know of it. When Dr. McClure broke the news to Edsel and me he urged us to do everything we could to relieve the patient of his business worries—in fact, he really should retire from active work. This was easier said than done. The elder Ford demanded to see me every day and called upon me for more detailed information than he had ever done before. Mrs. Ford cautioned me against worrying her husband with Ford Motor Company matters, but it was difficult to evade his questions. Edsel and I were the only ones permitted to see him.

Dr. McClure went to Fair Lane every day to give a checkup. Much to his indignation, Mr. Ford summoned his chiropractor, Dr. Coulter, for daily treatments. Dr. McClure threatened to take the patient to Ford Hospital, but Mr. Ford laughed at him. If he went to the hospital he'd put his chiropractor on the staff. He was tired of being confined, he said. He was tired of doctors, and if they didn't get him out of bed quickly he would chase them. He really had the medical men worried more than he was; and, almost before they knew it, he made a rapid recovery and within a month was up and around again, more aggressive than ever.

Nine years of opposing New Deal and resisting union pressure had worn down Henry Ford. Finally, by terrorist methods, the UAW was able to pull a strike at River Rouge.

From my diary: "Wednesday, April 2, 1941, home Towers. Rouge plant closed during night by strikers, C.I.O. Plenty of rioting at eight this morning by outgoing workers. Met Henry Ford at Willow Run at 10 A.M. He feels strike could not be averted. It would do more good than harm. Stayed away from the Rouge plant today. Phoned Helen twice. Edsel flew back from Florida."

I followed Ford's instructions to stay away. So did Edsel. One strike demand was for a union closed shop. Henry Ford had to assume the responsibility for dealing with that demand. Bennett was taking his orders from him and from him alone. So I went to Miami Beach, where my wife was staying. On April 11, I wrote in my diary: "Henry Ford called me tonight. Strike settled. Said I should go on my trips. CIO lost everything."

It was not clear to me what he meant by CIO losing everything. The strikers went back to work because Ford Motor Company agreed to discuss a union contract. It was also agreed that the National Labor Relations Board would soon hold an election at which Ford employees would decide whom they wanted to represent them in drawing up a contract.

Ten days later I returned to Detroit. I went directly to Bennett's office, where Henry Ford met me, and we talked over the new plant situation for an hour. Only 79,000 workers were back at work whereas 91,000 had been there before the strike.

Henry Ford avoided the whole matter as much as he possibly could and began spending quite a lot of time with me—just as he used to do. We were building Pratt & Whitney airplane engines, and Willow Run was now in the making. I understood Ford's state of mind and did everything I could to keep him off the labor subject.

Meanwhile, the National Labor Relations Board held a plant election. UAW-CIO received 51,866, or 69.91 per cent of all votes cast. The American Federation of Labor got 20,364 votes, or a percentage of 27.45.

Votes for a no-union clause resulted in 1,958, or only 2.64 per cent. This was crushing news to Henry Ford, perhaps the greatest disappointment he had in all his business experience. He had been certain that Ford workers would stand by him. This was the last straw. He never was the same after that.

These election results stimulated UAW's contract demands. A committee headed by Harry Mack of the Ford sales department and J. A. Capizzi, the company attorney, met with a committee of the union. Bennett was available for conferences on important issues but did not participate in the routine discussions, which dragged on for nearly a month.

By June 18 a formal contract had been drawn up. Bennett showed this to Ford, who when he got the sense of the document walked out, refusing to have anything to do with it.

The next morning Mr. Ford telephoned me to see him at Dearborn. When I got there he told me how he had had a look at the CIO contract, and that was all he had to say. Then he said, "Charlie, let's take a ride."

We rode the rest of the day, looking over pretty nearly everything that was going on in the plants. After I dropped him at his office, I had been back in my office only a few minutes when I got another call from him. Don't go home, he said, he was coming over to see me. He also wanted Edsel in my office, for he had something to say to both of us.

It was about 5:30 when he came in. It soon became evident that he was in a bad frame of mind about the union contract. The more he talked about it the bitterer he became. Finally he exclaimed, "I'm not going to sign this contract! I want you and Edsel both to understand that as far as I'm concerned the key is in the door. I'm going to throw it away. I don't want any more of this business. Close the plant down if necessary. Let the union take over if it wishes."

I pointed out that we had large contracts with the government; if the plant closed down, the government would step in and tell us what to do.

Mr. Ford simply replied, "Well, if the government steps in, it will be in the motorcar business and it won't be me."

It was almost seven o'clock when we left. I went home for a late dinner with my wife and told her about what was about to happen. I went to bed very much disturbed. After a restless night I woke up rather late, not knowing whether I would go to the office or not. I switched on the radio and heard it blasting out the news:

"Ford grants the CIO union shop and checkoff." I was dumbfounded. It couldn't be true. When I got to my office, Henry Ford was waiting for me. Of course, I expected he was going to confirm the news, so I didn't ask him.

We sat for about fifteen minutes discussing things in general. Not one word from him about what had happened. Then Edsel came in. The elder Ford continued talking idly for another fifteen minutes, then left us sitting there.

Edsel looked at me and said, "What in the world happened?"

"I was just about to ask you the same thing," I replied. "I've been here a half hour with him and not one word about what occurred last night."

We gathered at the Dearborn for lunch as usual. Nothing was said at the roundtable about the mystery. All that I got out of Bennett was that he got the word from Mr. Ford that the contract should be approved.

I didn't stay at Dearborn long, but I got back to my office as soon as I could. The afternoon newspapers on my desk carried more details.

After having battled unionism for years while competitors were forced to sign contracts, Ford had created the biggest sensation in the history of labor relations, said the news articles, by going the whole way with the CIO United Auto Workers. Under the contract terms, all the 120,000 eligible employees in thirty-four Ford plants across the country had to join the UAW. New workers must do so after being hired. Union dues and assessment would be deducted from Ford Motor Company paychecks and turned over to the UAW treasury. Moreover, Ford agreed to match the highest wages paid by competitors in each job category. From being the outstanding foe of CIO, Ford went to the other extreme by giving the union the most favorable contract in the automobile industry. Thus the news. What had started out as a controlled discussion with the union ended up in a full rout. It was open acknowledgment that Ford was giving up the powers he had wielded for thirty-eight years.

No one could understand this fantastic shotgun wedding. Here was the outstanding independent manufacturer who fifteen hours earlier had told his son and me that he would have nothing to do with a contract with any union. I felt that I knew Henry Ford's innermost thoughts. I could not be wrong here. Something had happened. But what? I went around with him daily for weeks without getting the answer. He stayed away from the plant. At luncheon, which I had with him every day at the roundtable, he would rush in and out. He was a different person. Edsel had the same reaction. So did Campsall, Mr. Ford's secretary.

One morning about six weeks later Henry Ford called for me at my office. We got into his car, and I drove him out to Willow Run. After a few questions about how the plant was going, he said, in an apologetic way, "Charlie, you and I have not been the same in our relations for a while."

"That's true," I said. "I've felt it and I can't understand the reason. You've never acted this way before. What's wrong?"

"I don't want to go on this way," he said. "Charlie, let me explain what did happen. Remember the night I left you and Edsel in your office. I went right home and told Mrs. Ford about the talk I had with you and that I had instructed you to close the plant and I would not sign that contract.

"Mrs. Ford was horrified. She said she could not understand my doing anything like that. If that was done there would be riots and bloodshed, and she had seen enough of that. And if I did that, she would leave me. She did not want to be around here and see me responsible for such trouble.

"She became frantic about it. She insisted that I sign what she termed a peace agreement. If I did not, she was through.

"What could I do? I'm sure now she was right. The whole thing was not worth the trouble it would make. I felt her vision and judgment were better than mine. I'm glad that I did see it her way. Don't ever discredit the power of a woman."

Those were his final words on the subject.

Now I understood, and I was in complete sympathy with Mrs. Ford. Henry Ford never referred to the contract again. Mrs. Ford never mentioned it. And I never told this story to anyone until after both were gone. It was not my place to reveal such a secret, but I tell it now to show how both Mr. and Mrs. Ford were always in tune and aware of real responsibilities they had to the community.

Henry Ford was never the same after that. A few weeks

later he had a stroke similar to the one of 1938. Then came the attack at Pearl Harbor and entry of this country into a war which Ford had sworn would never be.

He was now in his seventy-eighth year. For nearly ten years he had fought governmental invasion and union domination. From now on his previously set opinions about Wall Street and international bankers, the Roosevelt New Deal, scheming motorcar competitors, foreign wars, and his son Edsel's quiet determination to live his own life hardened into an obsession which occasionally flared into hallucination.

This had a tragic effect upon the great industrial empire that he headed and had built up during his prime. But not even Henry Ford could destroy it.

19

The Biggest Challenge of My Life

ORATORS, columnists, professors, preachers, and propagandists performed magnificently with the theme that World War II was a war between two ideologies. But whatever inflamed people's minds in warring countries, victory was on the side of the heaviest-armed battalions. The conflict became one of two systems of production.

The Axis powers turned out more human robots than war machines. Although Hitler's armament was formidable and fearsome, it would have been more so had it come from mass production Henry Ford-Detroit style. The seeds of United Nations victory in 1945 were sown in 1908 in the Piquette Avenue plant of Ford Motor Company when we experimented with a moving assembly line. Thirty-five years later everything from artillery shells to giant four-engine bombers came off assembly lines in the same method that we first developed when turning out Model Ts.

Throughout 1940, Henry Ford was in bad health and worse morale. His memory was failing as rapidly as his obsessions and antipathies increased. His pet peeve was Franklin Roosevelt, but any mention of the war in Europe and the likelihood of this country's involvement upset him almost to incoherence. Edsel, who was suffering from stomach trouble, came in for unmerciful criticism. The elder Ford was not the decisive man he had been in Model T days. His emotional streaks wore one down, and late in May the situation became so unbearable that I took a fishing trip off the Florida Keys to get away from it all.

Meanwhile, Hitler invaded the Low Countries, the British evacuated their forces at Dunkirk, and while the Germans pushed on toward Paris, Washington officials were stirred to intensive defense measures. Heading up the production side of rearmament was William S. Knudsen, formerly my deputy at Ford and now president of General Motors. Edsel called me north to join him in Washington to look over an airplane engine the government had asked Ford Motor Company to build.

It turned out to be the Rolls-Royce aviation engine, one of the triumphs of British precision engineering. When I saw it I knew that its fine workmanship and high performance would appeal to our organization. I was enthusiastic about the project, for I realized that it was a challenge. With Knudsen and his able chief assistant in aviation, Dr. George Mead, one of the founders of United Aircraft, we discussed tooling and machinery.

I telephoned Henry Ford, who agreed that we should take the Rolls-Royce job, and when I returned he surprised me by accepting a contract on the basis of the British getting 60 per cent of the engines. This was surprising because he had declared earlier that Ford Motor Company would not make war supplies for any foreign nation and he had been severely criticized by the British press for his stand; but I believe the enthusiasm Edsel and I showed for the project influenced his decision. When I arranged for separate rooms to carry on engineering and tool designing, Mr. Ford expressed approval.

No one could have been more careful in keeping him informed than Edsel and I had been. Suddenly he reversed himself.

His action was set off by a tactless statement by Lord Beaverbrook that Ford had accepted an order for 6,000 Rolls-Royce engines and implying that he was now supporting the British. Actually, we had not accepted an order from England. Our dealings were entirely with American officials.

Mr. Ford knew that the United States would divert 60 per cent of the order to Britain, but "The Beaver's" statement was different from the way he saw it and he made a public denial.

Three days later I got a call asking me to come over to Edsel's office. Bill Knudsen was there. Henry Ford had sent for him, he said, and he didn't know why. Edsel didn't know either, and neither did I. In a few moments Henry Ford came in. He shook hands all around and then told Knudsen what a fine fellow he was. "But," he added, "you're mixed up with some bad people in Washington, and you're heading for trouble."

"I don't understand what you are talking about, Mr. Ford," Knudsen replied.

"I won't make any of those Rolls-Royce engines for England," Ford said.

"But, Mr. Ford," Knudsen remonstrated. "We have your word that you would make them. I told the President your decision, and he was very happy about it."

At mention of President Roosevelt, Henry Ford grew tense. "We won't build the engine at all," he said. "Withdraw the whole order. Take it to someone else. Let them build the engine; we won't."

That was the end of the Rolls-Royce for us. Packard took on the contract and built a fine engine. Knudsen left Edsel's office purple with rage. I felt sorry for him. To have to report this scene to the President must have been a bit difficult. Later in the day I saw Henry Ford. I never heard him shout louder.

He was wild about Franklin Roosevelt and people in Washington. "They want war," he repeated again and again.

We heard the same thing for days following at the roundtable at Dearborn. Roosevelt was tied up with the warmongers of Europe. General Motors, General Electric, United States Steel, and the DuPonts controlled Roosevelt. They had interests in European industries and they were bent on pushing the United States into the war. And so forth and so on.

An equally deep-seated reason was behind Ford's refusal to make these British engines. He admired their engineering excellence, but to manufacture them he would be making something to somebody else's design, and that thought hurt. When a man's work is merely mediocre, he is let severely alone. But when it sets a standard for all to see—and copy—he becomes an object of admiration and envy. That was Henry Ford's situation. The Ford car and its method of manufacture had become a standard for the world, and as long as he got the fame and credit for it he was satisfied.

In all my years with him I never put so much pressure on him as to persuade him to take part in the government's military aviation program. When Bill Knudsen suggested a few months later that Ford make Pratt & Whitney air-cooled aviation engines, Edsel was all for it. So was I, but the elder Ford said, "Don't make it."

It was not until I pointed out that we might set new standards in building them that I secured Henry Ford's consent to make 4,000 Pratt & Whitney engines. Then our organization moved fast—and dangerously. Without so much as a scrap of paper from Washington to show for it, and with the ever-present likelihood that the elder Ford might change his mind, we obligated Ford Motor Company for $30,000,000. We contracted on our own for quick construction of a building. We ordered tools and machinery and assembled a production staff. Ford accountants were on my neck because we had no order from Washington on which they could keep their records. "You know how to control records," I said. "You do that and be sure you have them in good order. Let me worry about getting the contract."

On November 1, 1940, Edsel signed a contract in Washington. Nearly two months earlier we had already broken ground for the Aviation Building, and after the ceremony Edsel spoke to me about his sons Henry II and Benson. "They've had enough school," he said, "and they want to go to work; I hope you'll help me place them where they may learn how our departments are run."

Both boys used to visit the River Rouge plant during vacation time. I saw them only on these visits and occasionally when they were with their grandfather. I had often wondered whether they would ever come into the business or they would turn out to be playboys like so many rich men's sons; but here they were, ready for work, and I had great respect for them.

Coming from a father like Edsel, it was a great compliment to be asked to help guide the boys. I suggested that they be attached to the Pratt & Whitney project where they could watch the planning and machinery placement. From then on they took their work like other Ford employees, and that's about the highest tribute I can pay anyone.

The blitz rained down over England. London-bound Nazi bombers were guided by the Thames; on moonlit nights, when the water reflected light from the sky, it was like driving up an illuminated highway. The Dagenham plant of the British Ford Company was a standout and was heavily bombed by going and coming German planes. I thought news of this destruction might have some effect upon Henry Ford's attitude toward a war program. But he heard it without uttering a word. Nevertheless, he was obviously of troubled mind and he would leave the luncheon table at Dearborn as quickly as possible.

Late in November Knudsen showed Detroit automobile manufacturers the government's all-out war program and left it to the auto makers to adapt themselves to it. Knudsen's idea was to tie all auto makers into an over-all plan. I spoke against it because too much time would be wasted talking about such things and that, instead of imposing, government should delegate certain plans to qualified companies. If it had a project for something it felt Ford Motor Company could make, I would take the matter up with our designers and give the government a proposal. Other auto makers supported me, and the meeting broke up.

When I reported this event to Mr. Ford, he promptly blew up. He had been in a bad mood ever since the Rolls-Royce episode; now he suspected a conspiracy to grab his business. Once again he warned me that Knudsen and his Washington group were after him. I was over the barrel. On one side a mightily determined old man racked by hallucinations; on the other hand, a Franklin Roosevelt Administration, able, even eager, should occasion arise, to take over Ford Motor Company. To avoid the latter, we should demonstrate our willingness to participate in the aviation program, with much of which I was in accord. That program was coming for sure, and I made ready to meet it.

My stand at the auto makers' meeting with Knudsen apparently bore fruit, for during the week before Christmas Dr. Mead and a cocky, likable little Air Force major named Jimmy Doolittle called upon us. Would Ford Motor Company, they asked, be able or interested to turn out 1,200 of the Army's large four-engined Flying Fortresses? Five days later Dr. Mead returned for further discussion of the plane program, and a group from Curtiss-Wright came the day after to urge that we look over the California airplane manufacturing plants. Henry Ford would not see the Curtiss-Wright group, but he sat in at the talks with Dr. Mead. He had high regard for Mead as a great engineer and asked me to bring him to Dearborn whenever he visited us.

As the government plane program shaped up, it was clear that Ford Motor Company was counted upon to be a part of it. I was keen for it, and so was Edsel, both of us being sure that Ford know-how was a key item. Surprisingly enough, Henry Ford offered no opposition. It was more to please our ambitions, Edsel's and mine, that he went along. "Those planes will never be used for fighting," he told me. "Before you can build them, the war will be over."

It was plain that the elder Ford was determined not to be involved personally in the project but would allow Edsel and me to try things out. This was the biggest lift for my spirits. I wanted to spend Christmas with my family at Miami Beach, and it was arranged that shortly after New Year's, Dr. Mead would meet me in Jacksonville and we would fly in an Army plane to Tucson and then to San Diego to look over the plant of Consolidated Aircraft, which had developed the B-24 bomber but was proceeding with production at a snail's pace. I didn't know it at the time, but within a few hours I would face the greatest challenge of my entire production career. A quick, spectacular flight over the mountains from Tucson brought us into San Diego early in the morning of January 8, 1941. Here we were joined by Edsel Ford, his sons Henry II and Benson and by Pioch and Hanson of my production staff. We spent the rest of the day at Consolidated Aircraft with its head, Major Fleet, looking, listening, and taking notes. I liked neither what I saw nor what I heard, for if the situation here was typical, the Air Force's aviation program was limping along on not even one wing and a prayer. Consolidated's goal was one B-24 bomber a day, or 350 a year. It was painfully evident that it did not have either the plant or the production methods to meet this quota. Even if it was able to do so, it would take three years to produce 1,000 of these four-engine bombers, and the Air Force wanted them in as yet unannounced thousands.

It was obvious that Consolidated's plant must be enlarged, but even if land was available, the Air Force people were opposed to further plant expansion in San Diego within range of attack by sea. And if the existing plant was revamped for more efficient operation, production would be suspended, a step which the Air Force also opposed. It wanted what it could get without delay. As Dr. Mead put it, a little bit then was preferable to none at the moment but great quantities later.

Inside the plant I watched men putting together wing sections and portions of the fuselage. The work of putting together a four-engine bomber was many times more complicated than assembling a four-cylinder automobile, but what I saw reminded me of nearly thirty-five years previously when we were making Model N Fords at the Piquette Avenue plant. This was before Walter Flanders rearranged our machines and eight years before we achieved the orderly sequence of the assembly line and mass production. The nearer a B-24 came to its final assembly the fewer principles of mass production there were as we at Ford had developed and applied over the years. Here was a custom-made plane, put together as a tailor would cut and fit a suit of clothes.

The B-24's final assembly was made out of doors under the bright California sun and on a structural steel fixture. The heat and temperature changes so distorted this fixture that it was impossible to turn out two planes alike without further adjustment. The Consolidated and the Air Force people talked about an order from Ford Motor Company for center and outer wing sections; but it was obvious that if the wing sections had uniform measurements, the way we made parts for automobiles, they would not fit properly under out-of-doors assembly conditions.

All this was pretty discouraging, and I said so. Naturally,

and quite properly, the reply was "How would you do it?" I had to put up or shut up.

"I'll have something for you tomorrow morning," I said.

I really did have something in mind. To compare a Ford V-8 with a four-engine Liberator bomber was like matching a garage with a skyscraper, but despite their great differences I knew the same fundamentals applied to high-volume production of both, the same as they would to an electric egg beater or to a wrist watch. First, break the plane's design into essential units and make a separate production layout for each unit. Next, build as many units as are required, then deliver each unit in its proper sequence to the assembly line to make one whole unit—a finished plane. To house all this and provide for efficient operation there should be a new plant specially designed to accommodate the progressive layout. I saw no impossibility in such an idea even though mass production of anything approaching the size and complexity of a B-24 never had been attempted before. But who would accept such a wild notion? And instead of one bomber a day by the prevailing method I saw the possibility of one B-24 an hour by mass production assembly lines. How could the aviation people take that estimate seriously?

As soon as I returned to my room at the Coronado Hotel I began figuring how to adapt Ford assembly methods to airplane construction and turn out one four-engine bomber an hour. Throughout the day I had made copious notes. I listed all major units of the plane and the subunits and fractional units required for their assembly, and I had gathered figures on Consolidated's labor force and job performance. From these I computed each unit operation, its timing, and required floor space as I saw them, and paper began to fly. Figures for each unit I kept together in a separate pile, and soon there were little stacks of paper all over the floor of my room.

I was back at my old game of sketching a series of manufacturing and subassembly operations and their orderly progression toward becoming major units—a game I had played many times since that morning in 1908 at the Piquette Avenue plant when we first experimented with a moving assembly line. Again I was practicing my production planning philosophy, which stemmed from my patternmaking days when I fashioned wooden models of Henry Ford's half-thought-out designs: "Unless you see a thing, you cannot simplify it. And unless you can simplify it, it's a good sign you can't make it."

As I look back now upon that night, this was the biggest challenge of my production career—bigger than any Model T assembly line sequence for Highland Park, more momentous than the layout and construction of the great River Rouge plant in which I'd had a part. It took eight years to develop Ford mass production system, and eight more years before we worked up to a production of 10,000 cars a day. Now, in one night, I was applying thirty-five years of production experience to planning the layout for building not only something I had never put together before, but the largest and most complicated of all air transport and in numbers and at a rate never before thought possible. Once again I was going on the principle I had enunciated many times at Ford: "The only thing we can't make is something we can't think about."

Through most of the night I set down figures and revised them. I arranged and rearranged the stacks of paper as it became plainer to me which unit came after the other in moving to final assembly and how much floor space was involved. At length the whole picture became clear and simple. I knew I had the solution, and I was elated by the certainty that the Germans had neither the facilities nor the conception for greater bomber mass production. Along toward four o'clock, I was satisfied that my piles of paper were arranged in proper order and represented the most logical progress of units to the main assembly line; and I knew I could prove a construction rate of one big bomber an hour. Now I had something to talk about.

Standing over the papers, I roughed out on Coronado Hotel note paper a pencil sketch of the floor plan of a bomber plant. It would be a mile long and a quarter mile wide, the biggest single industrial building ever. I still have that sketch, initialed by Edsel Ford, his two sons and others, and I still get a kick out of it. The result of one night's hard work, it is the true outline of Willow Run, which took two years to build and came through on schedule with one four-engine Liberator an hour, 18 bombers a day, and by the end of the war a total of 8,800 big planes off the assembly lines and into the air.

When I finished my sketch I went to bed, but was so carried away by enthusiasm for the project that I couldn't sleep. I was building planes the rest of the night. At breakfast with Edsel the next morning I was somewhat woozy as I showed him the sketch and outlined the bomber-an-hour proposition. He was in complete accord and assured me that Ford Motor Company would build such a plant. My high respect for him went higher than ever. We spent an hour together, getting set for a meeting in Major Fleet's office to shoot the works on a $200,000,000 proposition, backed only by a penciled sketch.

Edsel's sons, Henry II and Benson, accompanied us to the session with Fleet. One of the real kicks that I got at the time out of this trip was that the boys were with us and were so keen about everything they saw. They were a bit reluctant to go to the meeting but Edsel and I insisted upon it.

When I told Dr. Mead and Fleet that Ford Motor Company was prepared to build B-24's, Fleet's reaction was to repeat his proposal of the day before: "Why not make units for us, and we'll assemble them?" And he offered us a contract for 1,000 sets of wings.

"We are not interested in assemblies," I said bluntly. "We'll make the complete plane or nothing."

It is curious how little incidents stick in one's mind. I recall young Henry Ford, sitting in the background. When he heard me say "complete plane or nothing," there was the same flicker of the eye and quick smile of approval that I had seen so often in his grandfather.

"The reason why we want to build a complete plane," I explained to Dr. Mead, "is that we believe we can do a good production job. If the Air Force will give Ford Motor Company a contract and will spend up to two hundred million dollars, we will build and equip a plant capable of turning out one Liberator bomber an hour."

With that I tossed at him the sketch I had made the night before. The offer and estimate took Mead and his Air Force associates by surprise. They did not question our ability to go through with an undertaking of such magnitude, and the Ford group was all smiles when Mead said this plan was just what he wanted. Instead of perhaps 520 planes a year, it would give him 540 planes a month. Fleet agreed to give Ford a license to build the B-24 and would provide drawings for all parts of the plane.

"Let's leave it at that," said Mead. "Develop the idea as much as you can, and I will call you to Washington in a few days."

When Fleet ordered his engineering staff to produce a full set of blue prints, we were surprised to learn that Consolidated did not have detailed plans of their own bomber. "How can we get them?" we asked.

We were told that they could not get draftsmen to complete the drawings. This and other statements made around Consolidated gave me the impression that, while Ford subcontracting for B-24 parts was welcome, there was not much enthusiasm for our building the whole plane. "All right," I said, "we'll send out enough engineers and draftsmen to make a complete set."

No more attempts were made to hold us off until Major Fleet took me home to dinner, where he tried to hire me to take on his plant. "You'd better talk with Edsel about that," I said. That, I thought, was that, but it wasn't.

A short time later Fleet approached me again. Knudsen and the Air Force people apparently had been riding him about Consolidated's production, and he figured he needed someone who could handle Knudsen. He repeated his offer for me to take over management of his plant. When I repeated my suggestion that he talk with Edsel about it, he took another tack, suggesting that Ford Motor Company buy Consolidated. This I squelched on the ground that the government never would permit it, even if we were so disposed. Then came an amusing turn. Knudsen, after talking with Fleet, asked us to join a company made up of Consolidated, Douglas, and Ford. Fleet, I knew, would welcome that but I was sure that Douglas would not. I was sore all over at this, got in touch with General Echols and Assistant Secretary of War Patterson, who promptly killed the three-company plan.

Meanwhile, after my return to Detroit from San Diego, I had two immediate problems. First, I must have plans made ready for Washington. I had the architects lay out a cross section of the bomber plant high enough for a full plane sitting on the floor and with an overhead crane capable of covering the whole area. Aisles between machines and assembly were to be wide enough so that a motorcar might move down the line. I put Pioch and Hanson on studies of all metalwork and electrical equipment; and we broke the plane preassembly into nine different departments, one for each section—center wing section, two wings, two wing tips, nose and front pilot sections, then the nacelle and tail sections.

For location of this mile-long plant I had my eye on the

Ypsilanti area, where Henry Ford had a big acreage in soybeans, one of his agricultural hobbies. I knew this tract well, for I helped Mr. Ford acquire it from Ben Gottfredson, an old friend of mine. It had the perfect drainage essential for the plant's takeoff airport, and it was not too far from our River Rouge operation for me to keep an eye on production in both places. Then I was ready to talk with people in Washington.

Now I had another problem: getting Henry Ford's approval of the bomber program. I anticipated that this might be harder to accomplish than getting Washington's approval. I showed him my penciled sketch to explain what a properly laid-out plant could do, and I reported my San Diego ultimatum: "Complete plane or nothing." In return I got the usual long lecture against war, how General Motors, the DuPonts, and Franklin Roosevelt were conspiring to take over his business. This time, however, the lecture ended differently. "Make a complete plane only," he said; and this was my authorization to proceed with Ford Motor Company's—and the world's— biggest single industrial plant.

Years went into the planning and completion of the River Rouge layout. For Willow Run we had but months and days. This was our timetable of achievement:

February 25, 1941, project approved in Washington.

April 18, 1941, official ground-breaking ceremony.

May 3, 1941, first structural steel erected.

August 12, 1941, first machine tools installed.

November 15, 1941, first production man-hours.

July 12, 1942, first acceptance of knock-down units to be delivered over the road to San Diego and Fort Worth Consolidated plants. At this time Willow Run plant was 90 per cent completed.

September, 1942, first acceptance of B-24's completely assembled at Willow Run. From approval of project to building the world's largest manufacturing structure and delivery of planes—nineteen months!

Those nineteen months and the fifteen months following until I resigned from Ford Motor Company were the most fantastic of my career, which up to then had not been devoid of the unusual, the unexpected, and even in those days, the fantastic. I was in complete charge of production of the Ford company now geared for war. We were no longer in the motorcar business but were virtually a government subsidiary. I had launched my company on the assembly line, mass production of four-engine bombers—something never before tried—at the previously unheard-of rate of one an hour, and I had begun this $200,000,000 program before even a contract was signed, before even Congress had passed the Lend-Lease legislation which would provide the money for that contract.

Doing business with the government, treading through a maze of controls and frequently conflicting priorities regulations, vexed by wildcat strikes and labor and housing shortages, to say nothing of the erratic delivery of essential materials, was a frustrating experience. It would have been more so but for Merrill Meigs, who succeeded the able Dr. Mead as chief of the Aircraft Section of the War Production Board. Meigs was not an aviation expert. He was an advertising man who became a Hearst executive, and he was endowed with an uncommon amount of common sense.

Meigs was tops to work with. He could make any dark cloud look bright. There was not another like him in Washington. There were plenty of hell-raisers in that place. They did not help me. I could raise hell myself, but I needed something more. Meigs had that. From the White House down to the hell-raisers, Meigs was the balance wheel, and he did much to help me when and where I needed help most.

But Washington was not the least of my troubles. The

controlling owner of my company was an unpredictable old man unable to assume responsibility yet violently opposed to what we were doing and accusing me day after day of ruining Ford Motor Company. Titular president of the company was Edsel Ford, who was harassed by his father and his father's Man Friday, Harry Bennett, until he became a sick man, plagued first by stomach ulcers, and later by incurable cancer which took him to his grave. And to prevent the Ford empire, the greatest singly owned enterprise on earth, from falling apart, it was my duty to keep on until one of the third generation, Henry Ford II, who joined the Navy soon after our San Diego trip, could take over. All of which I did.

While building the plant and waiting for machinery we completed detailed plans for building B-24's. To accomplish such a major job, planning is the important thing. Someone with vision must start the plan moving, then there must be a frozen design to tie into. One reason why the aviation industry had not adopted the moving assembly line principle which prevailed in automobile manufacture was that changes were constantly made in new models, and thus prevented the frozen designs upon which assembly line operation depends. We agreed with Fleet of Consolidated and Air Force engineers that a plane design could be frozen up to the point where it was ready for radio, navigation instruments, and firearms design.

This understanding was reached after we made another trip to San Diego and a further look-see at Consolidated's work on the B-24. I had the wild idea that the bomber's fuselage from nose to tail, 66 feet, 4 inches, could be built up on end. This idea was suggested to me by a shop man in San Diego and was prompted after a B-24 had crashed and a crack test pilot killed. Investigation showed that the control mechanism had been locked by a loose nut dropping into a vulnerable spot. Under the on-end scheme, any loose parts would fall to the bottom of the assembly and would be discovered. After studying the proposal further, we rejected it because assemblers would be working practically on top of each other.

So we split the fuselage section. With that section in two parts, and wide open, we could install all the electric wiring and hydraulic piping, also install and check up the tail section. These sections could be set up on a conveyer, then brought to a point where the two halves would be joined by riveting. In that way the work could be constantly checked and inspected.

Consolidated people's method was the exact reverse. They made a unit, then dragged all wiring and hydraulic fittings through the door. Very few men could work in that space; and I described the pulling of wiring through the door as "like a bird building his own nest while sitting in it." So, we decided to continue fuselage assembly horizontally; more people could work on each unit and thus reduce assembly time.

Between helter-skelter production and labor shortages and union troubles, Fleet had his hands full with new problems. From a custom plant to large bomber production was a big jump. I made suggestions for a progressive assembly which was adopted later. Meanwhile, Consolidated was building plants at Fort Worth, Texas, and Tulsa, Oklahoma, its San Diego plant being rated as vulnerable to enemy naval attack. At Willow Run we would be able to turn out fuselage units before we would be equipped to build complete bombers. Consequently, I proposed that we ship knockdown units from Willow Run to Fort Worth. I had already gone into the question of over-the-road transport of these units with heads of big trucking companies. It was entirely feasible to build trailers big enough to accommodate even the largest units. They were the biggest things on the road, and when President Roosevelt saw them being loaded at Willow Run, he asked me if they were the ones he was getting complaints about blocking the highways. However, I had checked with Meigs in Washington and obtained the necessary authorization.

Even before Willow Run construction was completed, we were shipping knockdown parts over the road to Consolidated plants which made possible their production of 1,140 B-24's during 1942. This was one reason why Ford turned out only a few complete bombers in that year. Extravagant government-inspired publicity about construction of Willow Run produced flarebacks when there was no public announcement of completed bombers coming out of the plant. There were wisecracks about renaming the place "Will It Run." What was overlooked in all this was that we were making knockdown sections for planes built elsewhere. In other words, Willow Run was running even when it appeared not to be.

As soon as Consolidated balanced its parts production and we built complete planes, we did away with the trailers. But they certainly served their purpose in the 1942 program. The next year, 1943, Consolidated turned out 2,960 B-24's, while Willow Run's output was 2,184. In 1944, before cutbacks were ordered, the year's B-24 production was Consolidated, 3,817, Willow Run, 4,611. Even then we had not reached capacity production, which would have been 650 a month, or 9,000 bombers a year. "There's only one thing we need most," I told Meigs, "and that you in Washington can't give us."

"What is that?" he asked.

"Time," I replied.

As we became more and more involved in war production, streams of official visitors and other important personages called upon us—presidents of South American republics, the Duke of Windsor, General Giraud, and the like. Among our callers were several labor leaders with whom Ford Motor Company had been previously on rather distant terms. One was Walter Reuther, a former Ford employee. I used to see him in the toolroom, where he worked, and that was the extent of our acquaintance. Until he left to become a union organizer, I never knew he could make a speech. Afterwards I used to listen to him over the radio. As a spellbinder he was a wizard. After Ford was unionized, the only time I ever saw him was when he came with a group of Michigan state officials to look over our Pratt & Whitney engine plant. On that occasion he went out of his way to show me attention, reminiscing how "we" used to do things at Ford Motor Company in prewar days.

Soon after Reuther's visit came Philip Murray, head of the CIO. I took him down to Willow Run, which was then under construction. When I told him that we expected to employ 60,000 workers there, his eyes glistened. "Of course," he remarked, "we will take advantage of all our prerogatives."

He foresaw the new members and increased dues from that plant. So did I. "Charlie," he said, "I understand you still carry a union card." I passed that off with a laugh, for I quit the Patternmakers' Union shortly after joining Ford in 1905. Nevertheless, we had a friendly little talk. Murray spoke in a not too kindly way about Harry Bennett and said he wanted to see more of me. I put him straight on Bennett, that he was handling all union discussions and that I had all I could do with the manufacturing side of our war production. However, at a big union meeting that night Murray mentioned meeting me and assured his audience that I was a good friend of labor. Both with and without a union card, I am willing to agree to that.

Another frequent visitor was Charles Lindbergh, whom I later took on as a consultant at Willow Run. It was Lindbergh who, shortly after World War II broke out, persuaded us not to develop liquid-cooled aviation engines, a decision which later led us to undertake and then accept a contract for production of air-cooled Pratt & Whitney engines. It was with the approval of General "Hap" Arnold, the Air Force head, that Lindbergh was engaged by Ford Motor Company. Arnold told me that much of the Army's modernization of its air arm was the result of information Lindbergh brought back from Europe early in 1939.

For many years there was a conspiracy of silence to deny Lindbergh credit for this contribution. The Roosevelt Administration forced him to resign his reserve commission as colonel because he exercised his right to express, in peacetime, his opposition to our entry into the war. President Roosevelt called him a "Copperhead"—in plain language, a traitor. Secretary of the Interior Ickes declared him a mouthpiece of the Nazis. Yet all the time the Army was quietly making good use of Lindbergh's information on Germany's new planes and the extent of Nazi air power.

Denied a commission after the Pearl Harbor attack, he served, nevertheless, as a civilian adviser to our air forces. He developed a fuel economy system which greatly increased the cruising distance of some of our best planes. He helped teach Army fields how to land B-29's, and his service to his country has continued since the end of the war. No conduct of responsible American officials was ever meaner or more unjust than the campaign to smear Lindbergh; and the first official recognition of his wartime service was when President Eisenhower named him and the Senate confirmed him a brigadier general in the Air Force Reserve.

The middle of September, 1942, we got word that President and Mrs. Roosevelt would visit the Willow Run plant, and Secret Service men arrived to go over the schedule. When we laid out the plant we left enough room for driving an automobile down the main aisle, with the result that a spectator, riding in a car, could follow from beginning to end all operations in turning out a bomber. The route started where aluminum sheets were unloaded from freight cars. Next the sheets were followed into the press shop where the giant hydraulic presses were set in an aisle wide enough for a large truck. From the presses, the big stamped metal pieces of all sizes big and little were put on conveyers and moved to the different unit assemblies. It was a spectacular sight, nothing like it elsewhere in the world.

When this route was described to them, the Secret Service men were skeptical about having the President move through the plant with workers almost close enough to touch him. Then I took them over the route, and they were so impressed with the show itself that they agreed it was a must and arranged to station about a hundred guards along the way.

The afternoon of September 18 everything was ready. Plans were almost as detailed as laying out an assembly plant, and had been checked and double-checked to the minute. The Roosevelts' private car pulled into a siding at the northwest corner of the plant. An open automobile drew up alongside, and a ramp with hand rails was laid from the railroad car's rear platform to the door of the auto. The President, supported by a guard, came to the head of the ramp and walked down, supporting himself on the rail.

I had never seen him before, I was astonished to find him so helpless. He seemed to be in pain, and I wondered if he could make it. He moved slowly to the auto door, where his guard, a big strong man, lifted him into the seat in the right-hand rear corner. He was all smiles in a moment. Mrs. Roosevelt followed him. The two Fords and I stood by. The President asked Henry Ford to sit between him and Mrs. Roosevelt.

The Secret Service men had Edsel sit in the jump seat in front of Mrs. Roosevelt, and I sat directly in front of the President, so that I could turn and explain operations to him. Donald Nelson sat in front beside the chauffeur, and we got under way immediately along a route marked out with flags.

Mr. Roosevelt was extremely jovial. I had heard how easy he was to get acquainted with. Donald Nelson had introduced me as "Charlie Sorensen," and he called me "Charlie." He was ready and relaxed; this was his first look at an airplane plant.

Edsel was explaining the machinery to Mrs. Roosevelt. In a moment we were between the big presses. The workers caught the spirit of the occasion and put on a good show for the President.

Our car stopped between these mammoth presses for about five minutes. It was intended that we keep moving, but the President called for the driver to hold up. I pointed out how the metal arrived at the press, and after it came out of the press the man who took it out held it up for the President to see.

I was astonished at how he caught on to what we were doing. As we moved along, the President would point at something that caught his eye and shout at the top of his voice, "Charlie, what is that?" We would stop and I would explain. Mrs. Roosevelt was just as enthusiastic. She would see groups of workers on an operation that interested her. She would call, "Franklin, look over here."

They were like a couple of kids on a holiday. It was a good show, done for the first time in real comfort for the President of the United States, who for the first time was seeing an airplane plant.

The trip through the plant lasted about one hour and a quarter—about twice as long as had been planned. We drove out onto the ramp in front of the hangars, where we sat for a while watching planes come out of the plant.

All the while Mr. Roosevelt never stopped talking. He asked me if Bill Knudsen was around. I told him that I did not think he was, for if he had been I would have heard from him. I asked the President how he happened to choose Knudsen for the war production job. This is what he told me: The War Production Board was set up to handle the Army, Navy, and Air Force war equipment. To pick a man to head it was a problem.

Bernard Baruch, who had been head of the war production in World War I, came to see the President. Roosevelt asked him if he had any suggestions for a man to head up the department. He replied that he had the right man for the job. "Who?" asked the President. Baruch replied, "Bill Knudsen."

"Who is Bill Knudsen?" Mr. Roosevelt asked.

Baruch explained that he was president of General Motors. Mr. Roosevelt said, "I can't put him on that job. It wouldn't do to have the head of the biggest corporation step into that job. It would look as though I was prejudiced in favor of big business. Please think more about this and come back soon. I would like to find someone not associated with big business."

"Two weeks later Baruch was in my office again," F.D.R. went on. "I reminded him of our talk about a head for the war production department. I asked him if he had a man to recommend."

"Baruch said, 'Yes, I have.'

"Well, who is he?

"Baruch said, 'Bill Knudsen.'"

Roosevelt said, "I will consider him. My feeling is that a man like Knudsen should have a man associated with him in this, the biggest job in Washington."

"A week later," the President told us, "I sent for Knudsen and when he came to see me, by appointment, I had Sidney Hillman in my office."

The President told Knudsen that Baruch had recommended him for the war production job. "I have accepted you," he said, "but I want to put a man with you on the same level. I want you and this man to work as one."

Roosevelt then called in Sidney Hillman and introduced him to Knudsen. He then explained to them about his plan of working as one.

That ended our talk about Knudsen. Edsel and I were interested, for we never understood why Knudsen had been selected. Throughout all this, Henry Ford sat silent, but listening. It was evident to me that he was not enjoying the company.

The President and Mrs. Roosevelt were indifferent to him. Sitting between the Roosevelts, who were good-sized people, he was almost hidden. He could not enter into the spirit of the event. When Edsel or I turned to look at him he would glare at us furiously.

I am sure that the Roosevelts felt his unfriendly attitude. The workers responded to the President as if he were part of the plant itself. The attitude of Henry Ford was not apparent to the crowd. He was at a disadvantage where he sat. No one could resent others receiving attention as much as Henry Ford could. When he was around, the spotlight was for him.

We drove through a trailer park adjoining the plant, used by the plant workers. Mrs. Roosevelt criticized that form of home life. It was clear that a housing scheme was in her mind to replace it.

We returned to the railroad siding where the President made the painful journey up the ramp and into his private car. I remained in the auto while Edsel and Henry Ford went in with the President. In a few minutes I was summoned. The President, not seeing me, asked for me and in his jovial way thanked me for the trip which he said he knew I had arranged.

It was a nice friendly response to a great day. Henry Ford was gloomy, even in the final few minutes. The two Fords and I drove away in our separate cars. It was one of the worst days, up to that time, that I had ever spent with Henry Ford.

Even during the hard days of the battles with his stock-holders he had not been so gloomy or mean. He had spent a few hours with the man who was running the country and a war. Ford hated him, and he was furious because Edsel and I were giving all we had to a cause that was not his own. From then on he became even more difficult to work with.

This visit took place nine months after we were at war. Four days after Pearl Harbor, we were at war with Germany and Italy. This intensified our war material effort. Knudsen phoned me—wanted to double production, but when I suggested an order that would put up more buildings and buy more tools and machinery I found that he was merely handing me one of his pep talks. He never mentioned the subject again. Washington was like that the first week we were in the shooting war.

The normal economic system of the United States was completely upset. All civilian requirements were on a controlled basis. There was price control on supplies, priorities on travel, and a mobilization of labor and materials on a scale never seen before.

With it all, public morale was good, but Henry Ford remained aloof. He mistrusted officers of the armed forces in the plant and had hallucinations that he was being spied upon. He kept a crew doing special work for him. Among his projects was a five-cylinder motor which got nowhere, also a new lightweight car. This work, of course, was not in accord with government regulations, but I knew that, if there was official objection to this small diversion of priority material, I could assure Washington that the vehicle Mr. Ford was experimenting with might be used for light transport.

The basic idea was a tubular body and framework, light but strong where strength was needed. He showed it to me, hoping that he could divert me from the war program; and he hoped to divert Edsel the same way. So long as he was actively engaged on this project, it was a godsend to me, because it diverted Mr. Ford, too. Unfortunately, not for long.

I find this entry in my diary for January 18, 1942: "Had a call from Mr. Forrestal, wanting me to come to Washington. Said he would send his plane to New York to meet me. I'm a little suspicious."

I had no idea who Forrestal was. He caught me just as I was leaving for Boston and, though he spoke rather familiarly, he would not tell me what he wanted. I remember I told him he didn't have to send me a plane; I had one of my own. I put him off with "I'll be in Washington soon."

While in Boston I had a call from Meigs. I asked him who Forrestal was, and I was surprised to learn he was assistant secretary of the Navy. Meigs laughed when I described my cold reception of his invitation. "You must see him," he said. "Jim Forrestal is a great operator. Go see him and meet the Navy people."

Well, I did see him later, and my respect for him was as Meigs predicted. I have always been keen about anything that floats, and I've sailed yachts of my own big and little. My first craft was a raft on the Niagara River. When a boy of sixteen, I tried to join the Navy in the Spanish-American War but was rejected because the tips of two fingers of my right hand were gone—the lack of which was the occupational badge of the woodworking patternmaker. Then, in 1942, forty-four years later, I was sitting in with the top boys of the Navy, discussing matters in which two missing finger tips did not disqualify me.

The most annoying feature of our bomber operation was change in design during production. We would agree upon freezing a design, then be ready to go ahead. Back from the fighting fronts would come complaints or suggestions regarding certain features; and the plane designers came through with alterations in design with no consideration for the production program. Meigs and Knudsen were howling for planes, yet they tolerated these changes which slowed up our output.

I went to the mat with them, begging them to spend some time in Willow Run and see for themselves what we were up against. I never had much trouble putting changes into effect after they had been finally decided upon and passed. It was essential that we take advantage of what our pilots learned during their bombing missions. As General Arnold said, "I'd feel as if I had blood on my hands if I ignored these boys' suggestions." But what discouraged our organization was the need to halt or slow down production while waiting for Air Force decisions regarding proposed changes.

Eventually we got an Air Force committee on bomber design, which had headquarters in San Diego, to come to Willow Run and whip into shape a more speedy procedure covering changes. Briefly, the plan was to incorporate changes at certain stated intervals; and until those periods came due planes without those changes would be accepted. General Arnold built fires under officers charged with design changes and got quick decisions.

After that I was troubled only once. Apparently the new procedure had not penetrated to some self-important underlings at Wright Field, for one morning I had a telephone call from Dayton and an officer whose name I promptly and willingly forgot. He told me peremptorily that delivery of ships from Willow Run would not be accepted until certain changes were made; and he proceeded to tell me how to handle those changes.

I asked him if he had his recording device turned on; if not, I said, be sure to switch it on because I had something to say. "Now listen," I told him. "Authorized improvements and changes are being put through in double-quick time. Come and see for yourself. A pattern is set for bringing in changes that has been passed by your superiors. Go see them if you have anything to say, but don't sit down there in Dayton issuing orders, because I won't pay any attention to them."

I never heard from him again. We built the planes on schedule, and when I resigned in 1944 we were ahead of schedule.

CHAPTER

20

Henry Ford's
Greatest Failure

Henry Ford's greatest achievement was changing the face of America and putting the world on wheels. His greatest failure was his treatment of his only son, Edsel. And this treatment may have hastened his son's death.

The elder Ford wanted Edsel to be like himself. What he forgot, or ignored, was the fact that *his* father wanted *him* to be like *himself*. William Ford, Henry's father, was a strong-minded, domineering farmer who did all he could to make his son Henry become a farmer, too. But Henry hated farm work, which accounts for his later interest in tractors and other farm machinery. He wanted to—and did—live his own life, and that is what he would not accept gracefully and understandingly in Edsel.

Although Edsel was a more dutiful son than his father had been, he might have had an easier life—and probably a longer one—had he deferred more to the elder Ford and his ideas. In two important respects Edsel was like his father: he was an individualist who wanted to live his own life; and, like his father, nothing could move him once he had decided upon a certain course he felt was right. His decisions, though, were unlike his father's. The elder Ford was guided by hunches and intuition. Edsel reasoned out his problems after listening to and tolerating the opinions of others. He wouldn't compromise between what he thought was right and wrong, but he would seek adjusted agreement between extremes. What Henry Ford was unable to realize was that his son could not be a second edition of himself without being a mere copy of the original.

Edsel realized that he had a strong-minded father who was a world-famous figure. He knew he could not live up to his father's expectations. He knew his own limitations and did not hesitate to say so. He saw the lack of harmony between Henry Ford and James Couzens and other directors of Ford Motor Company and he could not be happy where there was discord. Yet discord followed him or involved him the rest of his fifty years of life. Henry Ford's idea of harmony was constant turmoil. He wanted his son to get experience the hard way, yet always tried to shield him—wanted him to be both steeplechaser and harness horse.

For all their ambition for Edsel to make a name for himself, Father and Mother Ford never wanted their son to grow up. They wanted to keep him close to themselves and to guide his every thought. When Fair Lane, the Ford mansion on the upper River Rouge, was built, the Fords had added a swimming pool, bowling alley, stables for riding horses, a garage full of fine cars, and a small golf course—everything they could think of to retain Edsel's interest at home. Of course, as the world knows, such lures do not hold real boys. Like all normal young people, Edsel wanted to be on his own to see and experience the world.

Edsel Ford, the only child of Henry and Clara Bryant Ford, was born in 1893 and named for Edsel Ruddiman, his father's boyhood friend. He was not born to wealth and a large retinue of servants. His father was chief engineer of the Detroit Edison Company at the time and tinkering in off hours with combustion engines. Edsel was one of the first passengers in his father's initial car of 1896. Thus, he grew up with the automobile and Ford Motor Company.

During school vacations he often visited the Ford plant, occasionally with his father, sometimes with boys of his own age. He liked to drop in at the pattern shop, where I was making wooden models, and tell me about things he was making at home or in school. After he went back to school, we seldom saw him; but when I was in the plant on Sundays his father would come over and bring Edsel with him.

After grammar school, Edsel went to the privately owned Detroit University School which prepared boys for college. Although a college education seemed the natural next step for a young man in his position, Edsel decided to forgo it. It was his own decision; he would remain at home and enter the Ford factories. He didn't want to spend in college the time that could be spent in fitting himself to stand beside his father. So began what seemed to be an ideal father-and-son partnership.

Late in 1912 or early in 1913, he went to work on the second floor of the Highland Park office where James Couzens and Frank Klingensmith held forth. Here he met the sales managers and their branch staffs. Henry Ford naturally expected great things from his son, but Edsel showed little interest in the engineering and production side of the business. Why should he? He was nearly twenty and without his father's lifelong mechanical background. There was some feeling on the part of the elder Ford that the front office people tried to keep his son out of the plant, that they wanted him for themselves. Actually, Couzens and other directors resented Edsel's coming into the company, and at times they were brutal about it. But Henry Ford's attitude was typical of his jealousy toward his son's friends and associates and their possible influence. Once in later years, when he was in a faultfinding mood, he accused me of being in sympathy with Edsel and such "riotous" living of his as attending cocktail parties. I took exception to this and replied that I felt toward Edsel as I did toward my own son, Clifford.

Frank Campsall, Ford's secretary, was in the car and heard me express myself so strongly. Next morning he telephoned me to say that I had made a mistake in talking to Mr. Ford like that. But that's the way I felt. I did have a fatherly feeling toward Edsel. Many a time when he was with me he threatened to resign, and I pulled him out of that mood. I was devoted to him, and he knew it. The only possible fault I ever found in him was that he was too kind. When he became president of Ford Motor Company he never did treat me like a boss; but I always worked for him as though he was my boss.

In 1915, just before sailing for Europe on his vain and much-ridiculed "peace ship" mission to "get the boys out of the trenches by Christmas," Henry Ford and I moved from Highland Park to Dearborn to begin farm tractor production. This move and gradual acquisition of land for the River Rouge plant set off another quarrel with Ford Motor Company directors. Canadian-born Couzens resigned as an official of the company in protest against Ford's pacifist statements during World War I but remained a director until late 1919. Edsel succeeded Couzens as secretary-treasurer and became a director.

While the elder Ford reinvested most of Ford Motor Company's profits in the company for expansion, other directors —the Dodge brothers, Couzens, and Rackham—demanded dividends. Henry Ford refused to attend board meetings, and here 22-year-old Edsel received his baptism of fire.

In 1916, Edsel married Eleanor Clay. Instead of living with

the elder Fords or nearby in Dearborn, the newlyweds understandably wished to be by themselves and made their home on the other side of Detroit. This was the first crack in the breach between Edsel and his father. Edsel on his own was a shock to his parents, who never expected he would go away and set up his own home. Soon the young Fords had their own circle of friends nearby. Grosse Pointe was the colony of wealthy, old-family Detroiters who then looked down their noses at newly-rich automobile makers. Henry Ford professed to despise them and their social, country-club life. As time went on, Edsel acquired a summer home in Seal Harbor, Maine, and a houseboat in Florida. He loved yachting and trips to Europe.

Actually, Edsel Ford and his wife lived comparatively simple, well-rounded lives. Edsel worked hard and was always on the job early. The elder Fords were teetotalers, and when they heard that Edsel took an occasional cocktail or highball, they were shocked and lamented the "evil influence" of his Grosse Pointe friends and surroundings. I never saw Edsel smoke; and nonsmoker and teetotaler that I am, his personal habits always appeared to me as those of any normal, well-behaved person. He made friends all over the world, and I never heard anyone who knew him speak of him except in the highest terms. I am told that there is no word corresponding to "gentleman" in other languages. Edsel Ford was a gentleman in the finest, fullest meaning of the word. He was gentle, considerate of others, unsparing of himself—and he was a *man*.

A year after his marriage, the United States entered World War I. Much of American industry had been producing war materials for the Allies; now Ford Motor Company took part in the expanded war program. Although Edsel was now an important factor in the company's over-all operations, he was torn about deciding whether or not to enlist. Edsel, I feel sure, could never have passed the Army's rigid physical examination, and his associates begged him not to sign up.

After the Selective Service law went into effect, I prepared his draft deferment papers, signed them, and showed them to Henry Ford, who sent me a note of thanks. When I took them to Edsel, he would not let me file them. He said he preferred to decide that matter himself. I argued hard that he should let the papers go through, that he would be serving his country more effectively by pushing our war-production program than by doing his bit in uniform.

The next morning I saw him again and then he gave his consent to file for exemption. It was granted in Washington with favorable comment, but a country-wide storm of public criticism broke over his head. Henry Ford, the pacifist, had finagled his son out of danger while other people's sons would fight and die. I never knew anyone in the Ford organization and with full knowledge of the facts who felt that Edsel was wrong in his decision, yet I was never positive that Edsel was sure he did what was right. I know that the furor and denunciation over his exemption hurt him deeply. I believe it was the all-compelling motive behind the enlistment of his two older sons in World War II, and it lay behind the continued insistence of Henry Ford II to remain in the Navy when his father and I needed him so urgently in the greatest of all war-production programs at Ford Motor Company.

In 1919, Edsel became president of Ford Motor Company. Henry Ford resigned, ostensibly to bring out another car in competition with Model T, but actually to frighten the few last lingering stockholders to sell out, which they did. From then on until the Ford Foundation was formed after Henry Ford's death in 1947, the company was owned outright by the Ford family. Although Henry Ford held no office when Edsel became head of the company, his word was law. Everybody in the organization was aware of the situation and governed himself accordingly, Edsel included, and his bearing throughout earned him respect where otherwise there might have been humiliation. Even so, a breach between father and son was appearing.

For this the Henry Fords continued to place the blame upon the Edsel Fords' Grosse Pointe friends, but their deepest suspicion and animosity was directed at Ernest Kanzler, who had married Josephine Hudson Clay, Mrs. Edsel Ford's sister. When I returned from a wartime trip to England late in 1917, Henry Ford told me that I would meet a new man Edsel had sent to me at the Dearborn tractor plant. He was Kanzler. I learned that he had studied law at Harvard and had spent a year or so in a well-known Detroit law firm. Otherwise he had no practical experience, but I was impressed by his direct manner and apparent willingness to do anything. I put him on following up materials requirements, and he did such a good job that I also tied him into our tractor sales program. It was a good lift for me to be relieved of that work, for which there were not too many young men available.

Again he did well, but he was overly ambitious; and that stirred up trouble. Being related to Edsel by marriage, he had easy access to the front office of Ford Motor Company at Highland Park, where staff began to believe he was taking advantage of that relationship. In doing so, Kanzler could not have done worse had he tried, for Henry Ford soon heard of it and he was looking for exactly that. It had always been our policy at Ford for everyone to start at the bottom. Kanzler was one of the few exceptions and largely for that reason, I think, Mr. Ford avoided him.

At the Ford mansion one day Mrs. Ford opened up on Kanzler to me. Too many people, she said, were taking advantage of Edsel, and of these Kanzler had the most influence over him. To make matters worse, Kanzler began talking about Henry Ford and how unfair he was to Edsel. He spread this among the staff, and after I overheard him saying the same thing to a tractor agent, I did not hesitate to correct him. He admitted that he had made a mistake which would not happen again.

One Sunday afternoon in 1920, Mr. and Mrs. Kanzler called on my wife and me at our home. To this day my wife remembers how shocked we were at their unrestrained tirade against Mr. Ford and the way he held Edsel down. There was some justification, as I have already revealed, for that point of view, but it did not justify wild talk.

Monday morning I told him I did not want anything more to do with him. He was free to go to Edsel at Ford Motor Company and air his views but he was through working for Henry Ford & Son.

Henry Ford came in as I was finishing. When Kanzler had gone, I explained what had taken place. Mr. Ford's only comment was: "You have not seen the last of him yet. He will be on Edsel's lap now."

That was just what happened. Kanzler was welcomed with open arms at Highland Park and went to work for Ford Motor Company. There was no doubt about his ability and drive to make his way but he could not understand that the elder Fords disliked his involvement with Edsel. They wanted Edsel to be independent of everyone but themselves. I pointed out to Edsel on several occasions that Kanzler was coming between him and his parents. He did not resent my mentioning the subject, but when he learned that Henry Ford wanted him to drop Kanzler he defied his father and had Kanzler elected a vice-president and director of Ford Motor Company late in 1923.

By this time I was back at the Rouge handling production. We were having rough going then with Henry Ford. The

American people apparently had outgrown Model T and preferred a more modern-looking car. Edsel could get nowhere in persuading his father to bring out a new car. Every suggestion he made was ignored.

Apropos of the situation he was facing I told Edsel this story: A certain man never had a happy moment with his wife. Everything he wanted to do, she would do the reverse. If he preferred his chair in one place, she put it in another. Then he discovered how to get his way—move the chair opposite to his preferred spot, whereupon his wife would place it exactly where he wanted it.

But Edsel could not practice subterfuge. One day after lunch, during a discussion of Model A, the proposed successor to Model T, Edsel criticized his father for not releasing new designs. Henry Ford got up and left Edsel and me standing at a drafting board. I could see a storm coming. In a few minutes Campsall came in and said, "Mr. Ford wants to see you at once in my office."

In Campsall's office, the elder Ford told me to tell Edsel to take a trip to California. "Make it a long stay," he said, "and tell him I will send him his paycheck out there. I'll send for him when I want to see him again."

Nearly twenty years later, as I shall relate, Edsel received from his father the same instructions about his two sons, Henry II and Benson. This was typical of the Henry Ford approach to personal problems. He never handled them himself, always delegated someone to carry his messages; and I carried many of them. But I could not understand this message to Edsel, who surely wouldn't accept it either from me or from his father. So I waited a couple of days before seeing him. Then I told him that his father had spoken to me about Model A and that it was useless to press him. He would do the job his way and assume full responsibility for it. I asked him if he didn't think we would get on with the job if we left it to his father. Well, that was one of Henry Ford's ways of getting his own way. Edsel and I went to lunch with him, and father and son were friendly and jovial. The cloud had passed.

Henry Ford felt that Kanzler was behind Edsel. Mrs. Ford would get hold of me and weep about Kanzler, who, she said, was creating discord between Edsel and his father and mother. This continued until Kanzler planted himself in an office adjoining Edsel's. That was the last straw. Staff and branch managers avoided Edsel. It was so apparent that Edsel was embarrassed. The only way he could see me or his father would be when he came to Dearborn for lunch. Then it was that I had a short session with Kanzler. It resulted in his sending in his resignation, on August 2, 1926, from all Ford companies and affiliates.

But this departure did not erase Kanzler from the minds of the Henry Fords and fears of his influence over their son. Within two years he had become executive vice-president of the Guardian Detroit Bank, which previously had taken over the Bank of Detroit that James Couzens had dominated until he went into politics. Edsel was a Guardian director and the bank's largest depositor with his own and Ford Motor Company funds. From 1932 to 1933 Kanzler was chairman of the board of Guardian and Union Group, Inc., a holding company for banks and trust companies, including the Guardian banks and with three-quarters of all bank deposits in the state of Michigan. Edsel was also the largest stockholder in this organization.

By the beginning of 1933 the entire banking system of Detroit was like a house of cards, which toppled when affairs of the Guardian group, particularly of Union Guardian Trust Company, became shaky. This was followed by the Michigan bank holiday, which was declared on St. Valentine's Day,

1933, and closed every bank in the state. The day after his inauguration, President Franklin D. Roosevelt declared a national bank holiday, and every bank in the United States was closed for nine days.

The Guardian group had been taking risks that sound banks would not touch, and it soon became apparent that they would be unable to reopen. All over the downtown Detroit banking center were huddles throughout the day and night.

In the middle of this complex situation, Couzens, Ford's old partner and now a United States senator, made political capital with Edsel and Henry Ford as a target, blaming them for the Detroit banking situation which touched off the bank holiday.

It was a bitter experience for the Fords. Henry Ford blamed the bankers—particularly Kanzler—for getting Edsel involved. If Craig, the treasurer of Ford Motor Company, had been a real banker he would have kept the company, as did other auto manufacturers, out of the trouble that finally came. Craig was honest in performance of his work, but he was treasurer in name only; Edsel dominated him completely. Edsel was a long time getting out of his difficulty and at a cost of between six and seven million dollars. But it cost him more than mere money; his health went with it.

Also, from then on, Henry Ford went downhill; he had a stroke in 1938. Six months after the 1933 bank holiday had come his defiance of NRA and New Deal threats to close down his plant. Then came labor troubles, with Edsel, although company president, on the sidelines while Harry Bennett was empowered by Henry Ford to deal with the unions. Edsel was determined to alter the company's labor policy but was up against a stone wall.

Relations between Edsel and Henry Ford were now

strained almost to the breaking point, and it became increasingly difficult for father and son to work together on anything. Neither could settle down to plant interests; there were too many problems of their own to be concerned about. And because I had been able to steer clear of this family discord I had a virtually free hand to build steel mills, tire plants, press shops, glass plants, make imitation leather, and set up new plants both in this country and in Europe. I was rewarded with a salary and bonus which made me one of if not the highest salaried man in the company. Nevertheless, the next ten years were a nightmare.

Although Henry Ford confounded the doctors by recovering from his stroke in a month, all of us were apprehensive about the future. Edsel spoke to me about bringing his two boys, Henry II and Benson, into the plant for some training. He wisely wanted them to know the foundation of the business. While Edsel's family was growing, his three sons, Henry II, Benson, and Billy, were with their grandparents a great deal. Just as in Edsel's boyhood, Henry Ford gave them everything they could wish for. He built miniature autos, tractors, and farm tools, even a small steam engine and threshing machine. Henry II was thirty months old when we blew in the first blast furnace at the Rouge plant. His grandfather lifted him on his shoulder and with a torch the youngster started the fire on the hearth that smelted iron ore for our foundry. This furnace was christened the "Henry" furnace. Benson did the same to a second furnace, which was named for him.

Edsel's plans for his boys to buckle down to work were not realized until late in 1940, a year which brought new problems. There was war in Europe, and war loomed on the horizon for the United States. Ford Motor Company became involved in a government armament program that would take us through plant expansion for planes, aviation engines, tanks, turboblowers, gun directors, jeeps, tank armor, steel and magnesium wastings, and construction at Willow Run of a mile-long bomber plant, the world's biggest industrial building. By the middle of 1941, a few months before Pearl Harbor and this country's entry into World War II, we were completely out of the automobile business; everything we had was thrown into war work.

Henry Ford had nothing to do with this program. He was far removed from the Henry Ford of Model T days. From 1906, there was first Couzens, then Edsel and me. He never did assume responsibility for operating the plant or the commercial end of the business. With these matters in safe hands, he went along as the glorified leader, which he was. After his stroke he became a querulous, suspicious old man. He scented conspiracies to grab his business. Often his memory failed him. Late in 1942 he said to me, "Charlie, there's one man I don't want to see any more. You must get rid of Knudsen."

Bill Knudsen had not been with us for twenty years, and he left the presidency of General Motors to head the government's war-production program. After I left the company in 1944, Mr. Ford used to tell his chauffeur, "Drive me down to the Rouge; I want to see Charlie." At other intervals he would be more like his old self; and my respect for the real Henry Ford, the man who was, and my gratitude to him never faltered and never has since. This must be borne in mind when I describe my hectic and harassed last few years at Ford.

Beginning with World War I days, I kept a diary consisting of short daily notes. My entries for 1940 show the tensions between Henry Ford and his son and grandsons. They show the burdens Edsel and I were bearing from day to day. They show how the great Ford industrial empire was kept intact, also my long, hard struggle to bring Henry Ford II to direction of its destinies. They trace events leading to my resignation from the company and my final refusal of the suggestion by the wartime administration in Washington that I supplant the man for whom I worked and to whom I owed so much.

It was late in 1940, just after Ford Motor Company accepted a government contract and built a plant for production of Pratt & Whitney airplane motors that Henry II and Benson came to work for us. When I mentioned to their grandfather that they were going into the plant, he first said he didn't want them around, then showed complete indifference. Young Henry was just out of Yale and married in July. Both young men were assigned to our aviation program. They watched the progress of negotiating a contract and I kept them posted on details.

Early in January, 1941, I met Edsel and Young Henry and Benson in San Diego, where we inspected the Consolidated bomber plant preparatory to committing the company to a plane-production program. We saw B-24 bombers being put together by laborious, time-consuming methods; and that night I sketched a plant layout capable of turning out by mass production methods one B-24 an hour. The gigantic Willow Run project was the result.

Edsel was not well. He was under constant observation by Dr. Mateer and had to spend much time at the hospital. It was a real effort for him to get around the plant. Over and over again Henry Ford told me what a problem Edsel was to him. Again and again I tried to impress upon him, without success, that his attempt to drive Edsel into line by using Harry Bennett to annoy him and check his every move was breaking down Edsel's respect for him. Bennett was merely following instructions.

A couple of months after Henry II, Benson, and I returned from our San Diego trip, Edsel came to me in great distress. He had come direct from a session with his father, who told him to see me and tell me to get rid of the two boys. He did not want them in the plant—send them to California, anywhere, the farther away the better. I should keep them on the payroll but be sure they got out at once. History was repeating itself. Those were the identical instructions Henry Ford had given me ten years earlier regarding Edsel.

Over this latest, Edsel was in tears. How could his father do such a thing to him? And why? Edsel knew of my liking for his boys and thought I might know what was behind his drastic order. I soon made clear what I would do. I telephoned Campsall to see if Henry Ford was there. He was. The response was evident; he was expecting to hear from me. I said I wanted to see Mr. Ford at once. "Come over now," said Campsall. "Mr. Ford will wait for you."

I turned to Edsel and said, "Let's go and see him together." When we walked into the office, Henry Ford was surprised to see Edsel with me and a look of hatred came over his face. I had never seen that expression before. (The only other time I saw him look even remotely like this was three years later when President and Mrs. Roosevelt visited Willow Run and Mr. Ford was sandwiched between them and almost hidden on the back seat of the automobile.) He had always been frank and kind to me, but this was different; I was interfering in a family matter. Nevertheless, that expression spurred me on to say what I had in mind, and did he listen! He never expected me to defy him as I did. "Edsel has given me your message about Henry and Benson," I said. "I am opposed to any such action and if you have any idea that I'll carry it out, forget it. I refuse. Furthermore, if you do this yourself, I am through. That's all I've got to say." I got up, and without looking at him I walked out with Edsel.

Next day when he came to my office he was the usual Henry Ford, nice and friendly. Nothing was ever said again about the incident. Although I never discussed it with Edsel, I knew it was on his mind.

Henry Ford saw that I was doing anything I could to help his grandsons get on, but instead of approval, his attitude was that I was assuming too much. Perhaps I was. I began to feel that I was in rather dangerous territory to be continually forcing this issue with him, but I decided that I would continue to do everything possible to help young Henry even if it meant a break with Henry Ford.

In the fall of 1939 I reached an understanding with Mr. Ford that in 1941, when I would be sixty, I could retire to an advisory position. This agreement was confirmed in the presence of Frank Campsall, Henry Ford's secretary.

But when 1941 came I could not ask for release. Our actual entry into World War II seemed imminent, Edsel was a sick man, Henry Ford was failing both mentally and physically, and throughout the whole organization there was uncertainty where the control lay. Ford Motor Company was now completely engaged in war materials production, and I had double responsibility—to the company and to Washington for carrying out this program. Consequently, I felt it my duty to remain until Young Henry took over and the matter of who was to be in control was settled. So I told Campsall that I would defer the plan that had been laid out for me in 1941 and would stay on the job.

In July, 1941, I was elected executive vice-president and a director of Ford Motor Company. Back in 1919, when Henry Ford resigned from Ford Motor Company and organized Henry Ford & Son and took me to Dearborn to build farm tractors, we had agreed that we would not act as officers in the company. But when Mr. Ford told me that Edsel had decided to give me official title he also said that he was in full accord.

For many years I had acted in official capacities though without title. With Edsel in Maine or Florida or abroad and with Henry Ford in upper Michigan or Georgia, these frequent absences gave me absolute freedom of action over Ford Motor Company's production. Now, in the war program, official Washington was dealing with me. Hence I was given an official title.

Then came Pearl Harbor. Ford Motor Company went on a seven-days-a-week basis. The normal economic system of the United States was knocked galley-west. All civilian requirements were controlled by Washington. There was price control on supplies, priorities on travel, and a mobilization of labor and materials on a scale never seen before.

From all this, Henry Ford remained aloof. The great pacifist remained passive; nothing to do with war preparation interested him. He would have a look at how things were going at Willow Run, but talk about its problems went in one ear and out the other. Mr. Ford had the feeling that he was being spied on, and he mistrusted Army and Air Force officers stationed at the plant. He was obsessed with the idea that he would be attacked by a government agent. I was astonished to find an automatic pistol in a holster under the cowl of his car. His chauffeur also packed a pistol. When I spoke to Mr. Ford about this armament, he could not explain why it was necessary, merely said he was pistol-practicing on his farms. Thus we went all out for war.

In January, 1942, Edsel was operated on for stomach ulcers. I had known of his trouble for some time and I was frightened to see the pain he was in at times. On one of our trips to Washington, he was suddenly taken ill after a seafood dinner. I got him back to our hotel rooms and called a doctor. Edsel was in such agony that I sat up with him all night, afraid that he was dying.

When his ailment was diagnosed as ulcers brought on by stress and strain, the doctors strongly advised him to quit work for a while and get away from his worries. Edsel promised that he would consider his health and become less active, but he never did. Had he done so, I believe he would be alive today. His father doubted anything was seriously wrong with Edsel's health. He kept preaching that Edsel must learn to eat right and live right—"right" being what the father ate and his mode of living.

"If there is anything the matter with Edsel's health," he told me, "he can correct it himself. First, he will have to change his way of living. Then I'll get my chiropractor to work on him, and if the hospital can't cure him, I'll get rid of the whole bunch."

The first time I ever saw Henry Ford have any concern over his son's illness was the day of Edsel's operation. I was no good around the plant that day, so I spent it with Mr. Ford, who was plainly worried.

"Edsel ate lunch for the first time since his operation," I set down in my diary March 2, 1942. "Doesn't look good to me." I was probably more worried about his health than he was. He was head of Ford Motor Company. If he had been in good health and able to be on the job, that would have been enough to balance matters so far as I was concerned. Instead I was between father and son, one of whom was unwilling and the other unable to assume full responsibility. Everything seemed to be conspiring against me. The more war material we turned out the more was demanded. I was knocking myself out with work. Twice I landed in the hospital and two other times I fainted dead away.

What hurt most was lack of organization to cover the top brackets. If Young Henry could have been with me, that would have relieved Edsel. But both he and his brother Benson decided to enlist, as was natural of any young men conscious of obligations to country. I tried every way I could to persuade them that they could render greater service to their country by remaining in the plant. I told them their father

had been in the same situation in World War I and that I
had worked out his deferment.

I got nowhere with my argument, for their father had
smarted for years under unjust criticism of that deferment.
Henry signed up with the Navy, Benson went into the Air
Force.

By July, Young Henry was commissioned a lieutenant j.g.
and detailed to Great Lakes Naval Training Station just outside Chicago. I had little hope that he would come back to
our war program. He certainly was entitled now to apply
for duty in the Ford plant. It would have given me peace of
mind and would have been a great thing for his father. I knew
full well that neither the elder Ford nor Edsel could be
active in the future of the company. The only solution I saw
was for Young Henry to take over. To me, he meant the
future of the company.

Once again I brought up with Ir. Ford the subject of making Henry II a director and an officer of the company. I
begged him to bring this about. It was useless. The old man
just didn't comprehend what I was talking about; but my
mention of Edsel stirred him to the old, familiar refrain. Once
again I heard how Edsel must change his living habits and
drop his present associates.

In November Edsel was in the hospital again with what
was diagnosed as undulant fever. This was caused by milk
which came from the Henry Ford farm and was not pas-
teurized, nor was the herd given regular tuberculin tests. The
elder Ford and Dr. McClure had many a violent discussion
over this omission, the former stubbornly contending that
pasteurization was unnecessary. Now Edsel was laid low by
this neglect, while his father attributed the illness to his son's
living habits.

When Edsel returned to the office after his hospital bout

with undulant fever, I noted in my diary that he "looks bad. Something wrong with him. At lunch with us, Henry Ford did not seem very sympathetic to Edsel."

Both of them were in a bad mood, which became worse almost every time they were together. Edsel's wife and sons wanted him to quit. They saw no likelihood of his getting well so long as he was harassed by his father and by Harry Bennett. Benson, who was home on leave, was particularly bitter. He burst out to me about his grandfather, who, he said, was responsible for his father's sickness and that he, Benson, was through with him. I began to feel this was a hopeless situation. From then on, events moved with the inevitability of a Greek tragedy.

On April 15, 1943, a day before I was to leave for a short rest in Florida, I noted in my diary, "Edsel came in at eleven o'clock. Looks like a sick man to me. I am worried about him. Tonight Henry Ford called me, wants me to see Edsel tomorrow morning and change his attitude on everything in general. Some job!"

While Mr. Ford was talking, I made these notes (I still have them) at the telephone:

  a. Discord over handling labor unions.
  b. Wibel and his attitude on Bennett, says Wibel is through.
  c. Bennett in full accord with Henry Ford. Henry Ford will support Bennett against every obstacle. Seeing labor leaders.
  d. Bennett's job, no one else.
  e. Change relations with Bennett.
  f. Kanzler relationship—wants it broken up.
  g. Regain health by cooperating with Henry Ford.

My first reaction after leaving the telephone was: What a brutal thing to do to one's son! To send me to him to tell him this! It was plain who was the inspiration for all this; Bennett was having his day. Still, I felt that I could help both father and son in this affair, and that was my approach when I saw Edsel the next morning.

I explained that I was on delicate ground. I showed him my notes and told him how his father had telephoned me. "I feel I can be helpful," I said, "but if you wish, I will go no further. It's evident where Mr. Ford is getting these ideas; but to me that is not so distressing as would be a break between you and your father."

"The best thing for me to do," said Edsel, "is to resign. My health won't let me go on. But, Charlie, I want you to know I appreciate what you're trying to do. It's a kindly act, and I'm grateful for it."

He was in tears. I sat on a couch with him and told him when he calmed down, "If you go, I go too. I've had enough of people resigning."

By that time we could talk more dispassionately about Henry Ford's message. The part about Kanzler and "cooperation" with the elder Ford was old, familiar stuff. References to Bennett, though understandably infuriating, had little meaning; Edsel had bowed long ago to his father's will that Bennett handle labor relations. The really serious item was "Wibel is through."

A. M. Wibel came to Ford Motor Company in 1912 as a machinist. He advanced through the organization and in the 1930's succeeded Fred Diehl as head of the purchasing division. That always was a tremendous job, but it became a supercolossal one with World War II. Wibel's work was beyond reproach—and that in a field where critics hit hard. Edsel, Wibel, and I had the full confidence of Washington. Wibel had dealt directly with Henry Ford for many years, and until his dismissal was ordered, I never had heard Mr. Ford find any fault with him; and he was one of the few I could say that about.

Edsel explained to me that he and Wibel had a hot session with Bennett over some supplier Bennett favored. Edsel told Bennett to keep his nose out of purchasing and stick to personnel and union negotiation. So it was plain to see how and by whom Henry Ford had been stirred up against Wibel. Wibel was one of the Ford Motor Company greats; yet now he meant nothing to the man for whom he had worked more than thirty years.

After two hours of persuasion, Edsel promised he would not resign. Then we went to lunch, where he and his father were all smiles. I suspect that Bennett had checked my activities during the day and had reported my long session with Edsel to Mr. Ford.

Immediately after lunch Henry Ford and Bennett came over to see me, fairly twitching with curiosity. Mr. Ford was plainly disturbed when I told him that Edsel was prepared to resign. I added that if that had happened I would have left also. I described how Edsel had rightly pulled up Bennett on his behavior and I announced that if Bennett ever interfered in my work he would be stopped the same way.

"You're right," said Mr. Ford.

"Very well," I replied, "is Harry Bennett immune to correction by Edsel?"

Whereupon Mr. Ford sailed into Bennett, and I got up to go. "I'm leaving for Miami," I said, "and I don't know when I'll be back."

My parting remark was: "And when I do come back, I want to see Young Henry here."

Satisfied that the Wibel matter had blown over, I left that night for Florida. I had delegated work at the bomber plant to all the superintendents. A report on daily operations was in my office every morning, and while I was away I got by phone the results of the previous day. The day after I left, I heard, Edsel walked through the Willow Run plant alone.

It was to be his last look, for immediately after that he took to his bed and never got up again.

The fifth day of my Miami stay, my office phoned me a note from Henry Ford instructing me to get Wibel's resignation. After the scene in my office and his call-down by Mr. Ford, Bennett had his hooks in Edsel again! I finally located Wibel in Jacksonville and explained the situation to him. He understood perfectly and without hesitation sent in his resignation. And so we lost one of the best men in the company. He was not the first to go this way, nor was he the last. Knudsen was in Miami on a short vacation and was shocked when I told him about Wibel.

Back in Detroit, the first week in May, 1943, I found that Edsel was at home ill. His operation of the year before had not been successful. A serious stomach condition had developed and another operation was being considered.

"May 10," I wrote in my diary. "To bomber plant, met President of Bolivia and party at ten-thirty. Henry Ford came to my office at five and said Edsel is much better."

When is Henry Ford going to realize what has happened to his son? I asked myself. Edsel's condition had been found to be incurable cancer. His father had not been told, for he continued along the same old line: Edsel must mend his ways; people like Kanzler were taking advantage of him. I never before had a case of nerves. I could take anything—but not any more of that.

On May 18, a month after I had taken his ultimatum to his son, Henry Ford was told that Edsel was dying. Even then he refused to believe it. He insisted that the Ford Hospital and doctors must bring Edsel back to health, and he was bitter about their failure. That was his conclusion to the end. Nevertheless, he was suffering severely and seemed to want to have me around. Dr. McClure, Mr. Ford's wise and patient personal physician, was seemingly unmoved. "Henry Ford is a sick man, too. We must expect him to say and do unusual things. He should not be around the plant or have anything to do with the business. But what more can we do?"

"May 26," I entered in my diary. "Edsel Ford died one-ten a.m. Dr. McClure phoned me one-twenty. To office nine-fifteen. Henry Ford phoned me ten-fifteen, very well composed. I cracked up."

Edsel's funeral was held two days later, and my wife and I were the only ones outside the immediate family who went to the cemetery. "Thank you, Mr. Sorensen, for your many kindnesses," Mrs. Edsel Ford wrote me. "I do appreciate them and it all does help, but it is still very lonely."

The night before Edsel was buried, Mr. Ford telephoned that he had decided to take Edsel's place as president of Ford Motor Company. My immediate reaction was "impossible." Mentally and physically he was unable to handle the job. I have wondered ever since why he told me this, for usually he did things his own way, never asking for advice. He said that his taking the title would end all speculation. But why tell me? If he did so to end any speculation in my mind about inheriting Edsel's office, it was unnecessary, for I never had any such ambition.

The morning after Edsel's funeral, Campsall phoned me to come to his office to meet Henry Ford, who wanted to talk to me about reorganization matters. I replied that Mr. Ford had already told me that he would become president of the company. I reminded him of the agreement I had that I could retire when I became sixty on a consultant basis and salary for life. I told him I wanted to take advantage of that now; Mr. Ford could do his reorganization without me.

Campsall was upset. "Consider Mr. Ford and his condition," he urged.

"Yes, I do," I replied, "but I want him to bring in Young Henry at once. At once! Mr. Ford can't assume any responsibilities. All must now be tied around Young Henry, who will look after the family interests.

"That's all I've got to say. Will you take this up with Mr. Ford as soon as you can?"

Apparently this scared the daylights out of Campsall, who said he didn't know how to bring that up to Mr. Ford. I left and went to Willow Run bomber plant. Shortly after I arrived there, Bennett and Capizzi came in, as eager as bird dogs. J. A. Capizzi, who handled the legal end of Bennett's union negotiations, said that he'd just been talking with Henry Ford, who had sought his advice on taking over the presidency. "But," added the lawyer, "you should be president, and Mr. Ford should be chairman of the board!"

I listened a long time so as to fathom what was on Capizzi's mind. It seemed strange for him to discuss this matter with me, and also very much out of order. As I pieced out the situation, Capizzi must have talked with Campsall after I had left his office; and Campsall, disturbed by my announced intention of retiring at this time, intimated that Henry Ford wished me to be president. I, of course, knew differently, so I quickly cleared up any thought or suspicion my two visitors might have had that I wished to succeed Edsel. Only a fool would have sought to dethrone Henry Ford. Years after I left Ford Motor Company there were stories that I was president of the company for a day, all of which, I gather, was something dreamed up by Bennett.

The next morning's directors' meeting would have scotched that story before it was so industriously circulated had minutes been kept of such gatherings. My diary is probably the only true record. "Monday, May 31: Henry Ford called me to meet him in his office at the Rouge. He arrived at ten forty-five. Henry II and Benson with us, together with Craig. We held a meeting, electing Henry Ford president, and me executive vice-president, Craig, vice-president and treasurer,

Moekle, secretary. Mrs. Ford called me, asked me to see Mrs. Edsel [who] is rowing with Henry Ford. Settled her down."

The directors' meeting did not last more than fifteen minutes. Henry Ford II, who later told me he had not known the purpose of the meeting, objected to election of a president so soon after his father's death. He expressed himself strongly against his grandfather's taking over the presidency, but he was overruled. When the meeting broke up there was none of the usual congratulations and best wishes. Most of us were stunned.

Henry Ford pulled me along with him on his way out. He wanted to keep me away from Henry II. I got into his car and drove it. His chauffeur followed in my car.

"You've got a job now," I said, adding for emphasis, "now *you* run it!"

"Charlie," he replied, "everything is going to be the same with you and me, just as it always has been."

"You've taken on a job," I repeated. "I know you don't realize what that means, but this time you've got to. Edsel did. I can work with anyone who understands his responsibility. But you don't."

Mr. Ford just didn't comprehend what he had done—an 80-year-old man taking over the active direction of the biggest single production unit in the world's biggest war. His promise that things would be the same was impossible with Edsel gone. The future of the company was at stake. Again I mentioned Henry II and Benson. The only proper thing for the elder Ford to do, I insisted, was to make Young Henry president and Benson vice-president. That would work, I assured him, and I would go along with it 100 per cent.

"We have much to do today and for the future," I continued. "We must organize for that. As things stand now, we're slipping. These boys will be some foundation for the future. Better give some thought to that."

"You're right, Charlie; you and I will settle that," he replied, but after nearly forty years of association with him I could read his mind and I sensed that what I had said had made little impression on it.

At home that evening, Mrs. Henry Ford telephoned me that her husband had had an argument over the telephone with Edsel's widow. Would I please see her and calm her down?

I called Mrs. Edsel. "Come right over," she said. "Glad to see you."

Young Henry and Benson were with her. It was as I had suspected. Mrs. Edsel resented that morning's board meeting; its unseemly haste showed no consideration for her or her family. She had suffered an irreparable loss, yet her judgment was sound and reasonable. I agreed with her about the board meeting and repeated my conversation after it with Henry Ford. Nothing, I told her, would reconcile me to Henry Ford as president of Ford Motor Company. I only asked her to consider wider aspects of the situation. It was imperative that Young Henry come to work, and I implored her to bring this about.

A few days later Henry II came to my office and promised he would come into the business. At last things began to look up! This was my happiest day in a long time, and I got in touch with Merrill Meigs in Washington regarding Young Henry's release from active duty with the Navy.

The elder Ford, however, continued petulant about his grandson—didn't want him in the plant, was too easily influenced, had changed his religion when he married a Catholic. All the same line, but somehow I detected a difference; Clara Ford had been reasoning with her husband and taking the part of Mrs. Edsel, Young Henry, and his wife. Now Henry Ford might talk himself "goofy," as I phrased it in my diary, about Young Henry, but his wife would see to it that nothing should prevent their grandson from taking a hand in the management of the company.

Late in July, 1943 came Young Henry's release from the Navy. On August 10 he went to work. I asked him to get around the plant. Let the workers see him and let him get acquainted with the superintendents. That would help change the atmosphere. Something had to be done to save the company, and the more the elder Ford got rid of key men in war-production work the more insistent became rumblings from Washington. Because of his bad health, his mental condition, his age, and his pacifism, Henry Ford was a natural target for Washington officials to shoot at. I got this from General "Hap" Arnold, from Knudsen, Donald Nelson, "General Electric" Charlie Wilson, and many others in the know.

Young Henry moved into his father's office. He took over Edsel's staff and began to see a side of the business he had had no contact with before he went into the Navy. Things were not pleasant for him at first. His grandfather used Bennett to harass him, just as had happened to Edsel. In the face of such trials and attempts to belittle him, I took Young Henry with me on visits to New York and Washington and meetings with government officials. This gave him his first look at the heads of big business, bankers, and top men in the armed services. It made a real impression on him, and wherever this 25-year-old young man went he, too, made an impression— a good one.

One morning I was with him when he got a telephone call from Bennett. He was getting an earful and could hardly get a word in. Not wishing to listen, I stepped into the outer office and went back when Henry II put down the receiver. Not a word was said about the phone call. He was under fire —I could see that—but Young Henry was composed and resumed his talk with me as though nothing had happened. The boy can take it, I said to myself happily; everything will work out all right.

By now I had decided I'd had enough. The picture was clear: the team was breaking up. The captain was a sick man, unable to call the plays. The line coaches were gone. Anyone who made a brilliant play was called out. That had happened to John Crawford, Edsel's trouble-shooter who defied Bennett. It had happened to Wibel. It had just happened to Sheldrick, who for fifteen years had been in charge of engineering. Finally, out went Gregorie, the clever designer— "stylist" is today's word—who drew the lines of the Lincoln Continental, which is still sought by lovers of fine cars and rates with the fine old Rolls-Royce.

Production was in the capable hands of Mead Bricker at Willow Run and Rausch at the Rouge. But whatever plans there were for resumption of civilian production after the war were being kicked to pieces by Mr. Ford. It was plain that a postwar program called for complete reorganization of Ford Motor Company. But who would do it? Certainly not Henry Ford. I would not be there. Edsel was gone.

There was only one thing left for me to do: see that Henry II stayed on, make it impossible for him to leave by passing the responsibility to him. With New Year's less than three months away, I told Mr. Ford, with Campsall present, to relieve me January 1, 1944. I wanted to take advantage of the retirement plan that had been agreed upon for 1941. I would go to Florida and not come back to the company. Again I advised making Henry II president. I warned that Washington was concerned about the loss of key staff men and to be ready for trouble from that quarter. To this day I don't know whether Mr. Ford fully understood what we were talking about.

My last days with him were rather formal. The day before

I left for Florida I went over to Dearborn to say goodbye to the staff there. On my way out I ran into Mr. Ford. I told him I was leaving in the morning and not coming back. He made no response except to say, "I guess there's something in life besides work." He followed me to my car. We shook hands, and I was off. I never saw him again.

This was easier than I had anticipated, but it was not over yet. I had asked Mr. Ford for my release. Any announcement about it should come from him. But it never did.

"House looks more wonderful than ever," I wrote in my diary upon arrival at Miami Beach. "I love it very much. Wish I could stay here always, need the peace of mind. . . .

"What a hectic time I have had with Henry Ford since Edsel passed away! The fine, cooperative relationship I had with Mr. Ford for thirty-nine years is gone. His heading the Company as president did what I anticipated. He is surrounded by a bad group, but they only carry out his wishes. I can't blame anyone but Mr. Ford. I know his whole family, Henry II, Mrs. Edsel, all the children, are heartbroken. I made the mistake of being ambitious to help him in his great trouble when he lost his son, for which I can blame him, Henry Ford, only."

Russell Gnau, my secretary, phoned me from Detroit about rumors there that I had resigned. All production operations were going well. Bombers were coming out of Willow Run still ahead of schedule. That was good news. "If one builds well," I said, "he won't be missed too much." Russell reported that Henry Ford was on his estate at Ways, Georgia, and that Campsall had been phoning to learn when I was coming back.

Meanwhile, I was fishing and swimming every day and getting plenty of rest with it. A chronic sinus condition cleared up from sea bathing and sunshine. Many friends dropped in for lunch with us. Time was flying and very pleasantly, for the first time in many years. Also extremely pleasant was a lot of newspaper publicity about record production at Willow Run.

Also meanwhile, there came messages from Ways, Georgia. When was I going up that way? Again and again I told Campsall that I was remaining in Miami Beach. "Please get a release from Henry Ford," I repeated. "You know what I want. If I don't hear soon, I must issue a statement of my own. Is Mr. Ford sick or unable to settle this?"

Campsall couldn't answer. Of course, I knew why.

"March 2, 1944: Campsall called this morning, said Henry Ford felt that I should resign—his excuse, I am ambitious to be president of his company. Well, he can't treat me as he did his son and made a nervous wreck of him. I will live longer, his tactics are killing. Am very happy about it."

I was happy because here was a simple, quick end. Accordingly, I wrote out the following:

Mr. Henry Ford
Dearborn, Michigan

Dear Sir:
Please accept my resignation as vice president of the Ford Motor Company, Dearborn, Michigan. I expect to remain here until May 1, returning to Detroit May 5. I will sign any documents necessary to go with your acceptance of my resignation at that time. Will you please allow Russell Gnau to handle until I return.
Yours truly
Charles E. Sorensen

Then I telephoned Campsall and read it, adding that I would give it out in forty-eight hours and would be glad to add anything Mr. Ford wished. He did not call back. Later, when I was in Detroit, he told me why: Henry Ford was too ill to talk to me or decide anything. My trouble with him had him down, and he could not pull himself together.

Mrs. Ford finally got the full picture from Campsall and

his call was in response to her instructions. From then on Mrs.
Ford virtually took over for her husband, and I am sure she
was right in doing so.

I doubt that Henry Ford ever knew what had happened.
When he returned to Dearborn he thought I was still with
the company and repeatedly told his chauffeur to "take me
over to see Charlie."

After I announced my resignation I spent several hours
listening to telephone calls from Washington. Donald Nelson
wanted me to go to Russia and repeat my visit of the 1920's
when I tried to show the Communists what American mass
production meant. C. E. Wilson of OPA wanted me to come
back and take over Ford Motor Company for the government.
Merrill Meigs, my best friend through all this war-production
affair, urged me to come to Washington. I told him to come
to Miami Beach and we'd talk the whole thing through.

Charlie Wilson's call disturbed me. He said the President
insisted upon Henry Ford's removal from Ford Motor Company and all connection with the war production. General
Arnold, head of the Army Air Force, had been putting
pressure on the White House to get me to Washington to
take a bigger hand in the aviation program.

Wilson said Washington officials understood my situation
and approved of the step I had taken. Nevertheless, they were
going to replace Henry Ford. I tried to make clear that
the organization was capable of meeting all schedules. "Don't
disturb it," I urged him.

I was glad to see Meigs. I needed his help and advice, for
no one in Washington understood Ford Motor Company and
me better. But even he did not know all. He never knew my
troubles with Henry Ford after Edsel's death.

Meigs and I talked all day. I told him that if the government
forced the removal of Henry Ford, much as that removal was
desirable, I could not be either a party to it or a beneficiary

of it. I could not sully my record of loyalty to the man who had given me so much of his confidence—and friendship. Whatever years were left to me I had to live with myself. And I could not usurp the place of the man upon whom I had pinned my flag thirty-nine years before. I could not, that is, unless there were greater obligations to the country and the winning of the war. But Henry II was now at work. He had been elected a vice-president. Ford Motor Company was ahead of its wartime production schedules. Young Henry would see the rest through.

Finally Meigs said, "I can see it clearly now. Don't let the people in Washington involve you in this."

And they never did. For I had now found peace of mind. And in that state, which I had never before experienced for any length of time, I wrote the following letter to one of my most valued, candid friends:

My best friends are my critics. You say, "Why did I not develop a real successor?" Mr. Ford, like many men of his kind, never had a successor, they just can't acknowledge that such a thing is possible. Was his son even a possible successor? This war program which he, Henry Ford, never entered into, and which he would not take the slightest interest, got me in trouble plenty with him. Can't you use your imagination a bit? I was the only authority in the Company that Washington recognized. I am the victim of that situation. I got out on my own all right rather than follow his son. That is all. Now, tell me, how could I develop an organization that would live on after I am, or he is, gone? My only ambition was to do exactly that. His grandsons, three of them, coming along, I felt I was living for them. In the bottom of my heart I still feel that way. I would do anything for them because the business should carry on in their hands. I guess I was too ambitious for them. I have said a lot to you here, more than I have to anybody. I would feel rotten if I thought that you or anybody else said I was a quitter. The war program was up to schedule, and even ahead. I am in the best of health, and better prepared to render a service than ever. I can't say anything. If

I did, it would appear that I was attacking the man who helped me get what I have. I bear him no malice. Do you understand my position any better now?

I wrote that in March, 1944. Printers and proofreaders—and solvers of crossword puzzles—know a mark which means "let it stand." It's the best end I know of for my record of nearly forty years with Henry Ford.

Stet!

Index

Addison, Christopher, 238
"African Golf," 185–186
Akron Rubber Company, 211–213
Allison, Fred, 120
Americana, Ford's interest in, 20
American Federation of Labor (AFL), 268
American Peace Foundation, 150
Amtorg, 207, 208
Anderson, John, 166
Armed Ship Bill, 162
Arnold, Gen. "Hap," 292, 299, 328, 332
"Arrow, The," 71
Assembly branches, Ford, 170–171
Assembly line:
  in aviation industry, 288
  moving, 117–118, 125, 156
  wartime significance, 273
  see also Mass production
Association of Licensed Automobile Manufacturers, 119–121
Astor, Lady, 16
Automation, 103, 115
Automobile, low-cost, *see* Low-cost car development
Automobile industry:
  New Deal code, 258–272
  in Russia, 197–216
  wage policies, 147
  wartime program, 278–279
Automobile race, first, 70
Automobile shows:
  Detroit (1906), 84
  New York (1906), 80–81
Avery, Clarence W., 46, 130
Aviation Building, 277

B-24 bomber, 4, 279, 280, 281, 284, 288, 314
  production figures, 290
Bald, Eddie, 65, 66
Bankers, Ford and the, 166–168, 310–311
Barthel, Oliver E., 68, 74
Baruch, Bernard, 295
Batt, William L., 210
Beaverbrook, Lord, 275
Bennett, Harry, 8, 27, 146, 288, 291, 311, 314, 320, 321, 322, 325, 328, 329
  fearless personal courage of, 256
  in Ford labor relations, 255–272
  as peacemaker, 260–261
Berghoff, Breedo, 237
Bethlehem Steel Company, 174
Bicycle racing, 65–66
Birds, the Fords' interest in, 16–17
Black and Germer Stove Works, 61
Blast furnaces, 158–164, 170, 174
Bloomfield Hills Country Club, 226
"Bodies by Fisher," 81
Bonbright, Howard, 265
Botsford Inn, 20
Bowers, Joseph, 167–168
Brakes, Ford, 224
Breech, Ernie, 249
Bricker, Mead L., 234, 237, 329
Briggs, Walter, 264–265
Briggs Body plant, 263–266
Brisbane, Arthur, 27–28
British Ford Motor Company, *see* Ford Motor Company, Ltd.
British War Mission to the United States, 236

Bryant, Marvin, 233
Bryant and Berry pattern works, 68, 69, 72
Buffalo, N. Y., Sorensen's early life in, 61, 65–69
Buick, the, 218
Buick Company, 226
Bullitt, William C., 208
Burke, Edmund, 215
Burroughs, John, 18, 19

Cadillac, the, 116
Cameron, William J., 3, 142, 143, 176, 193
Campsall, Frank, 13, 245, 246, 270, 304, 309, 315, 316, 324, 325, 329, 331
Canton, Ohio, 98, 99, 102
Capizzi, J. A., 268, 325
Carlson, 195
"Cast-Iron Charlie," 4, 80, 107, 163, 243
Central Steel, Ohio, 235
Chamberlain, Neville, 29
Chapin, Roy, 68
Charity, Ford's attitude toward, 21–23
"Chauffeur," Ford as, 70
Chevrolet, the, 218
Chiropractor, Ford's, 318
Chorley, Kenneth, 185
Christian I, King, 60
Chrysler, Walter, 226
Chrysler Corporation, 91, 226
Churchill, Winston, 16
Coal, Ford sources of, 152
College story, Sorensen's, 63–64
Committee for Industrial Organization (CIO), 31, 268, 270
Communists, big-city demonstrations and, 254–256
Connecting rod, Model T, 105
Consolidated Aircraft, 279–280, 285, 288, 289, 290, 314
Consumer, Ford's attitude toward, 254
Consumer credit, 148
Conveyor system, 128–131, 170
Cooper, Tommy, 66, 69, 70, 71

Copley, Frank Barkley, 41
Coronado Hotel, 281, 283
Coulter, Dr. L. B., 18, 266
Couzens, James, 15, 32, 36, 43, 45, 48, 49, 72–79, 84–88, 94–95, 302–304, 310–313
as director, 160–161
efficiency incident, 39–41
in evolution of mass production, 119–123, 128–130
five-dollar-day development and, 139–140
Ford and, 86–87, 94
low-priced car development and, 85–87
resignation of, 152–154, 157
row with Sorensen, 188–189
stock of, 166
Cowling, Bill, 26
Craig, B. J., 311, 325
Crankcase, Model T, 105–106
Crankshaft development, 177
Model T, 105
V-8, 230
Crap-shooting, Ford and, 185–186
Crawford, John, 235, 237, 244, 329
Crowther, Samuel, 3, 52–54, 116, 142, 143, 193
Curtiss-Wright, 278
Cuyahoga River, 156
Cylinder block castings, 78–79

Dagenham plant, 277
Dahlinger, Ray, 151
Dancing, Ford's interest in, 20–21
Dearborn, 158
Ford farm at, 15
tractor development at, 154
Dearborn Laboratories, 19, 255
Dearborn-River Rouge area, 137
the Fords' affection for, 154
natural advantages of, 155–156
De Dion engines, 66
Deer, Ford's, 17
Degener, August, 52
Depression, Great, 174, 225, 253–272
Detroit, as automobile center, 68
Detroit Athletic Club, 226, 248
Detroit banking situation, 310–311

Moscow, 196, 199
Motorcycles, 66
Murphy, Frank, 255
Murray, Philip, 291
My Life and Work, Ford, 52, 129

Napoleon, quoted, 51
National Industrial Recovery Act, 258
National Labor Relations Board, 267-268
Navy, Sorensen's interest in, 298
Nelson, Donald, 209-211, 293, 328, 332
Newberry, Truman, 28
New Deal, 146
Ford and the, 253-272
Nijni Novgorod Ford plant, 198-199, 204, 206-208
"999," racer, 71
Northcliffe, Lord, 236

Ohio River, 183
Oka River, 198
Oldfield, Barney, 66, 71
Olds, Ransom E., 75
Oldsmobile, 67, 68, 75
Oliver Plow Company, South Bend, 29
Ore fields, in China, 206
Organization, Ford's sense of, 43
Osborn, Frederick, 182-185
Oscar II, 150

Packard Motor Car Company, 141
Parker, Mr., 120
Patent litigation, 119-121
Patternmaker, Sorensen as, 64-83
Patternmakers' Union, 291
Patterson, Robert P., 285
Peace Ship, 7, 25, 30, 150-152, 157, 304
Pearl Harbor, 231, 272, 317
Pennsylvania Railroad, 191
Perry, Lady, 12
Perry, Lord Percival L. D., 12, 16, 195, 240, 247
tractor development and, 236-239, 244-247

Pioch, William, 177, 279, 285
Piquette Avenue plant, 36, 42, 73-74, 126, 156
manufacturing operations, 118-119
mass production concept in, 116
Model T production in, 97-112
Planetary gear, Ford's interest in, 99-101
Plantiff, Gaston, 150-151, 167
Plow, tractor-attachment development, 241-250
Plymouth car, 226
Poles, free, in Detroit, 195-196
Pratt & Whitney aviation engine, 100-101, 268, 292, 314
Ford Motor Company manufacture of, 276-278
Putilov Steel Works, 200-203

Racing cars, Ford's, 70-72
Rackham, Horace H., 160, 304
stock of, 166
Radiator conveyors, 128-130
Railroads, *see* Detroit, Toledo & Ironton Railroad
Rausch, R., 329
Reuther, Walter, 147, 291
Ritter, George, 210
River Rouge-Dearborn area, 137, 154-156
River Rouge plant, 4, 5, 9, 37, 49, 286
basic concept, 151-152
B building, 170
blast furnaces and foundry at, 158-164, 173-175
development of, 156-157, 165-179
legal actions restraining, 161-165
model of, 160
plate-glass manufacturing, 172-173
production variety in, 176
river-widening and, 181-183
steel manufacture in, 173-175
strike at, 267-272
tire business, 212
traffic problems, 159
unemployment at, 255-256
Rockelman, Fred, 52, 195
Rolling-mills, Russian, 201
Rolls-Royce aviation engine, 274-276